Rwanda:
Work of God, Work of Evil

(A story and a diary)

out 11/09

by Brigitte Kehrer

To Pros,
may this personal
experience of humanity
give you strength and
hope! warmly Brigitte

Published by Destinée S.A., www.destinee.ch

Originally published as *Rwanda: Part de Dieu et part du diable*
© Editions L'Harmattan 2002

Cover photograph: Rural Rwanda near Byumba in northern Rwanda with permission of Joe Stajskal, 1999

All rights reserved by the author

Translated by Charles Akin.

Includes bibliographical references.

ISBN 0-9759082-1-9

Rwanda:
Work of God, Work of Evil

(A story and a diary)

PREFACE

The driving force for writing this book emerged during a visit to Lake Kivu in Eastern Rwanda. I was spellbound when I first saw it. Just one visit to this place will haunt you for the rest of your life. Lake Kivu calls to you, and its metallic hardness catches hold of you. Its reflection draws you in, like an abyssal attraction to the layers of collective unconsciousness.

Neither your senses nor your memory come out intact. It's like breathing infinity.

Yet, even though this splendid scenery spellbound me, I reflected as well the beauty of nature and its insolent right to overcome tragedy. This lake undoubtedly reminded the reality of what happened here such a short time ago. Genocide took place in Rwanda where over one million people were murdered in a few months. And Lake Kivu swallowed that horror like a cobra makes a mouse disappear along his digestive tube, without even chewing on it. Washed it out, decomposed the bodies carrying them along what Rwandan called the sacred Nile up to Abyssinia. In a way the water was the means to absorb the shock and the place were the bodies were thrown away like textile puppets. It was the dumping ground for thousands of corpses that were eventually carried away, dejected or eaten by crocodiles.

The images of this horror were attached to that lake like ghosts appearing in shades of mist giving desperate signs in its reflections. Yes the bodies were gone, but the souls were still screaming and wondering what had come across humanity to let innocent people being killed like animals. People gathered in churches, people praying, and people asking for mercy; all thrown in the lake, now.

There are no waves on that lake: only the hard metallic sound of the sulphur coming out in small smoke volutes. More then any other place in Rwanda, even though memorials or places of mass graves had deeply struck me, but this lake said something more about the genocide: maybe an archetypical

1

message of things being impermanent. Water comes and goes. There is tide and the moon comes and washed all the sins. Water is always the same and never alike.

Indeed, this lake touched me deeply and later that day, when I collected my emotions, I began to contemplate the surface and see through it to the ground.

I found myself thinking about Rwanda, looking for an answer to the simple question of how did this all happen? Why did all these events happen here in Africa, in Rwanda? Why such a frenzy in killing and perpetrating a genocide? Are we allowed to utter any judgment, as we have in Europe allowed and seen similar horrors, scarcely 50 years ago and we screamed never again? Are we all so blind and hypocritical? What does it mean to have a collective human responsibility for each murder perpetrated on one of us? Yes this lake was throwing at me much more questions than giving soothing answers.

I considered is there an inherent evil in mankind where we are all capable of enacting such acts. What are the causes for such enmity? There is a good and an evil part in all of us: we better acknowledge that and try to address the difficult shadow parts in our lives and countries, before uttering critics to other nations.

Is it inevitable that acts like this will recur again on a minor or major scale?

Looking at the lake by sunset, I thought to myself, I swear to me that I will not abandon these people if something happens again. But I did not exactly know what it could mean.

I thought of the peace-keeping forces. Just one little word maybe, by one of the generals... and the genocide could have been stopped?

And now, the Rwandans were in the middle of a very difficult process of reconciliation and forgiving. Who on earth can forgive to have lost 19 brothers and sisters and parents and children? Is there such a word meaning life after genocide?

Looking at this metallic hard and immitigable lake I discovered: It is this reality that appealed to me that I wanted to show: the nearly impossible task that the international community was ordering Rwandans to do: get together again, be kind, we pay for that and please reconcile.

I remembered my mother's words. She used to say even 50 years after Auschwitz: Why did we not prevent anything with theses monsters?

Is reconciliation really possible? Looking at the world's situation, only one answer came to my lips: time and a lot of goodwill and time and again time. Give them time.

So, I was compelled to consider all these questions and decided to talk about it in public, as I was keeping a diary.

On the lake Kivu that day, I then firmly decided to write the whole and true story of a nearly impossible reconciliation process. "Work of God, work of evil" was going to be a story about the life and emotions of Rwandans and the few international people in the middle of them attempting reconstruction, trying not to feel to guilty and not too aloof either. I though OK, this lake give me the strength to let everything come up again, my days and my fears here to do the wrong things: I would then see how the facts would emerge.

In this sense, only the author is responsible for this story, which seeks to be neither political nor polemical. The story reveals aspects of daily life in Africa, specifically in Rwanda from June 1998, four years after the genocide, to June 2001. The impressions are those of a European woman, a foreigner, who has sought to give special importance to the difficulties of rehabilitation without taking sides. The story also seeks to answer the question of how to reconstruct a society from its ashes by giving something else than just money or good intentions...

Using a diary and the testimony of Rwandans, an attempt is made to understand better what the reconciliation process takes for efforts. The relentless struggle of ordinary and well-intended people to survive is sincerely gripping. Faced

3

with an unprecedented collapse of society, the question of the role of religion appears in the background.

The wounds of this small African country have still not healed. After the war, reconciliation and pardon must be dealt with both inside and outside Rwanda. At the request of many Rwandan friends, many names of people have been changed. At the same time, the persons described represent various facets of a country that is trying to find national coherence and overcome its shame.

One unbearable reality has haunted me during my stay in Rwanda: most of the genociders are still around. Or living in neighbouring countries. The majority of them are comfortably installed in northern countries undisturbed: why is the international tribunal so slow, why is it so difficult to pursue them, those who have been carefully preparing the genocide and the propaganda? It certainly does give some understanding and forgiveness to the sometimes-harsh tone of nowadays-Rwandan authorities. They affirm their wish to go away from retaliation: can we give them a chance? The answer for me was really yes. We must, it is our duty to give confidence in a renewal and a breaking of the evil circle of vengeance.

The book is written more as journal than a reasoned story, but these experiences, little by little, begin to provide an overall image of the suffering of a people and their brave attempt to find reconciliation and meaning, like individual colours on a painters pallet that emerge into a lucid picture.

Names have been changed to protect many people who could face retributions if their identities were revealed. I have also not used the name of the international organization I was working for, in order to maintain professional confidentiality. At the same time, I can say that my assignment with this organization was to provide mediation services in the delicate rebuilding of Rwandan society. But, this is not my story. It is the story of modern day Rwandans and what they have experienced and how they face today's reality. It is a journalist's look into a work of evil and a work of God.

I dedicate this book to all those in Rwanda who are struggling to make possible a future filled with understanding and clemency.

Brigitte Kehrer
Switzerland 2004

Chronology

1885	Rwanda-Urundi became two German colonies under one administration
1921	The League of Nations created the Belgium mandate of Rwanda and Burundi
1931	A national identity card with indication of ethnic origin in Rwanda was introduced
1959	Death of the last reigning Tutsi king, Mutara Rudahigwa, and the end of the Tutsi aristocracy
1959	Social uprising of Hutu farmers with many deaths on both sides and massacre of Tutsis causing hundreds of thousands of Tutsis to flee abroad
1961	Victory of the Hutu parties in the first legislative elections
1962	Declaration of the independence of Rwanda and election of Grégoire Kayibanda, a Hutu, as president
1973	Military coup d'état by Major Juvénal Habyiarimana, also a Hutu
1979	Election of President Habyiarimana, who was re-elected several times until his assassination in 1994
1990	More than one million exiled Tutsis out of a total Rwandan population of seven million are still not integrated into society

1990   First military attacks of the Tutsi Armée
            patriotique rwandaise (APR) from Uganda

1993   First peace agreements at Arusha (United
            Republic of Tanzania) between the Hutu
            government of Rwanda and representatives of
            the Tutsi Front patriotique rwandais (FPR)

1994   On 6 April at 8 pm, an airplane returning from
            Arusha with President Habyiarimana was shot
            down near the Kigali airport. The Arusha
            agreements were to enter into effect. A long-
            planned systematic genocide began. Tutsis and
            moderate Hutus on prepared lists were
            massacred by machete. There were also barbaric
            assassinations of moderate Hutus, including the
            Prime Minister, Agathe Uwilingiymana. On 4
            July, Kigali was captured by the APR, coming
            from the north, killing civilians along the way,
            while the genocide continues in southern and
            south-eastern Rwanda. On 15 July, more than
            1.5 million Hutu refugees crossed the Congolese
            border and established camps in eastern Congo
            (former Zaire) at Bukavu and Goma. On 3
            October, three months after the beginning of the
            massacres, which had already taken the lives of
            more than one million Tutsis and moderate
            Hutus, the Security Council finally adopts a
            report qualifying the massacres committed by
            the former Hutu regime in Rwanda as genocide.

1996   Between November and December, 1.2 million
            refugees returned to Rwanda from the Congo

7

1997   Insecurity reigns, and attacks on the civilian population begin again from outside and inside Rwanda led by the Interhamwe militia of the former regime.

1998   Rwanda invaded eastern Congo in pursuit of the Interhamwe, among other goals.

TABLE OF CONTENTS

9

Brigitte Kehrer

Part I: Impressions, Nuances and Background

Chapter 1

My Initial Contact with Africa

A calling

     The story of my twelve years of working and learning in Africa is that of a calling and a return, as if I had already lived there before. My experiences answered questions about the meaning of life and about what we are doing that had been buried within me for a long time. My experience is linked to concepts of colour, the concept of race and the duty to serve humanity. All of this may seem pompous, but that is not my intention. Through my work in Africa, I discovered real life, where the contrast between European and African is more than that of a photograph and its negative with integration of all sorts of nuances. Africa has facilitated my reconciliation with myself, and Africa is now fixed in my life. What I had been seeking at the other end of the world was in fact lodged within myself. I was destined to meet men and women with curly hair and ebony bodies. They opened my eyes. I had been colour-blind.

     Africa has taught me about colours and nuances and also about the hardness and implacable side of the laws of nature. The continent that I fully embraced seduced me, and, then, I became part of it and then I again became a European with satisfaction and without any feeling of guilt, but with a slightly suntanned soul. Once many Europeans find a foothold, they usually talk with nostalgia about Africa. This is not a cliché. They find their lost customs. I was able to observe first hand the networks of solidarity and belief in ancestors, such as were practiced long ago and of which there are still traces in some parts of Europe. In the Alps of the cantons of Bern and

Valais, a storm can still indicate divine anger. Mountain dwellers don't joke about the prediction of an avalanche discerned in the menacing shapes of a cumulus cloud.

Just like in Africa, we have our secret practices. We still have inaccessible places where old healers converse intimately with the spirits. Africa makes it possible for us to appreciate our own customs and our own beliefs. For a long time, I have admired the work of Corinna Bille, a Swiss who writes about mysterious mountains and the dizziness of heights that release madness and desperation. Her descriptions of the fear of the mountains' threatening manifestations or the ghosts that live in the ravines and streams of the Hérens Valley are striking and vivid. I have also admired Rainer Maria Rilke, a poet who knew how to bring out the cracks in the magic mountain and the craze of the summits that he described at Sils Maria: Rainer Maria Rilke, the preferred poet. I love what cannot be said, to detect the unspoken and to find links with hidden realities. I stepped into Africa like an elephant, and I learned to become more feline. But no literature really prepared me for the thousand hills of Rwanda.

Mozambique

My first contact with Africa occurred in Mozambique, way down on the globe. At that time, in 1988, Portuguese specialists told me that when bathwater drains from a bathtub in the southern hemisphere it spirals anticlockwise, the opposite of what happens in Europe. So when I arrived in Mozambique, my first impulse was to check this aspect of terrestrial gravity. Leaning over water left from a bath in Maputo, I couldn't see at all how the water was draining. I drew another bath and slowly took out the plug. With my hand, I could sense the direction in which the water was draining; of course in the opposite direction from that in the Northern hemisphere. I was dumbfounded and asked myself how it was that Nature dealt with the fact of walking upside down. It was enough to

11

understand that reality here was different and to be wary of my initial reactions. Over time, I learned not to rely on my inadequate tools for interpretation and to check out things other than terrestrial gravity. I began at the bottom of the scale of questions. What is the African continent? What is the African aim in life? What is it like to be poor? What does it mean to want to aid Africa as a European?

Within a short time, it was I who was aided by Africa, reverting all the clichés. My initial curiosity was transformed into admiration of the differences. I looked around and began to observe the pace of life in the street. In Africa, a European always walks around with a specific purpose and during the day he quickly goes from one place to another. He is always in a hurry, even when on a holiday. He rarely wanders about. It is quite the opposite for an African, who always looks like he is walking about nonchalantly, wandering, taking his time. These two behaviours mark a clear distinction. There is an enormous observable difference to the naked eye from your first step into the street. In the evening, the European quickly goes back home, while the African begins to gather with members of his family. It's mealtime; sometimes the only meal of the day. Sometimes, ten, twelve, fifteen people are gathered around the table. The smallest piece of food quickly disappears without leaving a trace. No one puts anything aside for another time. Anyway, no one would know where to put it because there is often no electricity, running water or refrigerator.

Africa lives in the immediate present: from day to day. Every day is an obstacle that must be overcome. It is difficult to make long-term plans or to dream about a future beyond the immediate present. At night, everything becomes very dark. While we quickly lose our sense of orientation, the African comes to life. He walks off at top speed in the right direction. The darker it is, the better he sees and the faster he goes. He walks around as if guided by radar. The streets are usually poorly lit, and we quickly panic. We lock ourselves in our houses as though we were curling up. There are no Europeans in the streets late at night. On the contrary, it's in the pitch dark that Africa begins to come alive. People talk among themselves without seeing each other's faces. Darkness reinforces confidence and meets the need to be together in a community. At the beginning of the night, no one wants to be alone, which would be a real tragedy. Parents begin to speak in a whisper, and children don't go to bed. Everyone begins to tell stories: stories about their family, clan and village. Life at night is buzzing with intensity.

Quite often, villagers decide to try their luck in the city. If they find a cousin or someone from their clan or tribe, they can count on support. But many never find someone they know. Having left the misery of the countryside, they enter the hell of the city. They begin by building a roof, finding some materials, finding three sheets of corrugated paper. If they are lucky, they are able to dig out a small space for themselves in the slums. From being just poor they become very poor. Because they don't have any money, they wander about in search of a bit of work or a scrap of bread.

It's the other Africa: that of the uprooted, that where life in the villages is no longer sufficient. It is the Africa where the city attracts and people lose their orientation. These new African migrants are recognizable right away. They carry sheets of roofing, pieces of plastic and nails and with incredible resourcefulness are able to recycle everything that comes into their hands. It is a question of survival. They form another community in the swamps or on vacant land. They miss their village; there is no solidarity. Parts of automobiles, boxes, bags, everything is used. In Africa, nothing is wasted; everything is recycled. Among my first impressions of Africa were those of the network of alliances and clans and the absence of over-consumption.

My first stay in Mozambique was a real initiation. The incident of the bathtub that drains anticlockwise was left behind, and I came in contact with the enormous Indian Ocean. Long ago, the shores of Mozambique were often a stopover for

13

spice and silk traders, but sadly also for the sale of slaves. Water is a topic in which I have special interest. Because I am from the Lake Geneva area, I have been led to look at water and the way the wind is blowing the large water geyser (*jet d'eau*) in Geneva in order to predict the weather. I used to listen to the lapping of water, the background noise at dawn and wind blowing whitecaps on the lake. In my vocabulary, I long ago sorted out the names of the prevailing winds and the squalls. The winds are called *bise, bornan, fraidieu, joran, morget* and *séchard*, just like a panoply of pagan gods. In Mozambique, water is vital; everything has a hint of the ocean: the open sea, fishing, the coast, palms and emptiness. The offshore islands look like they were made from lace matching the turquoise blue of the sky and sea, joining at the horizon.

Immigrants are mixed with the inhabitants of Mozambique, along the lagoons, in the whitewashed stone houses, around the commercial neighbourhoods, all along the long coast, which is straight as a seahorse for more than three thousand kilometres. They have come from Goa or other places—Hindus, Pakistanis, Sri Lankans, even soldiers from Bangladesh—and have settled down. In all of East and Southern Africa, they are called Asians and tend to dominate commerce. Although many of them are very wealthy, they are careful not to attract the attention or envy of Africans. They lead a modest life, sometimes driving old automobiles with a tailpipe dragging dramatically from the back. They marry among themselves, frequent mosques and temples and buy, sell and speculate carefully as if they might have to move on from one day to the next.

My introduction to Africa took place in this coastal Africa, open to the winds, smiling and knowledgeable about how to enjoy life, despite the drama of fourteen years of fratricidal, chaotic and contradictory war. I do not know how, but everything seems to function. Mozambique is a mixture of many cultures, including Dutch, Italian, Portuguese, Asian, Arab and pirates, giving the landscape and architecture an air of obsolete rebellion and a pirates' den. Mozambique is a place for stopping over and chance meetings. It is crawling with people of all sorts and ilk. The country and its inhabitants also have amazing charm. Mozambicans are pleasant and accommodating; pleased to meet foreigners and fond of explaining their relationships with their colonizer. Their history is filled with events. The fratricidal war, a war between the forces of East and West, was one of the last political wars, so it is said, a result of the Iron Curtain that brought the country to its knees.

It was in the water, wrapped in a shroud, that healers (*curandeiras*), strong and inspired women, submerged me and rubbed me against the gravel at the seashore at Quelimane. After my kidnapping, they welcomed me and bathed me as if I had come back from the other world. They scrubbed me in the sea with gravel and sand like a corpse ready for burial at sea. They purified me of all the bad spirits. When these women completely wrapped me in a symbolic sheet of white linen, I knew that I had already been in Mozambique in an earlier life. I once lived there as a sugar plantation owner on the Zambezi or had been a clove trader at Pemba.

Mali

My life then led me to Mali, where I never bothered to check how the bathtub drained. The desert is immediate, and water is a commodity too valuable to be wasted. The importance of religion also changed. That was a Muslim world, very respectful of foreigners and guests with a long history related to the implantation of Islam. For instance, Timbuktu has its thirty-three saints and the library of the desert. Signs used to be read in the sand. There is a visible fracture between European and African, the raw, bright sand and the fertile black silt. The Bambara, Peul, Songhai and Turareg mark the difference between life and perception of the outside world. The vast area of the Sahel, from Mauritania to Chad over to Sudan, represents a change in colour and a change in values. All this is represented by shades of white, caramel and black. One day, black slaves huddled on the edges of this frontier said no to the raids, no to the men in blue from the desert. Integration is the only possible response. Mixing? Peaceful coexistence? On the one side, the kings of the desert, on the other, Africans tilling the land or grazing their cattle, for example the proud and nomadic Peuls. Anyway, our good-old God figured everything out: this border, the sand, the desert and the infinite spaces reaching into the Maghrib are a no man's land, a safe passage to the Atlas, Ghardaïa and Tamanrasset. Beyond that, it's Black Africa, which is like a teaming basket. The desert warns the traveller that he is crossing the frontier of colours. At Gao or Lere, I often asked myself whether I was European or African. The anachronistic dreams of the men of the desert are truly romantic but hardly realistic in terms of democracy and integration. To be a European does not necessarily imply support for the Turaregs. I kept changing colour. There is a wonderful, beautiful, serious and biting book by the Dutch-Belgian author Lieve Joris entitled *Mali Blues et autres histoires* that must be read to understand that Mali was a kingdom without rival: the cream of West Africa.

Rwanda

The Great Lakes Region was familiar to me only from the map, and I thought that the great lakes were near Canada. I chose to go to Rwanda. The only thing I knew about pre-1994 Rwanda was its gorillas and the famous Swiss woman who for a long time has run a hotel in the form of a chalet at Umutara. It was a neat and tidy hotel with chequered curtains where she prepared *rösti* (a traditional Swiss dish of fried grated potatoes) for herds of tourists who came through there to observe wildlife. All this I had learned second hand. The tiny speck on the map called Rwanda, where the name of the country is always larger on the map than the country itself, represented

16

Equatorial Africa for me: black, deep and ancestral. It was neither high nor low on the map of Africa. It was as though my destiny was now dictating that I had at last begun to deal seriously with Africa; right in the middle of the Black continent. I wanted to confirm the reports of generations of development workers that Rwanda is a beautiful country, a real paradise. The mountains are high and soft with emerald hills always crowned with sun and a peaceful, light haze. The valleys are bright, filtering a violet or purple light at sunset. Even the vegetation is warm and generous, shining under the pearls of morning dew lingering on banana leaves while the ground is red or ochre. Rwandans living in rural areas are very welcoming and very kind in their gestures and their manner of being. Rwanda has raised the notion of paradox to its height.

Genocide as told to our children

In Rwanda, formerly innocent, poor and manipulated men assassinated other completely innocent men without any reason, futilely. They were made to believe that by doing this, they would have more space and more wealth. Several witnesses have spoken of the presence of the devil in Rwanda between April and July 1994 when about one million Tutsis and moderate Hutus were killed by machetes; much more efficient than the gas chambers of the Nazis. In order to carry out the plan fully and do the work correctly, the entire community was made to participate in the plan to exterminate the Tutsi people, called "the cockroaches" by some Hutus. And that is what was done: everyone was implicated.

Full participation of the killers was meant to bring out a feeling of collective and federative guilt, creating enduring ties among Hutus. From then on, every murderer had the death of others weighing on his conscious and knew that he was at the mercy of the law of revenge. He knew that one day it would be his turn or the turn of his children. He would never know when. That possibility haunted him to the point that he ended

17

up wanting to forget that he had murdered. It is a method of self-persuasion adopted by many prisoners in Rwanda. Most of them deny any participation. If it had been any other way, they would have killed themselves right away. That would be too unacceptable and that's why they declared their complete innocence; at any rate they had done nothing serious. In order to kill one million persons in three months, at least double that amount had to have participated physically. And that does not include the architects or minds behind the genocide, the final solution, who left the country for calmer shores just as everything was beginning. Nothing can ensure us that the wounds have healed and that the madness will not begin again. We just have to hope that it never reaches such big proportions. The militia charged with carrying out the genocide, the Interhamwe (literally those who work together), continues to operate across the border in the Congo.

A quick review of the geopolitics of Rwanda

Rwanda has an area of 27,000 square kilometres. It is a small country located just east of the Congo (which has seventy-two times the area of Rwanda), south of Uganda and to the west of Tanzania. Its relief is mainly mountainous, with an altitude above 3000 metres at the summits of the five volcanoes. The geography of Rwanda is different from that of the neighbouring countries of Kenya and Tanzania, which have endless plains that roll on for hundreds of kilometres and a flat horizon. Rwanda, the opposite of the rest of East Africa with its large savannahs and soft plateaux, is characterized by its volcanic region and its thousand hills. This small country is an enclave located more than 1500 kilometres from the coasts of the Indian Ocean. The closest ports are Mombasa in Kenya and Dar es Salaam in the United Republic of Tanzania. While the Congo is inhabited by more than 300 tribes, in comparison, Rwanda has a single tribe: the Banyarwanda. This tribe is traditionally divided into three ethnic groups: the Hutus (84 per cent of the population), who are the farmers; the Tutsis (15 per cent of the population), owners of the cattle; and the Twas, related to the Pygmies, who primarily do domestic work. This system of society was created long ago. There is no written record; tradition is oral.

Several epic stories told by storytellers make it possible to fix the origin of this tribe without certainty in the twelfth century or later. What is certain is that since the fifteenth century a kingdom governed by a monarch (*mwami*), always a Tutsi, held power. He had very little contact with the outside world and did not organize conquests or became involved in the slave traffic. At the time of the political division of Africa at the 1890 Conference of Berlin, the colonial powers gave Ruanda-Urundi to the Germans. In 1894, Count G. von Götzen was the first German officer to reach Rwanda. At the end of the First World War, the Germans lost their mandate and Rwanda became a Belgian protectorate. The Rwandan monarchy, formed by a king surrounded by a group of aristocrats, resembled the former European feudal system. The monarchy in Rwanda lasted until the end of the 1950s.

The chief resource of the Tutsis was cattle: zebus, a breed of cows with enormous pointed horns that were considered sacred. Formerly, the king had the largest herd. According to long and expressive epic poems told at the time of celebrations, the cows passed in front of the royal tribune and the wealth and prosperity of the monarch was measured by the amount of dust raised. Like in Hindu India, cows were sacred. Rwandans drank their milk and blood in order to gain virile strength, collecting the blood by making a ritual incision in the carotid as is done with sheep in Mali. The blood is then poured into a recipient washed with cow urine (an antiseptic). Men do this purification rite because women are not allowed to touch cows.

As in many regions of Africa, a conflict over land existed between two groups: those who raise cattle and the farmers. Rwanda, a small and mountainous country, became the scene of a war between those who lived from cattle raising and those who farmed the soil. There was no place for them to move to graze their cattle. Pasture became insufficient and encroached on the already reduced fields of the farmers. Confrontation inevitably took place.

Until the end of the 1950s, Belgium depended on the Tutsis to govern Rwanda as a protectorate. An ambitious educated class desired independence, and then Belgium changed tactics. It began to support the Hutus, reportedly more docile, more conciliatory. In 1959, an insurrection of anti-feudal small farmers marked a definitive break in Rwanda. It took the form of a social revolution. The Hutus took back power and land. Tens of thousands of Tutsis were massacred, and tens of thousands were forced to flee the country to Uganda, the Congo, Tanganyika or Europe.

In 1962, Rwanda became independent with a young Hutu journalist, Grégoire Kayibanda, as president. The Hutus felt they had defeated their masters, throwing off forever the feudal yoke and definitively conquering power and yet they knew that they had not totally eliminated them. They feared that surviving adversaries and their descendants would one day seek revenge. The fear of vengeance is dramatically rooted in the African mentality. Fear can often be an instrument of madness, as has been shown by the recent history of Rwanda. In Africa, the law of revenge is, as in Corsica or Sicily, immutable and transmissible from father to son. It is known that this deeply rooted fear, diabolically maintained by corrupt politicians, was manipulated and transformed into genocide. There was a permanent fear of seeing the king's children return. We know the next chapter.

Kayibanda was the first president from independence until the end of the 1970s. President Habyiarimana overthrew Kayibanda in 1975 and held power until his death in 1994. During that period, he created a tighter and tighter government. Extremists invented the mad idea of eliminating the Tutsi race and meticulously prepared the genocide. It was unleashed at the time when integration of refugees driven from their native land during more than thirty years would have become a reality. During that time, the Tutsis driven out of Rwanda in 1959 saw the reality of Rwanda from refugee camps. They were poor, humiliated and forgotten and led idle, desperate and miserable lives. There were about one million of them that no longer had herds to graze, the symbolical basis of their existence. Their dream of returning to Rwanda, coupled with the impossibility of receiving passports in their host countries haunted them. The hope of seeing their hills became an obsession.

This would come to pass in 1994. During the genocide in Rwanda, a blood bath took place, of which Africa and the world are ashamed. Troops of the Armée patriotique rwandaise (APR) entered their country from southern Uganda. The 1959 revolution had divided the Banyarwanda into two opposing camps. Time only reinforces the mechanisms of disagreement and exacerbates conflict. For years, fighting took place on the borders. Pogroms and massacres took place far from the eyes of the world but were quickly forgotten. Repeated and bloody clashes finally led to an apocalypse. It was never easy to live in Rwanda. The villages had mixed populations, and the two camps lived side by side, mixed with each other and sometimes worked together. A climate of suspicion was difficult to overcome. There were many religious sects. The tradition of clandestinity and secrecy was widely perpetuated. Only a world of modern development and a solid effort to promote reconciliation will allow slow change. Perhaps the wounds can be healed, but the human and social destruction has been enormous.

The trap of using an ethnic identity

To speak and think in ethnic categories is misleading and illusionary. Categories such as truth or lies and dictatorship or democracy wipe out true and deep-seated human

21

values. Categories superficially reduce reality to a single confrontation. Rwanda is now trying to break out of these categories. However, they still exist and not to mention them is not easier than using them. It is as if a person were to have all positive or negative qualities because he or she is a Hutu or Tutsi. You could be considered worthless if you were not one or the other. This is useless and dangerous. Racial categorization has led to catastrophes elsewhere. The lesson is to make ethnic identity not a weapon for division, but a positive differentiation. Society should be based on the force of personal character, not on ethnic identity.

Surrealistic images

In 1994, television showed horrible and unbearable scenes of the genocide and dense, ragged crowds pushing and shoving in the camps at Bukavu and Goma. From a distance, it was impossible to understand what was going on. In Europe, sitting in front of my television, I was aware of a drama that was beyond any political analysis and any understanding. The pictures were so horrible that they lost their ability to portray reality. But why show Rwandan Hutus on television fleeing towards camps where thousands of killers were hiding? Why didn't television show us something during the genocide? Then, it could have caused an uproar. Why did coverage begin only afterwards, when everything was over? The media explained much later what really took place, but no one wanted to listen to them. That's why Rwandans harbour no illusions today. Everyone clearly advocates "Never again", but there will be no one to come to their aid if the unthinkable were ever to begin again. At least that is what they think. Are they right?

Responsibility

Five years after the genocide, Rwanda is completely different, now moving towards normalization despite having been torn apart. Before, it was a very peaceful place. Because everyone tried to make a big effort to explain to me that this was a paradise that became hell, I was confronted with a completely religious dichotomy and wanted to go there. To make amends? Above all, I wanted to see what was the work of God and what was the work of evil in this tiny corner of the world. And to understand. Very quickly, I became wary of the European's good conscious, the desire to want to help. I thought that to want to help could not be a valid reason. After the genocide, how can one correct what had already been committed? Only the question of the present is pertinent.

The question of guilt should be distinguished from that of responsibility. The words of Georgina Dufoix, former Secretary of State for Health in France, came to mind. It was a question of blood transfusions that had not been checked and that carried the HIV virus to blood-transfusion recipients. "Guilty? No!" "Responsible? Yes!" It was perhaps the beginning of a new attitude. I refused to go to Rwanda to whimper a false guilt. After all, I told myself, I wasn't there in 1994 and it was not me who killed people. They killed each other. The guilty are found among the killers. Even if there existed a whole chain of cause and effect, shared responsibility is a completely different chapter. I agreed to go to Rwanda because I felt that I shared responsibility in the sense that I was part of the international community, including those who had never been there, in the name of a universal chain of cause and effect. What finally made the big difference was to know that there were people in Rwanda, thousands of Rwandans, who had succeeded in putting their lives back together. They had tried to bury their dead and had the courage to confront reality. They were back together, for better or worse, and rolled up their sleeves to begin again to want to live and coexist. In Rwanda, I discovered another Africa located in the middle of the continent, land-locked, full of hills covered with forests and banana groves: there where absolute evil took hold of local spirits. Evil became justified, reverting all values, and was accepted in order to obtain what was supposed to be good: elimination of a race of people. Rwanda was a country where nothing could be said for many years, and all this was hidden behind an image of paradise. The subjugated small farmer had the right to plough his miniscule field peacefully, while more than one million Rwandan Tutsis fled to other countries. The Tutsis remaining in Rwanda were constantly harassed and did not have the right to study at the university or hold key posts. Their houses were systematically burned, and then they were killed.

The freedom to choose God

Immediately, I was confronted with a question of religion: Catholicism, Protestantism, Christianity, Islam, and animism, all religions that had so carefully and patiently worked to provide an education to all the population during more than thirty years, especially to the Hutu small farmer. The Hutus were the majority of Rwandans and those who quietly and piously went to Mass every Sunday dressed in multi-coloured cotton clothes. They dressed in clean and ironed clothes although they lived in shacks without a latrine. They went to church smiling flabbergastedly at the sermon of a priest who spoke to them about the love of God. It was a place where everything was all right although from the beginning of the 1980s they were also preparing the genocide. God was strangely silent in April 1994, granting complete liberty, including that of killing each other. In order to embrace this human liberty gained at such a cost, a whole region turned its back on God. Is Rwanda proof that a choice is given to man not to embrace God; even if there is a price to pay; even in a Christian country? Paradoxically, to spend four years in Rwanda is to rediscover faith and, for me, proof of the existence of a superior being, precisely despite the genocide; thanks to those who resisted this deluge; thanks to those who heroically fought against the rolling catastrophe. They were many, and history will never speak of them. Against all expectations, they do not dare speak of their acts of heroism, as if today they were still subject to human nature and to the orders that they had received. Recording history is always a question of reducing things to the essence. But the story of ordinary people and heroes in Rwanda who helped and sheltered those fleeing the genocide, risking their own lives, and that of the survivors and those who fled has still not been written. A history of acts of solidarity in 1994 exists. It is touching and disarming. For the people of Rwanda, the consequences of this tragedy are not measurable because they defy reason. Everything in their life is temporary, changing and precarious. Everything reflects only survival. Everything is subject to defiance. When something exists, they ask themselves for how long.

The genocide has left a violent taste of absurdity, anguish and uncertainty. Rwandans continue to feel threatened whatever their ethnical identity or personal experience in 1994. They are constantly frightened: frightened by a rent they cannot pay, by an increase in the price of rice or transportation, by an epidemic of malaria, by AIDS, arrests, the army, politics. Right or wrong, the vulnerability of the general population runs very deep. It is even more disturbing in several rural and distant regions where people were steeped for many years in a paranoiac universe criss-crossed by obsessing prejudices and ethnic aversions.

Ethnic hatred is also found in other African countries, but never on this scale, never to the extent of the horror that they now have after transgressing the worst of taboos: that of a plan to exterminate an African race. Often, rivalry among clans is the fiercest. Sometimes, rivalry is more cruel and intense within a single race, among women with the same skin colour and the same culture than conflicts between Europeans and Africans. In Rwanda, no one living on the hills ever asks himself whether a neighbour is wise, kind or evil. On the other hand, a question is immediately asked about a person's clan and his background. Where was he in 1994? He will be classified on the basis of his home hill and the background of his family: tacitly, but imperatively. This reality was very new to me.

The role of the cow in Rwandan society

Among the major remaining vivid symbols of Rwanda is the cow, and many people are still quite attached to it. For those who primarily raise cattle, cows remain their greatest treasure. A cow not only is a sign of wealth but also has mystic virtues. Its existence and presence link man to a higher and invisible universe. Both cow's milk and its blood are drunk. There is an indestructible link between animal and man. Every cow has a name, a personality and a character that its owner observes and knows. The highest compliment that can be made to a woman is that of comparing her eyes to those of a favourite cow. Even Rwandan dancers imitate the horns of cows, representing their strength. Cows also constitute the most important part of a dowry, just like a camel is offered to the parents of a young woman in other African countries.

Inner exile

I became acquainted with an Africa, that of the Great Lakes Region, where relationships are radical and dried up. The lakes are locked in a heavy chaos of metal and smell of corpses. In Rwanda, it is best to keep a good distance from an attitude of piety. Emotions and feelings are best kept for another planet. Rwandans often make fun of Europeans' melancholy moods and often have a painful look on their faces, but they look you straight in the eye. They will constantly remind you that on D-day there was no one to help them. There is also a hidden face of Rwanda; that of the vague reproach. You have the impression that that inexcusable abandon is always present in each conversation. It is true that the abandon was cowardly and difficult to reverse. Jean-Claude Guillebaud and the photographer Raymond Depardon wrote a very beautiful book describing their travels through the Horn of Africa and Abyssinia. They described how at times, wherever you are, something like a feeling of exile takes hold of you, sometimes like an invisible pain.

The new catechisms

Talking about God, I slowly realized that the humanitarian jargon can sometimes reflect a new end-of-the-century "good conscious". In a certain way, a vocabulary has replaced former catechisms and has been taken up by all participants in the development game as proof of their sincerity. If their humanitarian zeal is questioned, they are shocked. The terms "participation" and "partnership" have lost meaning and are often used with bad intentions. They are used to prevent questions being raised about real problems. There are often clashes between donors and recipients, who explain how the money must be spent in the best interests of the beneficiaries and the recipients who must administer them in their so-called common best interests. Donors are sometimes faced with great disparities of equity and seek more solidarity among their partners. They are very surprised that corruption exists and that poverty does not necessarily foment solidarity among beneficiaries. It's still a myth that must be erased.

Focusing

In Rwanda, April 7th is the day of commemoration of the genocide. In 1998, four years after the massacre, I was faced with this suspended time. I saw decomposing corpses excavated from common graves, reflecting the violence of a society that has had so much difficulty wishing itself well. Is there anywhere on earth where there is a still a bit of clemency or charity? But the word "charity" grates. Why is it used condescendingly with a touch of neo-colonialism? What right do we have to write about it? How do we dare study solidarity among peoples in the Great Lakes Region at a time when there are constant outbreaks of hatred? By observing too much, you can quickly go out of focus if you are not careful. Maintaining a clear and compassionate eye but critical discourse was my way to deal with a world filled with violence for which no schoolbook ever prepared me. For little things, however, I lived the ambiguity of anger and wonderment. Life always goes on after a tragedy, just like the grass that grows in cracks in concrete. A trend toward normalization has become apparent in Rwanda. But under the surface, a threatening fire has often burned. I had to re-learn to look at Africa in a different light by being the object of senseless hatred for Europeans. I sometimes felt rejected but, nonetheless, maintained the position that Rwanda had an obligation to undertake once again a difficult task; that of adopting structural adjustment measures and repaying debt. The task is doubly difficult because the debt is inherited from the disgraced previous regime. In Rwanda, chaos cancelled out the advances of modernization. Now, everything must be undertaken again, and tradition is often left in the gutter.

Roots

Rwanda is looking for its roots; its real roots. Is it because a whole family gives the newborn child its first name that there are still traditions? Is it their language, which is so very difficult and spoken on several semantic levels? The national language is poorly spoken by returning refugees because it was spoken on the sly during their period in exile. Is the act of taking an ember to a neighbour to start a fire in the morning a sign of true peace? Roots can be found only with the help of mechanisms of reconciliation in an integrated manner. Wars often contribute to fragmentation of a national identity. Wars are deadly for cultural identity and ring like so many bells of the traditions that could be healing.

Life at midnight on the hills

Who really knows anything about daily family life in Rwanda? What is known about the tensions among children and widows suddenly promoted to the head of families in the large sense, having welcomed into their clan all the survivors scattered around the country? How does daily life take place on the hills? Is it only the search for food for survival? No. There are still many living traditions that Rwandans hang on to.

In 1999, an international development specialist, Peter Uvin, stated in his excellent book about structural violence and public development assistance that formerly nothing was known about what was happening at midnight on the hills, but now, we are certain that we know nothing about life at midnight in the land of a thousand hills. Is that progress? It at least reflects the awareness that signs can be deceiving. I learned to interpret the euphemisms that appear in official speeches taken from all sorts of expressions of modernity: "poverty alleviation", "participation" and "democracy". This is a sort of verbal rhetoric that masks mechanisms of galloping corruption, which are difficult to stop. Differences in distribution of wealth have become alarming. Close supervision of the construction of a road, for example, becomes a difficult undertaking. The flow of humanitarian funds does not always have long-term effects. Furthermore, the real causes of the drama are difficult to detect. Structural distortions are constantly and endlessly grafted onto conjunctural problems. These cycles leave traces for a long time. Under this apparent existing order, however, there are precise ordered systems: those of improvised and recycled codes. I was able to observe the inflexible discretion that Rwandans know how to wear in order to confront the waves of misfortune, just like wearing a fur coat. I also discovered the relative degree of personal drama experienced, like a discrete and modest drop of water in an ocean of tears. Life starts out again on its course and despite the incredible imbroglio of relations reinvented among people. Day-to-day normality seems to recover its place. This is beneficial and helpful, at least on the surface. In Rwanda, you take relish in incredible simple daily things like the crowing of a cock, the meowing of a wild cat, the strong song of a bluish bird of paradise or the taste of a dish of manioc because of the genocide. For everyone, it is a new lesson about life. It is even more precious because it takes an effort to experience.

Rwanda taught me that reality is neither that which is seen nor that which can be understood, but the patient reconstruction of a puzzle formed by a thousand vague daily impressions on the screen of our imagination. Reality is made up of the looks and gestures of people who feel different but who are, nonetheless, very similar. Out of tradition and custom, they go to great lengths to hide what they really feel. They are the first silent and obstinate victims. Because of this, news, rumours and information are always both true and false. The question is to know how to form a clear and coherent idea of a country where culture works hard to cover the trail.

Reading between the lines

I had to create a whole new system of relationships and communication techniques by developing a sharp sense for nuances, details and intonation. I had to make an effort to understand what, despite clever efforts to sow confusion, might reveal a true thought. Rwandans practice a very interesting type of communication, at several levels and with the possibility of several interpretations. But communication is opaque, always opaque. I can recall having asked a Rwandan one day whether he preferred coffee or tea. After beginning to describe the benefits of coffee, he answered that tea was also good around five o'clock, but which was best depended. It was impossible to learn more about his preference. Rwandans force us, we Westerners impatient to jump to quick conclusions based on an assumption, to listen closely to what is not said. Above all, my stay in Rwanda considerably trained my ears. It taught me that something can be both true and false at the same time. Communication in Rwanda made me question my Cartesian approach. It changed my way of relating to other people.

Chapter 2

A Quick Look at Four Years of Working in Rwanda

During my four years working in Rwanda, I experienced many aspects of daily life quite different from what I was used to. This chapter attempts to give an insight into Rwandan character gained through my daily experiences.

My first visit to Kibuye

Just after the Runda roundabout in the centre of Kigali, there is the bus station. All the minibuses were waiting, bursting with both patient and exuberant passengers, too numerous, hanging out the windows and off the bumpers while other passengers waited. They piled in on top of each other as if it were the last bus to leave; a question of going somewhere together. The wait could sometimes be long. To travel by mini bus has a lot of meaning in Rwanda, a real suspension of time. That morning, Christmas Eve, the rhythm was very African. Time goes by, cowardly, openly, subjectively and flexibly, leaving an impression that time can be created only by man through an event; the sudden taking to life of something under our influence only when something happened. Time can, however, enter into hibernation, dark in eternity, if no event occurs.

Passengers were waiting for a bus to leave the capital. The first passengers sat down in the bus without asking when it was leaving. They entered, found a free place and fell into a deep sleep. They were waiting for time to begin moving again. They installed themselves as comfortably as possible, started to think, daydreamed or watched the bus fill slowly. One of the minibuses had only twelve seats but there were already thirty passengers. Inside, the welding used to keep the windows closed had rusted, the seats were all torn and were held in place by the passengers' weight. When someone left the bus, everyone shifted seats and a few fell on the floor like on a seesaw. If a passenger wanted to get off, everyone had to step off the bus in order to let him out. After two hours of waiting, the driver of the overcrowded bus started its engine. Bounced by the potholes, the passengers came back to life. One reached for a biscuit, another pealed a banana. The driver didn't stop talking; he looked as much back as in front. With one hand he held the steering wheel and used the other to gesticulate. Some passengers were already wiping perspiration caused by fear from their faces with a small serviette. Others decided to laugh about it and began to joke. A baby began to cry. There wasn't a drop of air circulating. The passengers were, nonetheless, happy. Usually, they had to walk barefooted kilometres and kilometres up and down hills carrying kilos of goods on their heads and sacks on their backs filled to the brim. That day, they were traveling by bus like the well-off.

Soon other minibuses would also be tearing off, screeching their unbelievably used tires and shaking on makeshift springs. They were taking their passengers to the four corners of Rwanda: towards Byumba, Ruhengeri, Kibungo or the Tanzanian border. In Rwanda, minibuses are real moving dangers. They cross through farm areas and towns at full speed going over the centre lines on the curves and giving no opportunity to cars wanting to overtake them. The minibus we were following was going in the direction of the town of Gitarama, a hard and harsh crossroads, a garrison and strategic town. We were following the minibus at a respectable distance towards the southern part of Rwanda, towards Kibuye and had to pass through Gitarama. Near the Ruliba brick factory, the route begins to wind slowly. After the brick factory, a creaking wooden bridge came into view. It was a fragile structure, which I had always crossed with reluctance. It announces the exit from Kigali across the sadly famous Nyabarongo River, which flows into the Kagera River and then Lake Victoria. Its waters can be considered the source of the Nile River. It is always filled with mud and floating vegetation, sometimes carrying a floating mass of white and green foam, as if it wanted to imitate the large Victoria Falls in Zimbabwe or Murchison Falls in Uganda. But here, we were really in Rwanda, where the Nile has only a distant importance.

Flying along, our car crossed the bridge quickly as if it wanted to forget that the river had also carried corpses in 1994, not so long ago. In 1994, this river, like so many others, was swollen with bloated flabby and misshaped corpses in an absurd way. They were. The proverb, "A lot of water will pass under the bridge, before that happens" can be taken literally for the Nyabarongo River. Water does flow under the bridge, and four years have passed. The bodies have left for the Nile. Events that have become memories still hit us persistently. Every time I cross this bridge, I shiver. This feeling is always echoed for an instant by a fleeting landscape, a slight smell or a sudden burst of warm wind. Crossing through a small village on the edge of town, I caught a glimpse of a bullet hole on an abandoned house, a collapsed roof, a sad and furtive gesture of a young girl with a pail of water on her head, her hair tussled by the effort of suddenly turning towards us. Her surprised look was fixed within me until the end of the journey.

I feel the incredible physical softness of this landscape, which insolently takes hold of the sadness created by the genocide. I was almost invaded by a diaphanous light, with a halo of hazy permanent fog that wanted to hide thousands of shades of green: bottle green, moss green, the silver green of the eucalyptus or the bluish green of the avocado trees. You could also see other greens: one that is more brownish, that of the upper branches of coffee trees or the soft streaked yellow green of the bark of the trunks of the banana trees. Nature breaks out in a state of madness, in an exaltation of proliferation. There is an overwhelming abundance of green vegetation in constant and exuberant eruption. Trees, bushes, lianas, pines and oaks reflect the altitude of more than one thousand metres that creates a temperate climate. But there is an internal order, a clarity where each biological species, close-knit and clinging to the side of the hill, has to grow together in order not to slide away. This inextricably interrelated and intertwined nature should inspire man, I tell myself while looking at these natural wonders. At any rate, it is a living reaction to the madness of the 1994 hecatomb.

Towards the top of every hill, there is a promise of another palette of shades of colour, which will disappear in the next descent. My eyes feasted on this mixture of the colour of dirt, the shades of green and this sky where a few clouds always pass. Cumulus clouds are dreamers. We were moving along with our noses in the wind at high speed towards Kibuye on Christmas Eve because I wanted to leave Kigali for Christmas and spend it with friends in Kibuye. I felt I had to leave the heavy atmosphere and harsh rumours of Kigali behind me. I had the impression that multi-armed pressures were sometimes trying to strangle me. From time to time, I have to get away; leave, breath and see something green. Nonetheless, I never leave without Prosper.

Prosper, a well-deserved name

Traveling with my driver, Prosper, was a constant promise of adventure. Every time he could take to the road, his eyes screwed up with cunningness, and he threw himself into the task as if it were a highly important mission. He wanted to show me everything about his country and would not renounce driving me to the far corners of Rwanda for anything in the world. For him, every trip was a gift from him to me. We probably visited every part of Rwanda. From the nooks and crannies of rural Kigali to Gisenyi on the edge of the lake, Umutara and Gahini. In my eyes, Prosper had almost all possible positive qualities: he is handsome, tall, wiry, clever as a monkey, intelligent, has several professions behind him, is handy with his hands, inventive, and is always in good humour. He had already effortlessly saved me from several comical situations with a simple snap of his fingers. He goes with me

35

everywhere, briefly explains what we have come to do whenever there are inquisitive policemen and adopts an Olympian calm when there is an obstacle.

During my four years in Rwanda, Prosper was my real bodyguard. He opened my eyes, cleared my ears and gave me advice during my talks on the hills. Translation was always necessary, and he did an excellent job. Sometimes, he was honest enough to say, "I don't want to translate that. It's no good," as if he were protecting his people, my opinion or my ears. But nonetheless, he translated the overall sense. When Prosper set out in the Toyota, it was a bit like he was transporting something precious. Straight as a ramrod, almost touching the roof of the car, he was convinced of his mission. While he was at the wheel of the car, Prosper commented about the news on the official radio and bravely gave his opinion on the real situation in the country. He expressed himself freely on expectations and hopes.

His family had left Rwanda for Burundi in 1963. In Bujumbura, the capital of Burundi, Prosper studied "humanities", as his puts it, and then became a small merchant. During the genocide in Rwanda, he lost three-quarters of his family that had stayed in Rwanda. He had met his wife in school in Burundi, and she came from the same hill as he in Rwanda. She lost all her family: twenty-four aunts and uncles. When they returned to Rwanda at the end of 1994, they began, as many other refugees, to roll up their sleeves. Prosper tried his luck at all sorts of small jobs and became a driver. Like most Rwandans, he is responsible, in addition to his wife and two children, for more than ten members of his distant family, including five children that survived. Among the many Rwandans that I met, he is rare in not wanting four children for himself in accordance with tradition. He wants to give a chance to his own two children and to his five adopted children and offer all of them equitably an education. In summary, Prosper ended up being my protector and an inexhaustible source of information and smiles. He often said that he had full interest in explaining and showing me everything about Rwanda, the things that were visible and the things that were hidden, so that I could understand and bring the help they needed. I was very wary at the beginning and checked everything he said. He never lied to me. Because he knew that I had a weakness for grilled sweet corn, we often drove through small villages from top to bottom looking for a small vendor. Often, it was our only midday meal. At the end of my stay as we drove back, he answered questions that I was going to ask but had not yet asked. He knew when I had a doubt or when I became angry about a problem. During all that time, he gave me a wonderful present: rich travels inside the history of his country and also inside his mind. When I first arrived in Rwanda, I had wanted to understand the slightest nuances of his people, both secret and ravaged. I wanted to understand fully in order to take sound decisions regarding each of his countrymen and, he often added, to distinguish truth from lies. Prosper dreamed about reopening cinemas in Kigali, "just like before". There we were on the road to Gitarama, beyond the bridge over the Nyabarongo, behind an overcrowded minibus.

Prosper is impressively calm. He tells thousands of jokes. Just to watch him drive is an impressive spectacle itself. He sweeps his steel-coloured eyes, just like howling spotlights, over the surroundings in a sweep of one hundred and eighty degrees. To the right, he describes a market scene, adding comments about what is being sold, the price of a kilo of rice and the quality of used clothing being sold. To the left of the road, he indicates a place called Nkurunziza, which means the place where cattle are guarded. Straight in front of us on the road he points out typical local trees under which sages come to prey to the god Imana (in Banyarwanda mythology Imana was the creator and supporter of all Banyarwanda people). The overcrowded minibus in front of us is called "En catastrophe". It had stopped on the uphill climb coming out of Kigali. Prosper patiently waits for his turn behind the minibus.

The minibus sputtered; the tightly packed heads of the perspiring passengers were all looking at the Toyota, as if a real battle were going to take place. The driver of the minibus calmly waited about ten minutes and then nonchalantly stuck his arm out the window and made a sign for us to pass him. A real first, if there ever was one. We turned around and made a small sign of thanks. All the passengers laughed. Prosper carefully passed his long and agile fingers over the gearshift. His skilful driving took me to Kibuye, where the Swiss have traditionally celebrated Christmas for many, many years. It is a chance to renew friendships, to look back with a bit of nostalgia. There is also another reason why I chose Kibuye. It is located in the extreme western part of the country, a small town that was isolated from the rest of the country on the edge of Lake Kivu for a long time, located among the volcanic rocks, a real jewel of paradise on earth. Just one visit to this place will haunt you for the rest of your life. Lake Kivu calls to you, and its metallic hardness catches hold of you. Its reflection draws you in, like the reflection of Narcissus. Neither your senses nor your memory come out intact. Like most visitors to this place, I am captivated by this lake and this town.

After Gitarama and another good hour of travelling, we took the road to western Rwanda. A road that once was just a track. Recently, the road was paved and now resembles a smooth carpet. It crosses granite plateaux and abrupt valleys, running through rust-coloured rocks, turned that colour by sulphate. To the right, there is a drop-off. Maize and sorghum are grown on terraced slopes. How do the farmers sow and harvest on such inhospitable slopes? The road goes on and on, approaching villages and markets filled with fresh vegetables and nonchalant women. Anyway, you have to be a real expert to find your way through the steep paths. You can catch your clothing on thorns and branches that scratch and cut. Sometimes, you can see an old man carrying a stick on which he leans and sweeps the path, frightening away snakes with his steps and his stick. We climbed up the hills of Gitesi, Kivumu, Mabanza and Muchubati in a long caravan behind other vehicles.

We were travelling along threatening, inhospitable and strikingly beautiful canyons. Along the road that winds dangerously, we saw cleared fields on wooded hills where there are often landslides during the rainy season. We drove pass people in their Sunday best who were coming out of church or walking to visit neighbouring families, scrambling up the hills like cats. I realized that the colours of their clothes are less flamboyant than elsewhere in Africa. But the *pagnes* are worn by the women with a care and conscious attention that refuses to recognize their real poverty and repulses any pity.

Near Mabanza, we passed another overcrowded minibus coming from Kibuye. It had stopped on the roadside but blocked the whole road. We turned off the engine and waited. All the passengers got out to let out a woman who was sitting at the back of the bus. She was wearing a green and yellow *pagne* and a scarf of the same colour on her head. She carefully and slowly got off the bus with her two children. A bit farther along, she bent down, grabbed the smallest child and heaved him onto her back and wrapped him tightly with a piece of cloth. The child continued to sleep. Then she squatted down, placed a small crown of straw on her head and picked up the omnipresent metal basin (made in China) full of red, white and green food. She made a precise movement, like an acrobat, sending the basin to the top of her head, then stood up and caught her balance with a little circular movement. The basin was wedged on top of her head, the baby hanging from her back still asleep. She took a step, gracefully caught her second child, who had begun to skip, by the wrist and set off downhill. Everyone watched her apprehensively. With regular and harmonious steps despite the steep slope, she went down the path majestically, light as a deer. Then she disappeared.

In Rwanda, houses are scattered about and hidden under banana trees. They are connected to each other by a maze of paths among plentiful vegetation, invisible to the untrained eye. You have to live in a village to know the true topography of the paths where the crossings are as secret as they are many. This form of dispersed habitat is not propitious to mixing and does not make meeting between clans easy. But the families want it this way because most of the time their ancestors are buried nearby in the garden, providing a reassuring presence. On the hills, belief in the spirits of the ancestors, their protective power, and their help is as alive in Rwanda as throughout Africa. Ancestors are consulted and often represent the hidden or sacred face of a decision. Rwanda is one of the poorest countries in sub-Saharan Africa. Three-quarters of the population live in rural areas. There is only one meal a day, in the evening. During the dry season, people sometimes eat only once every two days. When the family has an income, there is tea at breakfast, a piece of flat bread with an omelette and often *matoke* (a mixture of mashed green bananas with sugar cane). But everyone keeps good spirits. Each person contributes her share and accepts his fate. Although poor, the rural population is determined: there is no place for division, everyone seems to say, absorbed in deep thought and the struggle for survival. This ethnic division, so very fatal for the country, can it really be overcome with just a wave of a magic wand? No. It will require at least a generation. In the meantime, they are moving forward in order to eat and have a roof over their heads. However, there is a hidden family drama behind each face; each look reflects a horror scene.

The minibus started up again on a clear road towards Kibuye with thirty-eight passengers crowded into the back. All along the way, I saw a thick crowd on both sides of the road quietly going about their daily activities. Like a river that flows silently, ordered, well regulated, muffled, occupying every bit of space of such a difficult and tiny geography. Silence is sometimes a worrying factor in Rwanda. By observing the deliberate and slow movements of these people moving towards a small square of hope, I suddenly understood how dense the population is and how small Rwanda is. The pressure to use all arable land is a hard reality about which I suddenly became conscious. Then, after a good hour of right-angle curves and at the top of a hill, the horizon opens onto a body of water. It's a mirage, a startling sight, an opening on the world; a bit like Halong Bay in Vietnam.

Prosper stopped, fixed in awe, struck by the beauty. This is Lake Kivu, spread out like a moiré ribbon at the foot of the Ruwenzori Mountains. It is scattered with tiny islands that dot the surface of the water like a leopard skin. This enormous body of water open to the sky offers a remarkable spectacle. It is the result of the spewing out of ancient volcanoes. The earth, I tell myself, has been subjected to the flames of the past and the pouring out of aggressive lava, which left a landscape of prolific green vegetation in places. These are resources that we no longer know how to appreciate given their involvement in terrible ethnic wars. "Bitter beauty that my eyes do not know where to hide", once wrote a friend who is a poet. His words come back to me from far away. I barely heard Prosper's call as he carefully climbed into the car. The engine's purring was a noise hidden in the back of my mind. I hurried to climb in, my head filled with images of lava and persons from this magical place. I thought of Pompeii in Italy, petrified by a day of lava, where one lovely morning everything stopped because of a capricious Vesuvius.

The car accelerated, startling me out of my daydream. I said nothing and then suddenly because I am so happy and sad at the same time, I broke out in laughter, almost cosmic, and then Prosper started laughing, his laugh spreading out in exocentric circles onto the still sleeping shores of the lake, cutting through the enormous and invading pressure of the metal on the water. I have always considered laughter to be precious dynamite, an exit for an overflow of sensations. A real touch of humour often saves face in tragic situations. There were still two more big curves after that hill, and then we entered Kibuye. Every time I go there, Kibuye calls me, as if I were re-living an impression of déjà vu in a dream. But it is with a tuck in my heart that I always take this last curve just before reaching the lake, struck by thoughts of everything that we have not been able to prevent. It's here that the genocide really affected and decimated the population. There is a market at the entrance to this teaming little town on the edge of the lake, facing the shores of the Congo. There are all sorts of nationalities: Congolese coming to sell a variety of second-hand things. Rwandans sell their farm produce: exchanging beans and flowers for an iron or eggbeater. The market blends in with the lake. I can imagine it continuing on the other side of the lake. It spreads out the same smells, lively colours, ruby-red, incandescent violet, midnight blue, which only Africa knows how to combine with good taste and joy. Just under the hedge of bushes above the road indicating the beginning of the town stands the Saint Jean church. It was constructed from grey stone with a steeple. The windows have been broken. It is the first building at the entrance to the town and also the building that stands out. You can feel the ground shrink away. The air is still crying out with pain. The church has become a memorial to the genocide, and masses are no longer held there. Did the killing of approximately 14,200 persons really happen here on 17 April 1994 as a commemorative plaque states? In front of the church, there is a makeshift graveyard with stone-covered ground. At its centre is a Christ on a cross; silent.

We took the road along the lake, crossed the main road, went pass the Kibuye hospital and turned left down towards a small group of houses. I could see the *Maison des Suisses* coming into view at the edge of the lake where my friends were waiting for me. Prosper's face was shining like the silvery lake. He had delivered his precious cargo safe and sound. I took the steering wheel, and we glanced at each other without really looking. "Will you be able to find a ride back to Kigali?" I asked with a slight bit of concern. "No problem. There is always a bus, even if there is no schedule," he replied. I took him to the bus station just as an overcrowded bus was coming out of the parking lot. Prosper called out and the doors opened, revealing not an inch of space. Prosper jumped on to the running-board and began to talk with the driver. What a relief. He didn't have to wait long. He would be with his family for Christmas Eve. And just before disappearing into the bus already moving off, Prosper turned to wish me a Happy Christmas and asked whether I would be able to find my way back to the house and then to Kigali. Was he joking? The house was just two streets away, and there were signs pointing to Kigali every two metres. I nodded yes, very touched in the end that someone was trying to take care of me like that. He disappeared into the crowd of African heads and left to join his family. His long and tall shape all bunched up in order to enter the crowded minibus already leaning to the side even before setting off will remain a long time in my memory, and then I entered, or rather I disappeared into, the house on the shore of the lake.

A "lake of methane"

The welcome was very warm. They had been waiting for me since early in the morning. The long table was set outdoors for more than twenty persons with a view over the lake and the islands. Red candles decorated the white tablecloth. The simple single-story building has several bedrooms. It opens onto a large garden that descends a small slope to a small area of pebbles and the water. I rushed over to wade in the lake, where the temperature was just right. I'd have to go for a swim a bit later, I told myself. In the afternoon, a group of friends left for a boat trip on the lake with a boat with an outboard motor. For me, the lake is as important as yeast is for bread. It's like breathing in infinity. We sang wildly and splashed each other. Then, I began to contemplate the lake, and I found myself thinking about these months spent in Rwanda, looking for an answer to the simple question of why. Why did all these events happen here in Rwanda? Why a genocide?

43

Why was Kibuye one of the important centres of resistance, on Karongi Hill, on Bisesero Hill, but also the scene of the cruellest barbarism in the communes of Gishita and Rwamatamu?

The lake carefully keeps its secret. It also carried thousands of corpses and can't wash that fact away like the Nyabarongo River. There are dark and silvery reflections, like a layer of lead, refusing to serve as a refuge and life-source for fish and algae. This lake no longer wants to act as the origin of the marine world. It wants to provide only methane gas, making any boat trip hard and metallic. It lets only the toughest of insects into its waters. The cormorants along the shores search carefully for food. It's not the crocodiles that they are afraid of, but a sort of black hole, which seems to spin down to the centre of the earth. I spent a long time projecting my cares into this troubled water, and then my friends called me back to life. The boat roared, and we jumped out into the water near the shore. In the garden, friends were already busy preparing a barbecue, salads, hors-d'oeuvres, imported and local cheeses, as well as delicious desserts filled with chocolate. I joined in the preparations.

We sat down at the table just at dusk. Near the Equator, the sun sets all of a sudden abruptly going down like a theatre curtain at six thirty. There were still a few rays of sunshine that I savoured. We took time to sip well-prepared cocktails and enjoy the good company and the beauty of nature. Suddenly, Jean-Benoît decided to bring out a wonderful gift: we opened several bottles of sparkling wine one after the other. It was Christmas, and we are at the end of the world: about twenty Belgians, Swiss, Rwandans and Hindus, a wild assortment. Jean-Marc and Martin brought me back to reality. And what about dinner? We had to go for plates and serviettes. Now the night had become dark, and we walked around the garden in candlelight. Constance, Juliette and I brought out steaming plates of food from the kitchen. The tournedos Rossini were ready, and the pâté de foie gras was carefully placed in the middle of the serving plate. The barbecue was joyfully crackling away.

It was Christmas Eve, and I felt lost in time. Through the lapping of the water, I heard a troubling and strangled cry across the waters. Despite the uneasy feeling that griped me from being so close to a so-inhospitable and inexpressive lake, the surrounding landscape with its shrub-covered islands and the raw-coloured volcanoes winked at me. One of the volcanoes is called Napoleon's hat. It is thought to have the power to calm the spirits. Do the trees, bushes and rocks have a memory? Do they know how to feel suffering or do they just pretend to be indifferent? That evening, for the first time in since several months, I relaxed with pleasure. Young Vincent began to sing a blues song. The chords of his guitar bounced off the small waves of the lake and made our thoughts mellow. I also heard another concert, lively, just as lively: that of the locusts. Their melodious grating created a soft and smooth background to our friend's singing. I let myself relax into this happiness. The evening was a wonderful, simple pleasure for us; that of being together at Kibuye for just a moment. "And if we completely relaxed in just one big sight?, whispered Martin just as we began to eat. He slapped me on the back. "Let's live it up."

He was right. Sometimes you just have to sit back and enjoy life, enjoy being alive and able to experience happiness. Even if the lake whispered to us that we did not have the right to drop everything including the lake and all its mysteries. One day we would have to go and explore its depths to learn a bit more; but not today, Christmas. On a distant hill, you could hear the religious chants of children preparing for Christmas mass. We had made a promise to go to that hill to pray with them and reunite our split souls.

My stay in Rwanda was a bit like those troubled waters. I never knew whether to interpret the signs positively or negatively. That's the big secret of these people in a country of eight million inhabitants. They reveal only a small part of their secrets. They are fighting to regain an identity and are moving towards a sort of reconciliation. You have to combine suffering, cling to hope and joy—in the present and the future—in order to live in Rwanda. Inevitably, visitors always asked me the question, "How is Rwanda doing?" It's that question that everyone would like to be able to answer. There are two answers. If it were a question of quickly giving an opinion, you could say conclusively "Everything is alright and all wrong at the same time." What is daily life like in Rwanda after such a tragedy?

The next day, the sun tickled my nose from the first minutes of sunrise. The lake was calm, and I decided to go to mass. There was a collective, ecumenical ceremony on a hill where more than one thousand persons were gathered. Children ran about on the grass. Nuns began to chant songs. It was December 25th at Kibuye. Mass lasted for more than two hours. It was given in Kinyarwanda, and everyone found a moment of inner peace. Several government officials invited me to have lunch with them. There were quite a few of us, and the mood was relaxed. We ate goat meat on brochettes.

In the afternoon, I set out towards Kigali on an empty road. It was a wonderful moment, a good time to return home. The weather was warm and shining. Everyone waved as I passed. The valleys gave me a deep feeling of happiness at being then and there, sharing the concerns and problems of this country. The road continued to wind up and down hills. I dared to think that with every passing moment we were gaining just a bit of time, moving closer to the work of God and not that of evil. The beautiful shades of green make you think of hope. Memories of stories of reconciliation and solidarity began to cover over the indelible images of the massacres. Rwanda belongs to the Rwandans. They have to make it grow. And perhaps Kibuye and its mystery tied to the peaceful lake and the past will help them. It was on the shores of opaque and metallic Lake Kivu, reflecting the heat and the horrors of the past, reflecting the madness of men like the beauty of the sun, that I took the decision to write about the four years I spent in Rwanda. This lake served as the pump-primer, as if it had whispered to me that I could not leave all my impressions welled-up inside.

On the way back on the road from Kibuye, the lake was inscribed in my eyes, and the waves in the water were like so many tears formed in my memory. I was going to take my diary and tell the story about what I experienced in this so generous and cruel country. I decided to write about my impressions since my arrival in 1998. Although the diary and narration would cover June 1998 to December 2000, I spent a total of four years in Rwanda. At Christmas 2000, I decided to try to explain candidly my experiences because I had met so many wonderful people, madmen and wise men, the good and the bad. I had lived a real piece of life and had undergone a reinforcement of my religious beliefs. In Rwanda, there is real, visible, positive advancement towards solid progress. Progress is tangible, but there are also large patches of darkness, and the presence of Rwanda in the Congo is a big part of the mess. Even if the obstacles are numerous and the regime remains closed, the Rwanda of today is trying to promote solid reconciliation. All of us hope that peace endures. The situation is unstable, but it is improving, millimetre by millimetre. One step forward, one step backward, three steps forward... Progress is not linear. It is proportional to the basic problem that is that of overcoming hate among groups that have everything to unite them. As a very proud dignitary from West Africa said during an official dinner with humour and hope: "They are limping in the right direction." Little by little, the story is fitting into place, like waves on the water. But I should perhaps begin at the beginning with my arrival in Rwanda.

Chapter 3

Diary (1998)

Flashback: Learning about the Land of a Thousand Hills

The first shock is the sun, the intense, bright-light sun; then, the rolling hills, soft and peaceful. Every morning, a light haze covers the tops of the eucalyptus trees. Volcanoes rise in the distance. Under the volcanoes, the thick vegetation of the rain forest grows with lianas that have to be cut to open a path. This was formerly a paradise for tourists hoping to see the gorillas. There are soft slopes ready to slide and let the silt wash away after each sudden downpour, allowing the colours and smells to break out, creating an insolent reason for living. Rwanda is beautiful from the outset in its green clothing. The first impression is indelible: a perfect climate at a noble altitude, rising above the heat and the stuffy climates of West Africa. Birds are ready to glide over the branches of the avocado trees and hibiscus. But the people are truly sad. What a contrast. Each face encountered by chance in the central market or in the alleyways of Nyamirambo, a residential area of Kigali, reflects distress. I almost have the desire to take them all by the hand and show them how nature can sometimes be a balm.

The second impression is the colours: the colour of the landscapes, green-greys turning to yellow ochre, and the colour of the people. It is difficult to confront the relationship of colour between Europeans and Africans, which has to be examined with the right focus; with enthusiasm and reserve, a bit of distance and the right amount of drawing closer. These relationships are sometimes ambiguous and filled with awkwardness. At any rate, relationships are heavy with the weight of history and the past, going from slavery to the colonies, passing through the evangelization of all Africa. Nonetheless, the relationship of each person with his collective past immediately poses real questions. Promotion of awareness among the whole team for which I am responsible with our diverse expectations and varied experience in Africa was also a high point of my first days in Rwanda. Each of us has a different filter for looking at Rwanda, formed by our acquired attitudes. I have the feeling that it will be difficult to remain neutral. We have to combine the Europeans and Africans on the team, deal with our past experiences, our difficulty of understanding the present and our visions of an ideal future.

25 June 1998: A symbolic exchange

Byumba, Gisenyi, Kibungo: I made many trips to the hills to understand better the hard, poor, bitter reality of Rwanda. But it is there in contact with the local inhabitants, that my morale comes back all of a sudden. Rwandan women are especially magnificent. They take in orphans, till the fields, cut firewood and symbolically share their kitchen fires with their neighbours; even if she is an enemy and has a husband in prison. Reconciliation here is more than a vain word. It's an answer of silence in the face of an evidence: at any rate people are going to have to live together.

I visited the museum in Butare, where you can see photographs and drawings from the past: from William II of Prussia proudly offering a helmet to the Rwandan king at Nyanza at the beginning of the past century, up to the first outbreak of social revolution in the 1960s. The images are brief. The history of Rwanda is mixed with that of cursed kingdoms. I did well not to read all the literature on the history of Rwanda before coming here in order to avoid acquiring any prejudices. Nonetheless, a lot has been written about Rwanda. The photographs hanging on the walls of the museum in Butare speak for themselves. They evoke the 1950s, then the years of the overthrow of the alliances linked to an ideal of the small farmer and society, then the years of "apparent paradise" from 1972 to 1986. I read these descriptions of the history of

Rwanda only after having seen the country. They are often tainted with partiality.

The history of Rwanda has come to me mostly through the mouth of Rwandans, based on their perspective and their own experiences. But it is always in the past tense, like a sometimes-too-simplified retrospective. Formerly, there were kings, then vassals, and then everything fell apart when the vassals tried to become kings. No explanation is given, however, for the rise in surreptitious and predictable horror, which in a way was thought to be impossible; probably because it took place right before their eyes. Years are needed to talk about one's past. In Europe, the archives of the Second World War are just beginning to reveal their secrets; fifty years after the Holocaust.

This week, I met Abel, a journalist from Newsweek, who arrived from the Middle East. He makes an easy comparison between an exported war, the madness of surviving and the fear of deadly attacks. He has come to Rwanda for four days during which he saw, understood and decided that that is what it is. At this stage, I am just listening. Do I listen? Yes, I listen. I learn that Rwanda systematically attracts the rare intellectual kinds who come to spend several days. They come to explain to people living here what they should understand. The visitors have completely understood reality in three days. The contradiction is something completely obvious to them. They arrive with their minds filled with banalities. They usually leave with rough-hewn theories, bloated with certainties like frogs in the swamps in the spring. They are stuffed with thrown-together and well-lubricated, prefabricated explanations. In general, their final conclusion hinges on untenable ethnic simplification. What do our Rwandan friends think about these great theoreticians? Four years after the genocide, nothing has changed? You have to be honest. Here, no foreigner understands anything for a long time. The same can be said of Rwandans themselves; both those who returned to their country after many years of absence and those who stayed there. The other Africans also do not have the key to the solution. After a certain time, the *muzungus* (the white-coloured people) feel that they still understand nothing. They look for a logic in the course of events. That logic is often linked to that of hatred exploited by leaders thirsty for power through manipulation. When will there be a programme of applied psychology for African leaders that will teach them to let go? Finally, after much analysis, the visiting European intellectual thinks that he understands; but not everything. It was the complete opposite. The situation must be prudently analyzed.

27 June 1998: The first lesson for the newcomer

The first lesson for all newcomers to Rwanda is the following: all theories are valid as well as the opposite and both possibilities are valid at the same time. For example: the Armée patriotique du Rwanda (APR) considered themselves to be liberators in 1994 and respectful of human rights, but at the same time they killed many people. So much for the Cartesian way of thinking and goodbye to those who love cohesive theories. Amateur Manicheans trying to understand the course of history of a forgotten Africa, on your marks. Rwanda of 1998 represents a new challenge to any attempt to provide a simple explanation. There are a multitude of levels of understanding available to us. These levels cohabitate with codes commonly called "diplomatic euphemisms". The foreigner has to first check the level at which his Rwandan speaker is speaking. Then he has to ask himself whether what has been stated is not really the opposite. In Rwanda, no one speaks directly of politics. You have to first sound out the terrain. You have to weigh the reaction of the other person quite prudently. You have to know the position of the person you are speaking with, but you don't get involved. Once you have found the right channel, the access code is very easy. It's best to start with the nuances.

28 June 1998: A fully landlocked country

This Friday, we carried out an evacuation exercise with the Belgium Embassy. We live here a bit like on a razor's edge. Have we learned something since 1994? Even if everyone wants to believe that it will never begin again, a fear still exists that the latent conflict could break out. My priority is to try to understand Rwandans. I would like to have sufficient guarantees to be sure of really being able to help Rwandans without making mistakes that could have a repercussion on one side or the other. It's a difficult exercise: history always wants us to take a stand. But the last thing I want is to be dragged into a fatal ethnic dichotomy. I decided to think twice before accepting news from the man on the street, and I avoid listening to rumours and taking categorical decisions. It is even more difficult when you do not speak the local language. Sometimes, I find myself realizing that I am not exactly in focus, like when you have to adjust the zoom focus before taking a photograph. I must find my own way. But how can I create a network to verify information? It's not easy, and I have to learn to make things concrete by stages. Two or three years? My learning curve will be steep.

Already after only a few months, I am delighted to leave for Tanzania on Christmas vacation through Mwanza to the Serengeti National Park and Ngorongoro Crater. It might seem strange to begin a mission by preparing for a vacation, but that's what is in the back of everyone's mind here. If the situation ever became threatening, there would be a way out not far away. The surroundings are sometimes stifling, and the country is very closed, landlocked. This is probably true also because of the configuration of the hills. The landscape rises and falls constantly, influencing our perception of things. Definitely, we do not live on the wide-open spaces of the plains, like in Kenya. This impression of being closed in is linked basically to the fear that history can repeat itself and to the fear that we will be unable to prevent new massacres. Sometimes at night, I find myself almost feeling the souls that are all around us crying out their pain. They too did not understand why they had to die. Out of all the feelings we have in Rwanda, it's surly that of their abandonment that is the heaviest to carry. Did we really leave while the massacre was taking place?

1 July 1998: The sorcerer's apprentice

I spent a very instructive week. My real baptism is about to begin. First, my meeting with C. in a ministry. She was extraordinary, very calm. She lost eighteen people in her family. No comment. We spoke for two hours. I listened to the story of her wanderings since 1965: the refugee camps, the Congo, exile, humiliation, simply facts and no excuses. Only a Fanta orange interrupted our very intense conversation. Suddenly, I felt the strong conviction that you cannot be angry at a group that had been excluded since 1959 and then exterminated in 1994 that wants to take just a little bit of power at any price. Power was taken by force, it's true, whether we like it or not. But the infernal cycle should at some point be broken. Of course, some discretion is in order. I had been sufficiently warned about this before my departure from Switzerland. In the end, the injustices committed over so many years are there to give us an idea of what it means to be excluded. C. concluded the conversation with this beautiful truth: "No wrong has ever been set right or countered with hatred, but you do need time to forgive."

4 July 1998: Justifying the liberation

Liberation Day is celebrated every year in the Amahoro (peace) Stadium. It is fascinating to watch military parades; and that's true in all of Africa. Military parades are one of the founding myths of established order. It is not that I have become an unconditional supporter of the current government in the twinkling of an eye, but there is a certain and impressive discipline in the government's ranks. There are some devilishly intelligent and interesting persons at the core of the government who are seeking to promote true unity and reconciliation, while at the same time holding on to power. In fact, there is a mixture, like in any government.

Nonetheless, I fear that we have only limited influence. Let's say we are there, and we have to participate in this march forward towards African democratization. It has to be taken or left. The whole question is to know whether we forgive "the liberators who also killed many people", allowing them to live in a heroic memory on the ashes of a genocide; even if this memory is logical. We know that we have not finished keeping that hope alive. There is a willingness to forget, an appetite for happiness, and an understandable attempt to be carefree among the Rwandans. There is a real frenzy to show that it is their turn now to speak out on the international stage and to write their chapter. At the same time, I feel permanent pain in everything; a pain that is very slight but quite persistent. The African writer and statesman Leopold Senghor often said, "Warriors have a difficult time becoming rulers. Their mentalities are not the same. To take power through a military coup is sometimes more justified than cheating at the polls." He described how a certain Central African country succeeded in electing its president with 102 per cent of the votes. Without hesitating, the elected president announced that even the dead had voted for him. That's the real irrational Africa.

20 September 1998: The attack on Kivumu

I made my first professional visit to Kibuye. It was a baptism by fire because the authorities were full of expectations and they told me their stories; stories about their twenty years of exile abroad. They are also far from Kigali trying to repulse the enemy on all sides, which seems a gargantuan enterprise.

Kibuye, like before, remains a "cursed" region, and all sorts of recalcitrants are there. Now, things are changing a bit, but attacks by Hutu rebels still take place constantly. That evening, we were gathered on the shores of Lake Kivu with Chinese road builders, the local military commander, the prefect, the director of roads and bridges and their wives. We were sitting around a banquet table near this magical lake with the crackling of distant but persistent fighting coming from the forest all around.

The Chinese build roads for international organizations. They come and learn Kinyarwanda in two months. They converse rapidly with the Rwandans, as if it were a language as easy to learn as learning to eat with chopsticks. The Assimil method. Thrown into reality, the Chinese learn very quickly to speak, specializing in construction vocabulary. Curiously, their quick gestures and their smiling faces do not seem to clash with the solemn faces of their African partners. The Chinese use a small hotel in Kibuye as their base. They are in a closed environment, focused and working quickly as a unit. The individual seems basically to be at the service of a community. That evening, they prepared an extraordinary welcome. About fifteen typical Cantonese dishes, one after the other, flabbergasted us. Chinese music sang away from the loudspeakers. "It's a famous Shanghai opera," whispered a Rwandan who had probably asked the question before I did and had probably studied in China. We were received like kings. Because our hosts spoke only Chinese and Kinyarwanda, we could not carry on a sustained conversation. We had to communicate with onomatopoeia, indicating the amazing pleasure of our taste buds by "Oh!" "Ah!" and a "Hum!"

29 September 1998: Returning to Kigali in an armoured personnel carrier

Early in the morning of the next day, I left for Kigali. After having covered about fifteen kilometres, the car was

55

suddenly stopped in the vicinity of the Mukura Forest. A military riot was taking place. There were people running in all directions, crying "There was an attack, get out." Soldiers appeared, brutally pushing persons toward their homes on the hills. It was real chaos. The Interhamwe (partisans of the old regime who spread the genocide) had launched an attack at dawn on the Kivumu prison. Bodies were lying near the prison. Carts had been overturned; straw houses were burning. The rebels had silently come down from the forests and surprised the sleeping village. Suddenly, I was aware that some people were still killing out of hate, with the same mentality as in 1994 and that they were close by. The massacres were never completely checked. They were just contained. I saw some corpses cut into pieces under tall trees in the ravine around the prison. I saw persons weeping silently inward, as the Rwandans say. I discovered humble, poor and frightened people who were abused regardless of their ethnic affiliation. I passed empty eyes that did not understand why the violence had never stopped.

This event, which happened at the very beginning of my mission, undeniably contributed to transforming my fiction into reality. Yes, the enemy was still there at our doors, moving about, not hesitating to murder and hack with machetes in order to terrorize the local population. Several prisoners had been freed by force from the prison and taken into the forest. Have they agreed to take up arms again? How many of them are still there in the forests around Mukura, Gishwati and in the Congo? The prisoners taken away by force, did they have a choice? This episode on the road back from Kibuye opened my eyes to the reality of Rwanda four years after the genocide. Will it never end? How many people will die before things change?

The government officials were worried about me. An army lieutenant had come to my rescue. I finally returned to Kigali from Kivumu along trails below the threatening Mukura forest in an armoured vehicle. I watched the landscape go by at the speed of tank tracks and felt the cruel willingness of the rebels to sabotage peace, break the local population and continue the madness. Tens of persons among the mixed population had been killed at five o'clock in the morning by the Interhamwe in the village of Kivumu. They had come to free prisoners. Did it all make any sense? This attack had followed another attack perpetuated the week before against World Food Programme trucks in the North in the region around Gisenyi. When will this country be safe? How can a new society be built on a base so riddled with hatred? I have to continue straight on, I told myself. Don't panic. Give support to all initiatives promoting peace and reconciliation.

13 October 1998: The story of a priest

During that same period, another episode also struck me. It happened in a hospital run by nuns where a meeting was being held. I witnessed with extreme discomfort an attempt at division instead of an attempt at reconciliation. A priest gave a sermon that was very close to a hate-filled harangue; as if he wanted to rekindle all possibilities of disagreement. In the middle of the meeting, I rose and said that his words were creating a division between people like in the past. The European priest strongly insisted on the insurmountable gulf between the two ethnic groups, instead of uniting them and bringing about reconciliation. The audience, mostly Rwandan nurses and physicians, was petrified by this argument between two Europeans. That day, the priest took a step backwards, and my blood stopped flowing. I was ready to talk about the presence of the Church during thirty years; ready to talk about the church at Nyamata, about the corpses and the smell in the church. Finally, the priest let go, but an uncomfortable feeling remained. We exchanged glances filled with fire. I was sick to my stomach. I don't know whether my crusade was justified, but I was alone against a group of immobile and paralysed Rwandans in the presence of a European priest bothered by a woman who argued for the irrelevance of the use of ethnic affiliation. Will the Rwandans one day be on their own? Is colonialism raising its head again? Should the morphology of a person decide his destiny? Slavery and the slave trade did exist right under the eyes of the Church. Images of my first communion were buried in my anger. What had we made of God? Yes, this Rwanda is complicated. This country arouses many impulses, sometimes good, but also ugly. And the fact of my being a Catholic sometimes makes me angry, but what was going on here and in whose name? You have to be constantly on your guard against false certainties. I recalled the stories of Rwandans whose lives had been saved in 1994 because they were short and had a round face although they were Tutsis. It had been thought that because of their short height they were Hutus. How absurd prejudice is. You have to keep in mind constantly that you can be carried away by a false interpretation of reality. Just like before. You have to be detached and lucid, you must remain calm.

Since this unfortunate incident, I often do exercises in the morning to help me relax and step back, thanks to yoga, in order to balance the "for" and the "against" and the opposite. It relaxes me, but I carry a grudge against that priest; in fact against all forms of fanaticism. I am looking again at religion as it is perceived and lived in Mozambique and Mali. Have Christians and Muslims really overcome all the animist resistances on the continent? No, and fortunately. In Africa, there are crowds of Islamic mullahs and marabous, priests from various Christian sects and associations and thousands of shamans representing African cults and gods. But more than competition, there is tolerance. Mutual respect for the belief of the other is predominant. In the end, local rites prevail: those that make it possible to sort out the landscape, the symbols, flights of birds, tracks in the sand, forms made by clouds and the blood spilt by a sacred cow. It's on this basis that Rwanda can again find its roots.

1 November 1998: All Saints' Day

All Saints' Day is a time for contemplation. You think about your loved ones, those who have died: a courageous grandmother, a dark-skinned, dynamic mother. In our countries, we go to the cemetery to lay some flowers or a small bouquet. But in Rwanda, how do you remember a million persons? How do you recognize someone's tomb when there was no burial? Four years after the genocide, all the common graves have not yet been dug up. Several associations are trying to recreate a list prefecture by prefecture of the names of those who disappeared; but persons are missing in order to recall, complete and describe a block of houses or a clan that was decimated. Stories of mutilated corpses are really awful, and many prefer to remain silent rather than vividly recall the events. Nonetheless, here and there during my visits to the communes, sometimes just sitting on the side of the road, Joseph, Jean-de-Dieu, Marguerite or Yvonne have told me their stories. The pain behind the pain, the mad chase through the marshes, the chanting militants, the noise of the machetes hacking bones, the blood that didn't stop flowing, women with their stomachs cut open.

The survivors are a separate category of people in Rwanda. No one wants them; no one knows how to integrate them. And no compensation in the world can wipe away the nightmare, which comes to haunt them like a threatening sword night after night. Above all, it is the children who cannot express their past.

One day after a visit to her sorghum field, Marguerite told me, "When the Armée patriotique rwandaise (APR) came and called to me in the marshes of Kibungo, I didn't want to come out at first. I stayed there for almost two months crouched in the mud. Above all, I was afraid of a trap. I was also terribly ashamed, ashamed of what had happened to me, ashamed of surviving and ashamed of not having died with all my family. Do you think it's lucky to be a living dead person among the living? I am not so sure. Finally, when they arrived to liberate us, I slowly stood up and could see in the faces of the soldiers that they were embarrassed, downfallen. They didn't know how to behave in the face of such human tragedy. They threw me some clothes and I followed them. I could see that they hadn't the slightest desire to hear my story. Lamentations like mine, there are hundreds and hundreds. I continue to keep it to myself. From time to time, just with people from my hill when we gather around a bottle of Coca Cola, we talk about our lives. But we are forced to laugh in order not to cry outward. That is a little bit of relief and soothes me somewhat. That's all."

Today, Marie-Arménie rang me with all her tiny voice. Her voice still rings in my ears as a voice from the dead.

10 November 1998: Why hast Thou abandoned us?

You can gain strength by believing in an interpretation of the world run by the ancestors, whose spirits guide the actions of the living. And in Rwanda? How can religion penetrate local beliefs? When did the deep clear and natural ancestral solidarity give way to madness? Which type of fervour can still be practiced in the sullied churches? Many Rwandans have strengthened their religious conviction. Some have even joined obscure sects and speak untiringly of God's vengeance. These sects seem to be very strong and dangerous, as if they were exploiting human pain. They often speak of a sacrifice to be atoned for. Other Rwandans silently travel the local road to Sunday mass, nonetheless, asking in a low voice: "Why hast Thou abandoned us?" In Africa everything related to religion, ceremonies, the spirit, the supernatural and the invisible immediately releases a grave and respectful reaction. It's like a pause in a conversation. Everyone pertinently knows deep inside that to play with the supernatural and superior forces never ends well; unless recourse is had to the services of a mediator, sorcerer or healer.

To live in Africa and personally communicate also passes through an exchange of beliefs. I can recall a district health director in the prefecture of Byumba asking me one day, "Do you believe in God, Madame?" He was waiting for my answer impatiently, almost trembling. I realized that our future relations, his confidence in me and his interest and complicity depended on my answer. When I said yes, he visibly appeared very relieved, as if I was henceforth accepted into his world. The colour barriers were broken as well as those of age and social status. We could finally have a conversation. This dimension that I very quickly understood in the three African countries where I worked immediately created almost inseparable ties. Ties and contacts with what links the African to a superior spiritual level often allowed me to have access to a universal language, propitious to mutual confidence. It was never necessarily a case of a belief in a single god, but an unshakable faith in the existence of a superior force that gives a choice to man to have a spiritual dimension raising him above the visible universe, but which also leaves him free to not have a faith, of letting genocide happen.

15 November 1998: A climate of paradise

The temperature is almost a constant twenty degrees during the day and about eighteen degrees in the evening. We hear that the first winter frosts have occurred in Europe. On the Equator in Africa, the rainy season has caused a lot of damage to improvised houses, and the stubborn early-morning sun gives a desire to sing and hum. I'm beginning to feel good. I am less afraid of the reaction of Rwandans that I meet. I have perhaps touched here or there the indescribable and indefinable emotional dimension. I have begun to listen and feel sympathy. We share daily events, and that's quite a lot.

I wrote a detailed report on the situation in Kivu province in Eastern Congo. In reality, the frontiers of 1919 are being called into question. The situation is completely

61

confused. There is only hatred between all the groups that could be so close to each other. The hatred is stirred up by poverty and the lack of goods, although the soil in the Congo is so rich. The source of the problem, according to a Belgian specialist, is that the Congo is too rich and everyone wants part of its wealth. This morning at the Ministry for Foreign Affairs, we participated in a meeting where an album of photos was passed around with vehemence: photos of unacceptable horror that left us helpless: Tutsis cut into pieces, castrated, beaten and dragged through the streets of Kinshasa. Is there any humanity left? But to occupy another country is probably not the quickest and the most appropriate peaceful answer. In diplomatic circles, you often hear of the willingness to promote true democracy in Rwanda: "one man, one vote". This form of democracy is difficult to apply in this context. It means that the Tutsi minority would have few important positions because it is just a small percentage of the total population. This formula had already been an important factor in the dissensions and catastrophes. Political parties, democratic proportionalities and areas of competency need to be respected. There is still much to be written about the question of minority and majority in Rwanda.

21 November 1998: The role of heroes as models

Thursday was Hero's Day. We laid a wreath of flowers at the Remera cemetery in a Kigali neighbourhood in memory of a hero of the army of liberation, Fred Rwigema. Commemorations are heavy with political meaning. What creates strong ties and an identity for an African nation that will lead to an end of the cycle of violence? How can we pick up the broken pieces and recreate a true bond in a society so torn apart and so visibly divided? Here, there are extraordinary networks of solidarity that could be renewed and given new meaning. A Rwandan is above all a Rwandan: one language and a single belief. True sharing of the land will be the first tangible sign of reconciliation. In this way, ethnic divisions could be shown to be inappropriate.

I recall the work of an anthropologist that I read recently. He wrote about the souls of chiefs. In Africa, once a chief is chosen he becomes a sacred person. He no longer has the right to walk barefoot or sit directly on the ground. It is forbidden to touch him or to say something bad about him. He can be recognized from a distance because of an enormous, highly decorated parasol held above his head by a loyal servant. The anthropologist wrote of the attributes of power of the great African chiefs: "Every head of clan guarantees harmony among the two parties making up the clan: the world of the ancestors and the world of the living. He is an intermediary and a mediator. He settles disputes and resolves conflicts. He is also a judge surrounded by a council of elders and can take decisions only after having consulted the ancestors. Since the dawn of time, the chief represents a certain conception of democracy in Africa." Will the new head of Rwanda—an impressive person because of his sober countenance—know how to merge old myths with modern demands? According to the Rwandan people, the reply could be yes. If he provides security, peace, development, he will be given credit. If in addition, he succeeds in giving Rwanda a new image about which no one will be ashamed and an international and regional place and voice, then he will be praised.

29 November 1998: The sky is falling on our heads

Airplanes continue to fly over our heads. A bomb could fall on us any day, at any time. We listen closely to news from the Congo. Kindu, in the Democratic Republic of the Congo, is reported to have been taken by the Rwandans and their allies. It seems to be an important victory for the "rebels". The word "rebel" becomes quite flexible: who rebels against whom and why? Can any fighting still be justified if civilians lose their lives? Nonetheless, the official position of Rwanda does not

63

change: as long as the Interhamwe are helped in the Congo by the Congolese army, Rwandans will not leave the Congo. The Lusaka agreements remain for the time being the only platform for negotiations. The structure of alliances in the Congo is really complicated. Even specialists lose their bearings. In addition to the various military forces present in the Congo, including Zimbabweans and Angolans, there are mercenaries hired by those who pay the highest price. They are the Mayi-Mayi. The war in eastern Congo is both a war among brothers and a struggle for mineral resources. Sadly, it is always the civilian population that pays the price.

Those who know the Congo have begun to do something. Maps have been purchased and the advance of troops is monitored. There is speculation. All sorts of contradictory information is coming from NGOs in the field. Kigali is becoming a pivot. Everyone keeps running into everyone else. And depending on your point of view, the interpretation of facts can be diametrically opposite. You also begin to catch a glimpse of people from Eastern Europe in the large hotels; from Bulgaria, Russia and the Ukraine. Traders talk about diamonds passing through Kigali. The official media speak of chasing down the Interhamwe. According to the local radio stations, these former Hutu militants seem to have been rearmed by Kinshasa. Alliances criss-cross. I am apprehensive about discussions to be held the following week. Analysis of economic stakes is going to be difficult. Explanations of budgets and the distribution of government posts are repeated. The IMF is in Kigali, and the World Bank is carefully observing.

2 December 1998: The man on the list

One day, a man came to see me, furiously entering my office unannounced. "How come", he sharply demanded, "you can't even sort out what is true and what is false?" I dropped my pen and asked who in the world he was. "Mr. X", he

64

replied, "congressman, businessman, lawyer and survivor". It turns out that there is a list of perpetrators of the genocide circulating in all foreign capitals in order to facilitate justice. This man had disembarked at an international airport and was immediately arrested by a zealous immigration official who had checked the list of wanted persons and had thought that this man was on the list. The official had unfortunately come across a homonym, but had not verified the commune of origin. As a result, my visitor had spent a few hours cooling off, locked in a dark cell, before things were set right. He wanted compensation for that affront. I had to use all my diplomatic wits to calm him, explaining that Rwandan names are often very similar. I told him that he should be pleased to learn that government officials abroad are on the watch trying to arrest the perpetrators. It was very difficult to calm the man down. People here are still very sensitive in one sense or another. We are constantly asked to take sides and yet this was proof that situations are never black or white.

4 December 1998: Inactive volcanoes

Formerly, Rwanda was the pride of regional tourism. You can still find a gorilla and some volcanoes on the label of bottled mineral water, called Ruwenzori, produced in Rwanda. The volcanoes have emitted lava for a long time, and they continue to roar. Specialists in volcanoes do not exactly know what is going on, but the volcanoes attracted tourists and geologists, and the tropical forest was renown for its beauty. Nonetheless, since 1997 guerrilla forces have roamed north-western Rwanda and southern Uganda, preventing tourists from coming back to this magical region where gorillas welcome them with kind grunting. No one dares enter the virgin forest, and the gorillas are beginning to disappear. Given the Interhamwe's determination to come out of these forests below the volcanoes and take hostages and kill people in the villages of northern Rwanda, soldiers have been given orders to inspect the local inhabitants carefully. A group of tourists was recently killed in southern Uganda. The systematic hunting down of rebels has begun, and strategic places have been identified after repeated attacks on Ruhengeri and Gisenyi.

The Hutu population suffers from a lack of distinguishing between those who carried out the genocide and their global ethnic group. This generalization is very difficult to overcome and is unfair. Thousands of people have been forced together in the northwest for security reasons. The army recently gave the inhabitants living along the Congolese border three days to evacuate the areas of fighting. It is estimated that 500,000 persons have been moved to other areas and communal infrastructures. We were immediately sent by helicopter to those sites to survey the possibility of providing assistance. We discovered an apocalyptic situation. Again in the prefectures of Ruhengeri and Gisenyi at Nyaratowu, Nyamugali and Rwerere, people had been forced together for as far as we could see. We could see thousands of frightened faces in groups of 50,000 clinging to the hills. It was raining and plastic covers could not hide the extreme fatigue of these Rwandans from the north: exhausted, defeated, frightened, poorer than the poor and crowded together with a haggard look. They don't know in which direction to turn. The attacks and tensions have never really stopped in this corner of Rwanda, once the rich breadbasket of the country. Along the roads, beautiful trees have been cut down to provide security, while our main concern is the environment. The army, however, talks about survival. A dialogue between the deaf? Humanitarian aid is once again there to save the situation. In this crisis situation, it is difficult for us to measure the true roughness of daily life in the villages, on the hills and under the banana trees. Is daily life as humiliating for the local population as some people say? Do they really have so little freedom? Are they oppressed or are they really afraid of power? Do they have the right to circulate freely from one commune to another? Can you speak of human rights in a place that is so unstable? I am trying to understand better what is happening to the rural population.

Planes quite often fly low over our heads,. Peace negotiations in the Congo are not getting off the ground. For all the international community, the fact that the Rwandan army is present in the Congo represents a violation of international law that is difficult to justify. Rwanda is not well viewed abroad. We are in the country and are trying to help the local inhabitants.

18 December 1998: A wet tropical summer

There is a big difference between the European and African ways of thinking. My weeks are now measured in terms of official ceremonies, meetings with the international community and field visits. This Saturday, the United States Marine ball was a real joyous event. Even if the early official portion of that evening with flags and American songs meant little to all those who are particularly insensitive to these things, we had a lot of fun dancing. In addition to yoga for internal harmony, tennis for building muscles, I also take dance classes. Oxana, a Russian and former dancer from Minsk, gives us classical dance classes. In the middle of Kigali, we have the impression of being off stage at the Bolchoy Theatre. These courses are wonderful for me, even if I sometimes laugh when I have to execute creaking *entrechats* and soft *sissonnes* in Rwanda. The carpet is worn and smells a bit of mildew. The music squeaks. It is difficult to glide, and the leaps are too timid, but we try. This group of potential or faded dancers does not take everything seriously. These precious moments of dance counterbalance the drama of every day life and the noisy official receptions. This week was backbreaking. Among my activities I had to give a talk that was to be called "Cooperatives: success and failures". It is always delicate to speak in Rwanda of the past and praise new techniques. Political prudence must always take precedence over theoretical fiddling. I finally got around the problem by describing the tasks of the perfect participatory development worker. Nonetheless, the question of associations and cooperatives is very important for starting up micro projects. It is a whole chapter in itself. This question really merits going into further detail.

21 December 1998: The Iron Lady

Several of us went to see M. at the ministry in order to explain the international community's difficulty in accepting the presence of Rwanda in the Congo and to express our concern. We were very well received and were given a lesson on strategy. M. is a very beautiful woman with her head on her shoulders, who speaks well. She is a brilliant economist. Certain Rwandans have a radical way of showing their superiority. They take an interested distance and maintain impressive dignity.

She told me that there is a difference between occupying an area and pushing back the enemy that is always attacking and threatening Rwanda's security. She asked how should the Rwandan government act towards its people, to eradicate this hatred of the other ethnic group, this ancestral wariness, and to break the infernal cycle of vengeance that feeds vengeance. She seemed to ask for our sincere opinion. For centuries, Rwandans had lived together in harmony and now had to find reconciliation, but not as long as the Interhamwe continue their death raids. They had to go hunt down the brains behind those who want to continue to eliminate the Tutsis there where they are. And they are in the Congo. They had already stated that they wanted to welcome the others, the repenters, with open arms and had done so in 1997. One million persons returned from the camps in Bukavu and Goma. There was a noticeable silence in the audience. "I am not sure," I said, "what is justified or not in a war but I have the conviction that no one can occupy a foreign country. Right?"

M. stared at me for a minute and then said, "It is a question of priorities. I think that our troops can really make things move forward and promote peace," she concluded. "We have to work towards the resolution of conflicts in the region, including the conflict with the forces of the ex-FAR." She made a vague gesture. "Without your aid we won't be successful." This reality of the need to occupy the Congo remains, nonetheless, worrying.

24 December 1998: Christmas Eve

I spent Christmas Eve at an orphanage at Butambwa, located in rural Kigali on the road that goes up behind the brick factory. About eighty children were seated in a circle on the grass around the communal hall. Songs and dances were interspersed with small gifts that we had brought for them. But it was a cowherd of about ten years of age who with his small stick and his over-sized beret stuffed onto his head made us all laugh the most. Between two mouthfuls of rice and brochettes, he kept running out to check whether the cows had moved.

Part II: The Survivors' Pain of Existence

Chapter 4

The Story of Marie-Arménie

April is an especially delicate and nostalgic month in Rwanda. It regularly brings back memories of the madness and mourning in families. This mortuary flame is also fed by all the national commemorations held around April 7th. They take the form of systematic visits by groups to sites of the genocide. There are pilgrimages; something necessary, however macabre. These manifestations are indispensable, so that the painful memory of the genocide is not forgotten. They also revive rancour and strikingly remind survivors that compensation is taking a long time to come and that their claims have still not been satisfied. In fact, the "Survivors' Fund" has not been able to deal equitably with the problems of compensation and indemnity for all the damage caused by the massacres and pillage. Rwanda is a poor country. This compensation will at any rate be more symbolic than financial. You cannot erase a genocide. People cannot be resuscitated, but more substantial compensation would allow survivors to begin better again their lives. The question is delicate because the whole country and everyone has suffered from the hecatomb. Finally, only a global approach has been envisaged by the officials and the international community. For the survivors, these bits of compensation do not fill the emptiness of the horror. There is a basic moral wrong for which no indemnity can provide compensation.

This April Sunday evening, I was at the residence lighting a small fire in the fireplace with a few friends. This contrast between the always-temperate equatorial climate with a daytime temperature of 23 to 25 degrees and an evening breeze that is always a surprising pleasure is refreshing. The wind at dusk is wonderful. It caresses the avocado trees and bends the jacarandas in the garden, which are filled with multicoloured birds. Ibises squawk and large African hawks soar with the thermals. They sometimes fly high over the grass roofs of the houses descending in spirals to the ground with sharp cries. The climate in Rwanda is soothing. The difference between the heat of midday and the cool evenings is pleasant. This difference in temperature makes the fire in a fireplace especially enjoyable, and this reality is like a wink at clichés. Our idea of a sweltering Africa where only elephants and giraffes walk about contrasts with the lighted fires used in the winter to warm hands and feet of people in mountain chalets.

Several friends were sitting with me staring at the flames. We were listening to a CD of Afar music that a friend had just brought from the Horn of Africa. It was 8 p.m. when the telephone rang. That terrible portable telephone that makes you think you are needed at all times of the day by every one on earth. I answered the telephone, ready to brush off the person who had dared ring. The small voice at the other end was out of breath. "I want to say goodbye, because I am going to die tonight", said the small voice. I was paralysed and asked her to repeat what she had said. Then, I said, "Heavens above, hang on, please, make an effort, stay alive, I'm coming. Where are you?" I jumped into the four-wheel drive and grabbed a Rwandan friend who knows the Kigali Hospital Centre well. We rushed towards room 312, but the night guard stopped us with a movement of his head. No, you can't see the patients after 8 p.m. I looked at my watch and saw that it was 9 p.m. We began to argue, Sylvestre in Kinyarwanda and me with all possible and imaginable identity papers in French. The guard remained inflexible. Even a little bit of money (although he did look with interest at the bank note that I held out) did not move him. Suddenly, I had an idea. I told him that our visit was a question of life or death and asked him whether he had lost family during the "war". He nodded yes. Then I asked him whether he would have tried to save one other person? He

71

looked at me with apprehension. I couldn't tell in the slightest whether he was on one side or the other, which was disconcerting. It goes to show that the theories about ethnic identity based on physical traits is really a load of rubbish. I could not determine what this night guard was. But luck was with me. I had hit the right key. He had lost twelve members of his family during the genocide. He relaxed a bit, but kept a pained expression and stood his ground about letting us through. We asked him where he was from. We could sense that he wanted to talk. His name was Jean-Théoneste and he came from Butare. He told us about his flight in April 1994. Sylvestre and I sat on the stairs and listened to him. He wanted to talk about his personal drama without ostentation just so that we would know who he was. He looked into the distance. His voice was not whining. He added that he still didn't understand. "That's why I'm a night guard. It's easier to put up with at night." "What do you want?", he asked after a long silence that we did not want to break. I told him that we had come to see a woman; a friend of mine, who was dying and wanted to say goodbye to us. He stared astonished at us and asked whether we would be able to help her. I answered that I didn't know, but that the woman I wanted to see would die if I could not see her. I told a big lie by saying that I was a trained physician. Slowly, Jean-Théoneste told us to go inside and be quiet. We shook his hand and entered through the door. He took up his position as night guard, staring into the night. Standing straight like a soldier.

Marie-Arménie was lying with her back to the door facing the wall. She couldn't turn over, and she weighed about thirty-five kilos. Her mother was sitting at the bedside, motionless and without saying anything. She was resigned and had already lost seven of her nine children. Marie-Arménie was breathing with difficulty. Her eyes were glassy. The smell in the room was terrible, as if death were relentlessly stalking. I approached her and took her in my arms. She sighed. I asked her what was wrong. With a gasp she told me that she had never dared tell me that she was HIV positive. She had AIDS. And now meningitis and pneumonia. It was the end, she knew it. Her arms dropped, and I looked at Sylvestre. "It's like that", he said lightly, gnashing his teeth, in a tone the Rwandans usually use with a sarcastic laugh when they are in deep pain. No drama. Here, you never let go. I quickly calculated and said to Marie-Arménie that there was something wrong. This was impossible.

We got back into the four-wheel and took her to the King Faisal hospital and the next morning she was under tritherapy. Marie-Arménie was saved once again. She was weak, but she was fighting, fighting for her five children without a father. She wants to go back home and take care of her mother who has heart problems. Ever since the genocide, the mother of Marie-Arménie had become speechless, paralysed. She no longer felt anything and was moved by nothing. She was already living her next life. Marie-Arménie had become a friend, and her case is one of those that touched me the most in Rwanda. Her story is symbolic of all those with a cock-and-bull story that makes your hair stand on end. We ask ourselves how it was possible to live normally afterwards.

Marie-Arménie was born, just like the night guard, (there are coincidences) in the prefecture of Butare in southern Rwanda, a small white, welcoming town with a university and tree-lined streets. She was born in 1961, in a small rural commune into a middle-class family of nine children, Tutsi farmers. No, they did not just raise cattle, like in the cliché. They also farmed the land. The first seven years of her life went by well. She was well integrated into her family and got along well with her nearby friends (a term used to designate neighbours who are not from the same clan).

For reasons she never understood and which always surprised her, her mother asked her one day to leave the family. Marie-Arménie, the fourth of nine children, was to look after her grandmother who lived on a neighbouring hill. The little girl took it as an injustice and an abandonment, but also as

73

rejection by her mother. She often looked at herself in a small broken mirror in her mother's room. While it was true that she was a bit thin, when she grew up she would gain weight. She felt that she would become beautiful. Her body was becoming that of a lovely young girl, graceful, liking to dance, jump and sing. She was very easy to get along with. Was that a reason to be sent away like in a terrible fairy tale? With lowered head, she obeyed. A little bit like in a bad story by Roald Dahl, Marie-Arménie did all the unpleasant housework. She took complete charge of her frail grandmother. She had to carry water for three kilometres in a bucket on her head, walk barefooted up and down the hills on steep trails scratching herself on bushes, do the housework, scrub the ground, sweep the yard, plant potatoes, mind the calves and prepare the meals. From time to time, she was even allowed to go to school. Despite many hours of absence from primary school, she was the first in her class. She repeated her lessons out loud while she was sweeping. But because during that period people like her, in other words Tutsis, were not allowed to be first in their class, she spent the following six years at school with just passing grades. When she came home from school, she asked for paper in order to write her lessons, but her grandmother could not buy her notebooks for school. There was no money. The parents of Marie-Arménie wanted the boys in the family to study first of all. She began to climb into the trees to sing and write all the lessons she learned at school with a ballpoint pen on her legs. She sometimes imitated her teacher, disparagingly, from up in her tree. She began to find that from high up in the trees she had a vantage point to observe the world and look at the beautiful hills. The path was dark yellow and then as it moved away it slowly became ochre. Where the path entered the banana groves, it wound and became saffron, alternating with the green vegetation of the branches. Sunlight played on the interstices. Marie-Arménie dreamt about a colourful life. She loved her hill.

In 1973, she was twelve years old and began to realize that some people did not like Tutsis. She began to distinguish between herself and her family and other neighbours who began to look at them as plague victims. But she didn't say anything out loud, although the neighbours made her feel it in a thousand ways through pestering.

Violence set the whole prefecture on edge. Hundreds of Tutsi students were killed at secondary schools and at the university. Marie-Arménie wanted to enter secondary school, but she could see that it would be difficult, especially because her mother didn't see any point in sending her to school, and her grandmother had no money. One day she became very tired from working in the fields, climbed up into her tree and began to cry and pray to God to help her out of her predicament and her very difficult life. A great silence fell over her. For a while, she could think of nothing and then suddenly she had an idea that became stronger and stronger. It was beating in her brain. She had found it. She knew what she had to do.

Marie-Arménie, with all her twelve years, repeated to herself: since everyone was treating her as a pariah and distasteful young girl not even able to study, she was going to change the course of her life. She would marry a Hutu, and he would protect her and she would become rich. She had taken her decision and was unwavering. Her destiny was drawn. She came down from her favourite tree, calmed down and decided to begin her studies. She went to beg an aunt who lived under green banana trees on the opposite hill to loan her money for her studies. She promised to repay the money. Her aunt was her father's sister, whom she liked. She cleverly explained that she could not spend all her life sweeping the yard and taking care of her grandmother. She wanted to become a woman. Touched by her determination, the aunt enrolled her in the Ecole des arts et métiers. One of her own brothers, Eustache, seeing that she was gifted for studying, also helped her a little. He was already studying agronomy at the University of Butare. Thanks to him, Marie-Arménie was introduced into a group of students. She began to work furiously, often in the evening and late at night. Her brother had become an important agro-forestry specialist and had published several articles on questions of mudslides. He was killed in 1994.

The period of her studies at the Ecole des arts et métiers was a rather happy period in her life. The Soeurs Missionaires de Notre-Dame d'Afrique (White Sisters) personally took care of Marie-Arménie, who they found gifted and especially active. They gave her classes in drawing, language, general culture, French, literature and natural sciences. The little nuns were very thoughtful and carefully helped each student. Butare was an urban commune and even though Marie-Arménie had to travel thirteen kilometres back and forth every day and farm in the fields, she was well integrated. She learned French frantically because she loved that language. She recited the poetry of Jacques Prévert, acted in the theatre and learnt that her memory was excellent, having been trained by never having a notebook. Again, she became first in her class and stayed there for three years. The nuns proposed enrolling her at the university. Now, it was her aunt who refused. Marie-Arménie would have to take care of her nephews at her grandmother's, which her aunt thought would be much more useful. She had studied enough. Because her aunt worked at the hospital, Marie-Arménie had no other choice but to become the nanny for her children. It was a way of repaying her aunt the money she had borrowed.

But in addition to all the work, there was still the sick grandmother. She needed care in addition to the work in the fields, and there were always cattle to take care of. The teenager decided to let the storm pass by. She set to work, but did not give up. She visited her former teachers and went to see all the teachers that she had had at the Ecole des arts et métiers. She explained that she wanted to become a French teacher. A teacher named Siméon was attracted to her and let her know that, but she turned a deaf ear. In exchange for a few caresses, he gave her a few books to study. She began to work all alone in the evening by candlelight. She was now eighteen and no longer climbed into the trees, but worked day and night and wanted to prepare the university entry exam by herself.

Thanks to her hard work, she succeeded in obtaining the necessary forms and took the entrance exam. Then, the university administration explained that she could not study at the university. Her results were, nonetheless, above the average. No one explained why it was impossible. She still did not understand, but hid her disappointment. She tried again. Then she obtained work as a replacement teacher at a primary school far into the hills, but not because of the results of her exam, which were good. It was a place where no one wanted to go. She also had the right to continue to study all alone, if she wanted to. For the first time in her life, Marie-Arménie received a salary. She earned RWF 6000 per month (about 25 dollars). Her mother was not happy, and her father said nothing. She was still not accepted at her family's house, and she lived at her grandmother's. She asked her mother why she had been banned but was given no reply. Her father had nothing to say, while her brothers and sisters supported her a bit, but nothing more. She had to look after herself all alone. For Marie-Arménie, that was the way she wanted it. It was now time to get married. She was certain that with a husband she would be able to rest a bit at home and give French classes in the neighbouring commune. She thought to herself that her dreams were obtainable, observing the women around her who appeared to be comfortable at home. Other women, at least on the outside, appeared very happy. Her earlier decision stayed the same. She started to look around. The first man she met who would flirt with her would be him, she decided. Her destiny would decide her future.

A pickup stopped one day on the side of the road. A cheerful voice called to her and asked whether she would like to go into town. She looked at him. The man appeared to be strong; he was a Hutu, she could feel it. He didn't appear to be ill tempered, so she got into the car. They began to see each other often, as the saying goes. Alphonse was a driver and found this lovely woman graceful, gay and vivacious just like he wanted. Like in the fairy tales, Marie-Arménie was happy at the beginning. He took her everywhere in his green pickup, all over Butare, proud as a duck. She sat up front and saw everything from high up, like when she was up in her trees. She knew she was finally going to be like everybody else. Marie-Arménie's family was opposed to the relationship. Even more so when after four months the couple announced that they were going to marry. The mother of Marie-Arménie, Immaculée, foresaw only unhappiness. The father said nothing. He was weighted down by the financial troubles of the family. His sons cost him a lot of money, and he was worried. Furthermore, the harassments that the Tutsi family faced had become more frequent, which made him bitter. Marie-Arménie didn't expect anything more from her family, but all the same she was very disappointed. At any rate, she said to herself that her new life would be better than cleaning the floor at her grandmother's.

The announcement was made, and the marriage took place at the church. Not many people showed up. No one from Marie-Arménie's family bothered to come, and his parents also did not come. They were incensed that their son was marrying a Tutsi. What was he thinking about, with such a good job as truck driver? Why should they go to the marriage of their son who did not even marry a Hutu? At the beginning of their relationship, Alphonse said nothing to his parents about the origin of Marie-Arménie. He just talked about a young farm girl. Then they saw her and said no. It got off to a bad start on both sides, but the couple decided to lead their life as they pleased. Marie-Arménie received a dowry of a black calf from her family, which was a bad sign. The little calf lived for only a few months after the marriage, and Alphonse became angry right away.

A daughter was soon born. Her name was Marie-Angeline and she was very sickly. Her father found that she resembled too much her mother, who was too bony. Marie-Arménie did not have the right to continue teaching, but had to work in her husband's fields and stay at home. She received a total of RWF 500 (two dollars) from her husband per week for all her expenses: the baby, the household, food, water and clothes. She was unable to make ends meet. She complained to her husband, who began to beat her for her inability to manage her home. She didn't say a word. She just succumbed. For two years, she carried on a battle for him to let her leave the house. He became more and more violent and was more and more absent, drinking with his friends. He began to attend what she thought were political meetings, communal meetings. For the first time, she heard talk of the total elimination of the "cockroaches". After the beautiful words of the period before the marriage, life after the marriage was a different reality. Their house on the hill near that of her parents was very modest. The work in the fields never ended. The roof, the garden, the water cistern, everything was precarious. There was no electricity, and Marie-Angeline was growing up. She looked at her mother with respect and never cried. Alphonse changed jobs. He received a small promotion and became "the head driver" in a small company in the Gikongoro prefecture.

A second child was born named Pacifique: in order to sail away. There was never enough money. Marie-Arménie begged her husband who continued to answer only with beatings. Marie-Arménie found an argument that hit the bull's eye: if she could teach a few hours, since Alphonse was spending all week in Gikongoro or Kigali, she could earn a bit of money. She would give him half that money. He ended up not saying no, but asked for all the money and threatened to refuse his permission at the slightest provocation. What that meant she had not a clue. Marie-Arménie began walking several kilometres again with Pacifique on her back and leading Marie-Angeline by the hand. She taught as a substitute teacher, where she was underpaid because she was Tutsi and a woman.

She worked in her field planting potatoes, cabbage and beans. She worked very hard without stopping and slept just a little.

Alphonse, at any rate, spent all his time in Kigali. When he came home, it was always without notice and only to beat her. The first year, she even succeeded in selling a few vegetables. Her husband started sending his sisters from the city, who took away all her second crop. Marie-Arménie was now twenty-nine years old. One day, the school inspector came to see her where she was teaching all subjects for next to nothing to small children. The children's parents did not want their children to be taught by a Tutsi. He told her that at any rate, teachers no longer had the right to teach without a certificate. She showed him that she had passed her exams with good grades. She had the equivalent of a diploma but had simply been refused the paper. Ill at ease, he confirmed that she could no longer teach. Furthermore, the prefecture had decided that she had the equivalent of nothing. Marie-Arménie didn't budge. She also did not leave. The inspector was a bit embarrassed. After a short time, he offered her the possibility of teaching in a broken-down school for boys and girls twenty kilometres away, but not in a normal school like she deserved. But in order for that to happen, she would have to be just a little bit nicer to the inspector. Marie-Arménie refused categorically and rejected him. The inspector become furious. How could she refuse his offer? He hit her, beat her and threw her out. She had just the time to tell him that if she needed a diploma, she would get one at whatever price she had to pay. She would find the money. She knew that if she paid, she would have a pretty good chance.

She took her two children whom she had left at the door. Marie-Angeline was quietly playing with Pacifique. No one said a word. She went to all the hills to see her brothers, the nuns at the Ecole des arts et métiers to borrow money, beg, find and explain with dignity and with a plan. After six months, she succeeded in putting together the money to register for the year of study for a teaching degree. Despite jeers and many humiliations related to begging for money, she was rebuffed and turned back on all sides, but she succeeded; in large part thanks to a White Father who noticed her gifts in literature. He remembered the cheerful young girl in the theatre classes at the beginning of the 1980s and recalled that she especially loved to play angels in the sky in a religious play at Christmas. And she succeeded in obtaining her teaching diploma. She still asked herself how. Between studies late at night, she worked hard. Alphonse came and went. She didn't know his whereabouts. He no longer gave her money. He became taciturn, but continued to beat her. Often, she couldn't even go to classes, but she made them up thanks to a friend who copied the questions. A third child was born: Jean-Bosco. He closely resembled his father, she said secretly. She saw her husband less and less. She learned from one of her mocking sisters-in-law that he was leading a worthless life in Kigali. Another sister-in-law announced to her one day victoriously that her husband had found a very beautiful woman there. She later learned that the beautiful woman was a woman, also Tutsi like her, who sold her charms to everyone for almost nothing. She learned that this woman had caught a terrible disease and that she had transmitted it to her husband, who then passed it to her. The lady died. Her husband would also finish by dying in the throes of the disease in a damp cell where he had been tortured. She had become seropositive. In 1993, she had her diploma in her pocket and succeeded, thanks to miraculous help, this time from her brother, in teaching in a small primary school although quite far from her house, but where she was an official teacher. The commune organized a small celebration in her honour. She was the first woman to have obtained a real teaching diploma. Because Marie-Arménie continued her tendency not to see any bad intentions on the part of others, she gave the party and invited everyone. She felt that she had to forgive those who had mistreated her, but also according to Rwandan traditions she had to remain polite and maintain smooth and peaceful relations with neighbours and her family.

In that way, she told herself, no one could reproach her for anything. She felt that this time she had gained a bit of peace, but she was wrong. She began to teach and understand her pain. She was going to become disenchanted. Her work was perfect, but she was not paid. All sorts of excuses were given and she went from window to window at the prefecture where she was looked on with disdain and sarcasm. She wanted her diploma, but she had it and nothing else. Things were to become worse. For several years, lists had been circulating. First, the Tutsis were treated as "cockroaches" and madmen. They were arrested and interned in psychiatric hospitals, and then put in prison. They even disappeared. Marie-Arménie recalled the words of her husband sitting at a table with his friends around ten bottles of Primus beer late at night at the house. On the hills, houses were burned regularly like straw fires, and the police made no move. They explained that those were just accidents. At Sunday mass, everyone knew who burned the house of whom, but no one dared speak out in public. Everyone pretended nothing had happened.

Marie-Arménie became very concerned about her parents. Just in her home commune, eighteen houses were burned one night. The next day, no one had heard or seen anything. Furthermore, she knew it was best not to stand out. A militant replaced the gendarmes in her commune, and her husband became the head of the militia there. He came home more regularly and was no longer a driver. He said he was working on his business. It was impossible to learn anything more. Then there were rumours that all the Tutsis would soon be killed, but she had heard that for decades, and they were still there. They were only rumours, but at any rate that was impossible. The rumours became more persistent and more public, but no, they were just pieces of gossip.

Alphonse began to go out every night and came back drunk and exhausted the next morning at 5 a.m. He had stopped speaking. Marie-Arménie told herself that maybe she should run away. But where could she go with three children?

One day, Alphonse brought another child to the house without a word of explanation. He simply said that the child was his and was born to a woman in Kigali who had died. Marie-Arménie stared at the child, who was also half Tutsi, half Hutu. The child was older than Marie-Angeline, her oldest daughter. He was probably close to fifteen years of age. She told herself that her husband had probably known the woman for a long time, but she adopted the child right away. The young adolescent looked at her with sweetness and respect. His name was Vincent Hakezimana. Over the course of months, he became a big brother for her children. Vincent was also scared, especially about what was happening in Kigali. He had already seen a lot. She thought to herself that the boy had been born well before her marriage, but kept silent.

On 7 April 1994, grenade fire began. News on the radio was horrible. President Habyiarimana had been killed in an airplane accident. Everyone was requested to remain at home. Suddenly, Marie-Arménie realized. She saw the image in front of her of her mother, father, brothers and sisters who are going to be killed; she was sure. Despite the firing of grenades, she left her children with Vincent and ran to her parents' house. She crossed the hills, fell, became stuck in the mud but she ran faster than the wind. Bullets could not have stopped her. She finally reached her parents' house. Her father has just been killed behind the house by a bullet from a revolver fired by a delighted militant. Her mother was paralysed and begged her to return home. Marie-Arménie hesitated and threw herself on her mother's neck, crying hysterically. She had to make a painful choice between her mother, her own children, uncles and aunts and her family-in law. Her mother drove her away. On 19 April, her area was attacked. The roofs of the houses were on fire. Fires lit the sky; she hid behind the water cistern, a red bible clutched in her hand. Her youngest daughter, Sophie, wrapped in a shawl, was tied on her back. The four other children were hiding in a closet. Alphonse did not come home. He had disappeared. From her hiding place, she could see coloured clothes on the ground in the distance on the sides of the hills, like cloths drying in the sun. She could not believe her eyes.

The whole hill was strewn with bodies. She learned that her pregnant older sister had been cut into pieces that day in front of her house. Marie-Arménie entered into cataleptic shock. Some people came into the house. She heard them say that it was the house of Alphonse and that there was nothing hidden there. They left, laughing and splitting their sides. On 24 April, she heard cries outside the door. Alphonse was giving orders, and told the others to continue. One of them pushed him aside and opened the door. Marie-Arménie was there with her youngest daughter, Sophie, tied on her back. She was lying on the ground, slightly turned towards the wall, holding a red bible, which she had received for her first communion.

The other children were hiding. She exchanged looks with her husband. The militants loaded their rifles. Alphonse laughingly told them that there were other things more important to do. He stepped between them and once again led them outside. At that moment, she would have liked to have been killed like the others. She realized that to have children who were neither Hutu nor Tutsi was the worst gift that she could have given them. She could see the doors of hell. She was getting ready to run out with her children and ask for quick death from a bullet. She would have been ready to pay in order not to be killed by a machete. But a single thought held her back: her mother. Maybe she still needed her. Maybe that would be the opportune moment to reconcile herself with her, to ask her for forgiveness for the terrible choice that she had made to marry a Hutu. Perhaps, Immaculée would finally agree to explain why she loved Marie-Arménie so little. Alphonse did not come back. Days went by. Marie-Arménie and her five children fed themselves on grain and drank rank water. They did not dare move. One of their neighbours, a policeman and a friend of her husband, decided to take them into his house. He knew that he ran the risk of certain death if he were discovered, but he liked Marie-Arménie and her husband. She spent three months hidden during the day, quickly eating at night in the hut of the Hutu policeman.

In July 1994, Alphonse came back. He was unrecognisably thin. He did not say a word. He laconically ordered the whole family to flee because of the advance of the Armée patriotique rwandaise (APR). In a painful, heavy, oppressive, silent procession, the whole commune walked to the Kibeho refugee camp. Marie-Arménie no longer wanted to live, see or hear. In addition to the atrocities of the past few months, there was the added shame of being part of the group of killers. Three hundred thousand persons were piled into the camp. A stream separated the APR from the "French area", called "Opération Turquoise". The children were listless. They didn't move all day.

In the camp, an international organization realized that the graceful Marie-Arménie knew how to count, write and provide care. She became responsible for the nutritional unit of the international organization running the camp. As for Alphonse, he was just flesh and bones, the shadow of his former self: not a word, not a gesture. From time to time, because the camp was divided into sectors and cells based on origin, one of his buddies came to have a drink with him under the plastic sheeting distributed by UNHCR. He tried to cheer him up by recalling the good old days of cutting up everything that moved. Alphonse seemed to laugh a little bit less. He just pretended to agree in order not to make his buddy angry.

At dawn one morning, there was a riot. The whole western part of the camp was up in arms, bitter and really angry. They had just learned that Marie-Arménie was a Tutsi. They shouted that she was going to poison all of them, that she was working for the enemy and that she would kill all of them, strangle them, get rid of them with her "enriched powered milk". They began to throw rocks at her. There were more than ten thousand of them. A furious crowd. Without the intervention of the Europeans, Marie-Arménie would once again have been dead. She decided to flee to the APR-controlled area and asked her husband to decide right away. Listless, like a zombie, he mechanically got up and joined Marie-Arménie and their children in the lorry of the international organization. Her husband found work as a driver with a group of persons travelling every day to Cyangugu. Two months later, Alphonse was arrested at an APR checkpoint on the road to Cyangugu.

His destiny had caught up with him. A soldier had appeared and recognized him. They were from the same area in the same commune. They had been together at primary school. His arrest was violent with immediate solitary confinement. During several months, Marie-Arménie had to walk kilometres to take food to her husband in prison. She suffered embarrassment, gibes and jeers. He became bitter and lost weight because he was suffering from the effects of AIDS in addition to the torture marks. He started complaining that she did not come to see him often enough. He told her that he remembered the small white night shirt that he had offered her for their marriage. Marie-Arménie visited him out of duty. She did not feel any hatred, just great pity. She tried to tell him that she had spent years crying without his noticing. He did not understand and could not see what she was talking about. He was locked into total denial. Often he became extremely angry, forbidding her to belong to anyone but him. She made the journey twice a week during three months, taking him food, clothes, cakes and cigarettes that he had to share with his fellow inmates. He died in 1996, eaten away by illness and the humidity in the prison. He never regretted for a moment what he had done.

Marie-Arménie wisely turned the page without passing judgement. I first met her at Kibuye where she had found work to feed her five children. She sang and danced and wanted to give peace to people. What had changed the most for her was that now she was no longer afraid or embarrassed to be a Tutsi.

She dared eat with other persons. She always had her red bible with her and the small white night shirt. She taught her group of mixed schoolchildren to be tolerant and wanted nothing to do with politics. She then realized that she could move about without being afraid of being killed. She went to look for her mother, the only survivor in her family. Silently, Marie-Arménie and her mother learned to live together, as if they wanted to begin something again. But Immaculée was no longer in this world, even if she was alive. Marie-Arménie now had to fight against a new enemy: her terrible illness. In April 1999, her tiny voice came from the other side of death. He destiny is an example of that of many others.

Chapter 5

Diary (1999)

At the Heart of the Daily Struggle to Promote Reconciliation

5 January 1999: The new mosaic

This week, the Minister of Justice resigned. He was the second justice minister in two years. People are leaving. Is it because the government is so hard, so intransigent? What can you expect when twenty members of your family have disappeared? To be recognized from the beginning as indispensable? The survivors are unhappy and have begun to express their unhappiness. They represent a traumatized lost population that is difficult to integrate. The survivors are a problem because they do not feel understood by the Tutsis who have returned from Uganda and who did not experience the genocide. A clear break has been created in society. They would like to have tangible proof that their suffering is being seriously taken into account. Fortunately, they find it difficult to find their place in this new mixed society, where Rwandans from the Congo come in contact with those returning from Burundi, Uganda or Canada. Everyone tries to do things their own way and sees the future of his country in accordance with his education as an exile. A gap has been created between those who stayed and those who can no longer find their references and those repatriated Rwandans. How is it possible in such a poor country to ask other poor people to give compensation? Is the international community the only answer?

A census is being held. It is a difficult exercise, if you take into account the number of persons exiled in 1959, about one million, who returned to the country in 1994. The number of dead during the genocide must also be taken into account, between eight hundred thousand and one million. Then, there are about one and a half million refugees who returned from the Congo in 1997. Finally, those displaced from north-western Rwanda, about 500,000, who are no longer in their commune of origin, have to be included. The census of a total population of about eight million will be politically sensitive. Can we imagine the mixture of populations in this new mosaic that is Rwanda? Can we imagine the conflicts that will take place over titles to houses?

The horrors continue in the Congo. The massacre at Makabola was an example of a biased point of view. There was no detailed investigation, only accusations. Every time we visited the site of the fighting, we discovered wrongs committed by both sides. The press is often simplistic; placing the good people on one side and the bad on the other. But it's not like that in Africa and, in fact, nowhere else. Who killed 500 persons at Makabola? Was it the Banyamulenge (Tutsis who immigrated to Eastern Congo at the beginning of the past century)? Did Rwandans help them? All of that seems unbelievable. Almost no one protested in September 1998 when there were massacres of Banyamulenge. Why? The truth is somewhere in between the two extremes.

10 January 1999: The orders came from higher up

These are difficult times for Rwandans. With the stroke of a magic wand, it was decided that the country would suddenly pass from the status of a humanitarian emergency to the phase of long-term development. Everything seems to indicate, however, that we are in a grey area of transition and reconciliation. There are still pockets of population that are in dire need. The United Nations has changed its strategy and no longer gives money to NGOs. It favours other institutions and argues for reinforcement of institutional capacities. There is something like a stagnant air in Rwanda because fresh money is lacking. Development is probably the only factor that could accelerate reconciliation: working side by side in the fields and harvesting sufficient food for sale with everyone working together. But how can equitable development be promoted during such a difficult time? The disparities and injustices in Rwanda are still too great. While the economic programme is doing well, it does not sufficiently benefit the poor. Social cohesion and human resources are lacking. The middle class has either been destroyed or has left the country. There are neither sufficient human resources to carry out the reforms and restructure the government nor competent specialists. Some people—a small minority—are becoming wealthy. A complete absence of freedom characterizes everyday life on the hills. The harsh political system and the tradition of following orders from above were fatal for the country, making it possible to counter any opposition; and that situation still continues. Civil society has trouble forming an opposition. What does democracy mean here; more freedom, access to expression, more money more equally distributed?

26 January 1999: First prize, a Fanta orange

This Sunday, I went jogging with the Hash House Harriers, a group of runners led by the Americans, in the eastern part of Kigali around the King Faisal Hospital. We were a group of persons of all ages running full blast through the countryside before the startled eyes of the local inhabitants outside their little houses. It was a very American environment: quite well behaved. This strenuous exercise, running up and down hills, provides contact with crowds and a chance to escape. The very hilly landscape is beautiful, but the poverty of the local inhabitants is plain to the eyes. We were in the hilly slums of Kigali where the houses are precarious. Roofs are falling in, and doors often have no frames. Here and there, several chickens were scratching for bits of maize on the ground. The inhabitants of the alleyways watched us as if we were running the Paris-Dakar rally, but without any enthusiasm. What had these Europeans come to do in the poor neighbourhoods of Kigali?

An African can judge the life of Europeans only by the luxurious conditions they enjoy and we had no reason to be there. A small child of about ten years old came running down the muddy slope on my right and headed straight towards me. He ran behind hilariously shouting, *muzungu, muzungu* (white person, white person). He caught up with me and began talking to me. His name was Jean-de-Dieu. He was running faster than I could. He took my hand and shouted, "I'll show you how to accelerate." We began to run faster. He told me to breath through my mouth. I came in third, and he was first. At the finish line, the race official looked at him with admiration. His prize was a Fanta orange. He turned towards me and asked whether he could touch my blond hair.

Life is a song

How can I explain this fleeting feeling of time warp that I have? It's a sort of sudden and passing loss of my reference points. What was certain is no longer and everything else with it. I am sure that Rwanda is an initiation. Events take place day after day bringing problems to be solved; problems as large as mountains. Everyday, we pick up our tools and set to work. We deal with all the problems at once: such as those concerning education, agriculture and health. We participate in improving transportation and markets. We admire the cows. Where should we begin given that everything has been destroyed? I sense that this partnership with Rwanda and the sharing of the setting of priorities is important. It is a real learning experience about my own limits. At the end of the day, I will know better who I am because I will have better understood who they are. Rwanda doesn't allow for cheating. I don't want to hide behind humanitarian jargon or pretended indifference. I have to jump in. Relations between people are violent, rough, sincere, filled with love and hateful. We have our culture of justice, well-executed work and truth that frequently clashes with dubious intentions. It's a lesson in life. Never again could I not play a part in the world. It's as though I had been obliged through this difficult trial to accept myself as I am. I have learned to accept my contradictions, incoherencies, and search for meaning and have come to appreciate the honesty of doing minor things for the occasional persons with whom my destiny has crossed a bit by chance and with whom I share a moment. The positive is immediate: to accept mistakes is to first accept the mistakes of others. The Rwandans that I meet accept me and welcome me. I go along with them. I criticize them when I find that what they were doing is wrong, and they accept my criticism. It is a meagre victory: the course of events can be influenced whenever you succeed in understanding the logic of others. A point of view is closely linked to survival. During this time, we at the other end of the equation are drowning in over-consumption.

4 February 1999: Lunch in the country

This week, there was another field visit with the prefect. It was instructive and raised my hopes by seeing obvious good intentions in the rural area. Above all, I felt that the farmers wanted to move on and overcome their difficulties: to work, farm and put their antagonisms behind them. The prefect has an excellent attitude. Nonchalantly, he tirelessly visits the fields, houses and other areas. He observes, discusses and listens to people and tries to improve their daily lives. He is jovial and speaks several languages, but nothing prepared him for this position: he is an economist who returned to Rwanda in 1996. Exiled in 1962, he worked in the Gulf Emirates and has ten female children. We had a good laugh when he told me how he had given them names. The first were given names indicating positive events: Morning dawn, Day's happiness and then the names moved on to later parts of the day: Ray of sunlight, Light of the afternoon. The last girl is called "Oh, my

God, what have I done? Their names became inversely proportional to his impatience to have a boy. Whoever said that Rwandans have no humour?

We study the growing of pineapple, manioc, potatoes, goats, chickens and bees, receiving a lesson about agriculture from each local association. The ministry has published a small green book on appropriate seasons. All together, in the presence of the association, we read out loud the parts dealing with plant propagation. During talks to assembled farmers I always point out that I sincerely admire the association of energetic women. They always replied with a big hurrah and gave me a small woven basket. Then, we went to visit a model market offering tomatoes and cabbage. There really is not much offered at the markets. There is a lot of manioc cut into white pieces drying in the sun. A stray dog came up to smell the potatoes laid out in little piles. An African market is always a strategic centre. It's there that women gossip and earn a bit of money in order to buy their daily necessities. In the market, there is an enormous amount of third-rate junk, almost everything and yet nothing. There is almost nothing of value, but almost everything can be useful. Tin or plastic buckets and plates, hides and shoes, coloured cotton cloth, nylon dresses, spices and herbs, small bottles and charms against bad luck.

During the lunch in a cheap restaurant on the shore near Lake Mohazi brochettes of goat meat were served. The minister told me that he had trained as a veterinarian and that he had practiced veterinary medicine earlier. Right away, I sensed a certain tension between the minister and the prefect. I couldn't tell whether it was ethnic or political in origin, but there were moments of silence in the conversation. Each of them sees the future in their own way. One saw wells, bridges, markets and roads. The other talked about education, health and, above all, the children.

Throughout the country, there were still more than three hundred thousand children without families. Rwanda had done away with orphanages. Orphaned children are either the head of a reconstituted family or have been integrated into a host family. They have to do a lot of work and do not go to school. It is a generation of sacrifice. The little girls are forced to fetch water or cut firewood. Children have to confront all the problems of a developing country and at the same time live with the memory of a genocide.

18 February 1999: Baptism by fire

A little bit later, I was invited to a Rwandan baptism in a family of middle-class exiles who returned from Belgium in 1997. It was thrilling. The husband is a physician, the wife a nurse: Benoît and Marie-Angélique. Thanks to them, I better understand an old Rwandan custom: that of giving a child a name with a meaning. The name is fundamental in the life of the child. The child must fulfil its destiny and live out its name. There are no surnames in Rwanda. There is a Christian name and a name that indicates what the child should do and become in his life. Each person knows from which hill his clan comes, who is the head, who his father and grandfather are and, above all, where they and everyone else were in 1994. A child has two given names: one given upon baptism in Kinyarwanda and another, usually Christian from the Bible; for example Nepomuscène or Ezechias.

Let's take the example of the son of Benoît and Marie-Angélique. The enlarged family baptized him, giving him the name Rutikanga. The name means "He who fears nothing". His family, the local group and the school will remind him of it throughout his life. He must honourably fulfil this quality and behave in its light. At the time of his second baptism in the church, he will be named Jean-Baptiste. That day, I was invited to the baptism with the Rwandan name. I arrived at about 5 p.m. on Sunday at a beautiful recently repainted white house with a golden gate in the Remera section of Kigali. Children were quietly playing on the grass with a football made from pieces of rubber. On the terrace, close relatives were talking. They were wearing brightly coloured clothes and drinking either banana alcohol, Primus beer or Coca Cola.

The father and mother of the baby were quietly talking at the entrance of the house. Benoît and Marie-Angélique have three other children. Their little son was their fourth child. He was asleep, but his mother would bring him out in a little while. Samosas, little Asian appetizers made from deep-fried pastry with meat fillings, were being passed around along with potato chips and salted peanuts. I sat down next to a couple. The husband, an architect, had just found work with an NGO in the field of housing. His name was Faustin and her name was Atlanta. Atlanta knew Europe well because she had studied social science there. She had adopted five orphaned children in addition to her own three children. We began to talk about the new policy of modernization of villages. Faustin argued in favour of modernization and the need to exploit the small amount of land available in Rwanda. He felt its scattered habitat represented a danger and was inappropriate for solidarity and the forming of a community. He said that it would be impossible to pass in one year from traditional Rwandan reservation to the promiscuity of West Africa. He smiled at his wife. He felt that dispersed houses in the countryside and their isolation hidden under the banana trees greatly helped the work of the killers. We took up the topic of the way villages were to be regrouped with forced displacement of people. We mentioned the resistance of those who first wanted infrastructure, water, latrines and a health centre before moving to a new location. You have to take into account the grumbling of displaced farmers, I said. They have to walk kilometres to farm their land, and we know well enough the symbol of the land of the ancestors and family property. The new villages being built are sparsely inhabited. How can we harmonize the two tendencies?

But Rwanda is too small, Faustin burst out, for everyone to have a field. We are going to farm as a cooperative for the owners. That's our future, and we absolutely must learn

95

to live together. At that moment, Marie-Angélique brought the little eight-day-old baby and showed him to everyone. Because he had just been woken up, he was not happy and had a wrinkled face. But the cries and harsh treatment of the other children finally won him over and his bad humour slowly disappeared. He yawned. Benoît explained the custom to me of gathering around the baby, observing him, envisaging his future and suggesting names to the other persons. The guests gathered around in a circle. Dozens of names were suggested. First of all, the children made suggestions: "the one who watches over the cows", "the guide", "the loved-one of the forests", "he who will not tire of praising God", "the courageous", "the impetuous" and "he who fears nothing". That last suggestion made everyone silent, the conversation stopped. Something had happened. The right word had been spoken; like a breath of truth. The parents felt that it was the right name. In accordance with the custom, they chatted on during the night in order to ensure themselves that it was the right choice. We continued drinking, then everyone left, quite satisfied. It was the children of friends and the family that had given a name to the little boy eight days later, through intuition about his future. A current had passed, he was named and, therefore, existed. Then, the parents went to sleep. It is a beautiful custom. There are no family names common to the father, mother and children. This reinforces even more the impression that family ties are secret and difficult to identify in Rwanda.

23 February 1999: A Canadian obstetrician

He, the Canadian obstetrician, has been In Rwanda for twenty years. He invited me one evening to the "Caprice du Palais", the chicest restaurant in Kigali, it is said. In the form of a litany, he told me all about the 1990s: the arrival of the extremists, the impotent Europeans. He himself had found Rwanda worthy of a paradise, at least before, according to him.

Now, Rwanda was no longer a shadow of itself. "The stupid b.......", he shouted out loud. This put me a bit ill at ease. Those nostalgic for the past are not really my cup of tea. He had sent his Rwandan wife off in an airplane to Toronto in a remarkable premonition on April 5th, the day before that fatal airplane crash. At any rate, she was on the lists, he said. Then he offered me a pile of books and invited me everywhere. I had to explain kindly that I was very busy. It flattered me that he found me pleasant, but I thought that that was enough. One evening, while driving me home from my office where I had left my car, he made a mistake driving his old Ford and ended up with two wheels in a huge ditch for water pipes. All the surrounding night watchmen and ten other persons had to push back and forth. It took two hours to get us out. It was hilarious. I told him that for a gynaecologist, it was really funny for him to drive into a big ditch in the middle of the road. He didn't appreciate my bawdy remark, and I never saw him again.

27 February 1999: Mayi-Mayi at the gates of Rwanda

Things are not going well with the rebellion in the Congo. They are losing ground and are fighting among themselves. They have split into those in Equator and Kava provinces, as well as those from the north and those from the south of Eastern Congo. They are just mercenaries, the Mayi-Mayi, offering their services to whoever pays the most; fanatical combatants smoking marijuana that makes them feel invincible. They are an uncontrollable element in the Congo who kill without hesitation and support no cause. But at the moment, they are supporting the Rwandan rebels, the Interhamwe. They are very feared and don't hesitate to kill. We were quite worried that week. The fighting was tough at Bukavu. Very bloody it seems with a lot of loss on both sides. The Interhamwe were fighting on the side of the Congolese troops, the heavily armed Mayi-Mayi and other rebellions.

Bukavu in eastern Congo is right opposite Cyangugu, which is in south-western Rwanda. A bridge separates the two towns. The fighting is quite close. When will this hatred go away? How can a group of half-human soldiers in rags be stopped? Why does the population of the Congo have to suffer? I was still quite busy working on education and health.

4 March 1999: With kisses from Tanzania

Finally, three days of vacation. The visit to Tanzania is wonderful; especially the parks and Ngorongoro crater. I spent the night in a tent at the top of a mountain with an amazing view over the plateaux and the exuberant vegetation during the rainy season. It was like in a film. I felt an indescribable sense of happiness to be out in nature in Africa. The natural silence filled us with joy in luxuriant nature.

Tanzania is right next door to Rwanda, just to the east, but I had the impression of having crossed an ocean. There is a difference that is not only geographical but also human. There are no longer a thousand hills and you can see far away to the high mountains of Kilimanjaro and Meru. The local inhabitants react quite differently to Europeans. First of all, the European is not necessarily a tourist. That took me out of my role of development coordinator for a while. Second, Tanzanians have a sort of laziness, a laisser-aller of patient kindness that allows them to dream. How can the difference be explained? Has it been caused by different political systems, socialism, by inspired local chiefs, such as former president Nyerere or by ancestral mentalities and cultures?

Just several kilometres from Rwanda, there is a completely different Africa, a sandy, calcareous atmosphere and an ocean, a more relaxed rhythm. There are elephants and lions as in "The Jungle Book". There is a thriving handicraft industry tailored for the passing tourist: for example the Tingatinga art form of stylised paintings of animals and plants. I also sensed a certain indolence. Things must be difficult to get done here, I told myself. I then spent an evening in Arusha in northern Tanzania with some friends. They were participating in the peace negotiations for Burundi. John really impressed me. He told me about his time in prison with Mandela and described the struggle of the African National Congress (ANC). A White South African in prison for the ANC gave a different perspective to things. John also admitted that he was fed up with the endless sessions of negotiation about Burundi. He felt the talks were costing money and leading nowhere. The difficulty of carrying out peace talks with the Burundis should not be underestimated. They are extremely rough. The conference is made up of eighteen different factions and parties. One of the military groups doesn't stop shouting foul insults at the monarchists. John is English speaking and he has learned one basic word of French that the Burundis use all the time, but he can't repeat it to me. He deplores the absence of rigour in the talks and thinks that any progress will be difficult.

1 April 1999: Terrace houses

It's understandable. Rwandans are reluctant to talk about their pain and to speak of their past although they are confronted daily with its consequences. The importance of opening an outpatient psychosocial centre in the middle of Kigali has become evident. It is for all those who feel a need to consult specialists and be able to talk about their problems anonymously. This centre is available not only to those who suffered from the genocide but also to those who committed crimes. The question of trauma should be the object of all our concerns. The psychosocial centre will be inaugurated next week by the minister for health. This week was marked by a reshuffling of members of the government. I ran about everywhere trying to gain impressions, information and opinions. I also met with Cornelio, who is carrying out a study for the OECD on the effects of "political conditionality" of

99

public assistance. He has already written a book that had offended people. Now, he was continuing his crusade. He argued that no one has ever been successful at promoting something using threats.

I also went to Gisenyi in north-western Rwanda for the inauguration of the United Nations Inter-Agency Office. I was asked to represent the international community. The town is in a busy and hectic state of reconstruction and development. Business is booming with the Congo, and the soldiers appear calm. The 150,000 persons grouped around their sites of origin, especially in Rwerere, have begun to build their houses; sometimes under the threat of bayonets. Gisenyi is a beautiful town on the shores of Lake Kivu. You can see Goma in the Congo on the other shore a hundred metres away. You can freely walk about. But it's not the same as Kibuye. The attempt to force people to gather in villages is going to be a point of disagreement between the international community, United Nations agencies, especially UNHCR, and the government. I always try to talk about things first. What is most important is the opinion of local inhabitants: what they want and what they think. Because I have heard many jokes, sometimes really juicy, about the communal elections or rural associations, I can put the "new modern villages" into perspective, given the reality of the small farmers. The idea is doubtlessly good, but it will be necessary to proceed by stages and above all in agreement with those involved. Pilot villages for repatriates would make it possible to convince others. The problem is very complex. It is linked to the question of property and the cramped conditions of Rwanda with its hilly geography. Who has the right to own a house: the person who owned it before 1959, the person who returned in 1994, or the person who came back from a refugee camp in 1997? There is an enormous debate that is difficult to settle democratically.

7 April 1999: Bisesero, commemoration of a heroic resistance

We went to Kibuye with government officials who were visiting the provinces to know their country better. We were accompanied by representatives from UNESCO and visited the site of Bisesero, the centre of resistance where a large number of persons had been killed. This place is to be an international site for "Memory of genocides". The only difficulty is that the site is located an hour and half by car from Kibuye. Access is by a road that is almost impossible to use during the rainy season. Bisesero is perched on hills, a bit like sites of resistance hidden in the Jura Mountains that you run across by chance. We studied plans for construction of a future world memorial for genocide, which would at the same time be a place of prayer. A spiritual place based around a construction of posts with mirrors that reflect the sunlight at different angles. The slope of the hill is very steep. Reaching the summit requires a sort of painful climb up a volcanic mountain, like climbing Mount Calvary. At the base of the climb, there was still a communal grave on a sort of platform. Tens of thousands of Tutsi were killed here and their corpses are decomposing among bones, clothes and children's toys. The prefect begged us to help him. He wanted to keep the ground as it was, so that it would not be forgotten. He spoke a lot about revisionists who argued that there had never been a genocide and was quite worried. The odour was stinking, relentless. We could neither look at nor avoid this tragic scene. The prefect wanted us to send specialist to preserve the bones. Little by little the stench made us sick. It is impossible to forget the smell. At the beginning of the climb, there is a big book and I had to write in the visitors' book what I felt. I tried to speak in the name of all those who had lived and worked in Kibuye. I expressed my sympathy for the victims and tried to pay them a tribute. Can the dead hear us? Right after that, we were invited to eat brochettes at the edge of the peaceful lake. Everyone pretended as though they had felt nothing. For my part, I was unable to swallow a single piece of meat, and others followed my example. Rwandans hate pettiness and the compassionate looks of the Europeans who have regrets after the fact. They prefer dignity. I restrained myself.

10 April 1999: The opinion makers

It seems that our impressions from within Rwanda are different from those expressed outside Rwanda. To live here makes you see things differently. Our opinions are not more accurate; they are simply closer to a certain reality. A lot of theorists question this fact, holding that when you are concentrated on the steering wheel you don't see the road. I think that if you are forced to look at the road while pushing forward, you get better results. It's a question of your point of view. An ambassador commented last week that no one listens to us. He felt that even the most intelligent of analysts cannot understand the Rwandan and regional reality in a few days. There are specialists on Rwanda, even a lot of them, but they are often caught in the crossfire between the old and the new Rwanda. Just like the American journalist whom I met at the very beginning of my stay, more than ten professors, intellectuals, special envoys and eminent emissaries continue to pass through each week. They come for three days and ask for tailor-made opinions about what we experience daily. This dysfunction is fascinating. Just like the willingness of Westerners to package their rough, simplistic analysis, while any proper analysis requires fine-tuning and precise analysis. In general, we have already passed to the following stage when they make their own discoveries. Theories and words abound, although reality remains complex and the smallest thing can trigger hatred. The country is going imperceptibly forward each month. Progress seems to be in the right direction even if certain setbacks are necessary in order to take another step forward. It takes time to understand all the nuances of reconciliation. You can gain confidence only with tangible proof.

14 April 1999: Is arrogance the other side of shame?

Men make the world, but what role do their fears play? What are they afraid of losing? I am not a woman of power but of principle. I have to question my principles and accept other people as they are; especially when they are exactly as I think they should not be. This adaptation took months. It's not easy to be the head of a team every day. To be a woman working in an African country requires a great deal of modesty and conviction.

I said goodbye to Yolanda, my psychiatrist friend from Eastern Europe who had been working in north-western Rwanda. I was very sad to see her go. We had spent hours talking around the dirty and empty swimming pool on Sunday. Maybe they will send her back. She had been here since August 1994. Her stories continue to haunt me. It's unbelievable what Rwanda has been through during the past few years.

How can you begin at the beginning? How can you integrate one million persons in one year? How can the torn social structure be repaired? Sometimes, I find myself asking God not to let us make a mistake. And then, quite regularly when I am in the field, contact with the local populations gives me new hope. They don't seem free from their past, and yet they want peace at any price, even if it's in the small way of something different. The situation is often quite tense on the hills. The smallest incident can lead to madness. The local mayors (*bourgmestres*) do everything so that the violence does not go beyond the level of low-intensity violence. I also perceived that arrogance is often the mask and the hidden face of shame. Rwandans are very abrupt with other Africans, especially West Africans, because they think the West Africans are hiding perpetrators of the genocide. A new law has been passed in Bamako (Mali) requiring the arrest and trial of Rwandan criminals. Let's hope that that will improve relations between West and East Africa.

What a mess of permanent tensions. The atmosphere is often very heavy in Kigali, like the battery of a large torch. The only difference is that there is no longer any willingness to slaughter, except on the part of the Interhamwe. Last week, the authorities caught a member of the Interhamwe in Ruhengeri. He was only a middle-level operator. What is worrying, is that he was handed over to the authorities by the Hutu population. Has the period of denunciation come back? There is no reason to have any illusion about the apparently normal appearances of Rwandans, who often remain violent among themselves. They seem to have little clemency for each other. There is a harshness and a roughness in their relationships that seems to go far back. For me, it's a stark contrast with the gentleness of the Mozambican tobacco plantations and the palms, songs and dances of Mali.

28 April 1999: A Brahman woman

Living in Rwanda since 1996, she has the grace of an Indian woman who takes things with distance and wisdom. Her name is Shahaz. She brought her sari, knowledge about poverty and her basic spiritual values from Asia. Smiling maliciously, she told me that spirituality was not really the first Western value that you bring. You have to speak out and rise up against all injustice and vengeance. She promotes forgiveness, even if the prisoners swear it was not their fault. She is an important figure in Kigali because she says shocking things to the Rwandans in a melodious and soft voice. We need at least a generation to relearn to say thank you, she confided in me. She seems to be a person detached from this world, but at the same time she is very present. Her philosophy fascinates me. We often have tea on her flowered terrace at Kyovu where we talk about the best strategies to adopt for reconciliation. She is an upper caste Brahman from India, who fasts once a week, has a degree in biology and a doctorate in economics and three children at the University of Washington.

She is an economist and works in the reorganization of the Ministry of Finance. She warmly greeted me and asked how I manage to balance my dynamism, kindness and generosity in dealing with the international community. She also wondered how I manage to turn away the queue of men who purportedly are knocking on my door. I laughed and thanked her. I told her that more than anything else there were thousands of things that I did not know; starting with the importation of fertilizers, the property law and the growing of pineapples. But I have found a way to make Rwandans take me seriously. They understand that Europeans are not completely convinced of their good faith and that they have to prove it to us. Sometimes, an active and positive presence is more important that giving money. A search for a basis for friendship that links other people to Rwandans so that they can find their own voice on the international scene seems to me to be basic. That calls for patience.

3 May 1999: Burundi, a boiling pot

It's the story of a similar country that is not similar. It is a little bit similar, but with people who are different and at the same time similar; people who solve their problems in another way. It is as if as younger cousins despised by their bigger Rwandan brothers, they have to prove their ability to move forward differently from a new genocide. But to no avail as bears witness the many forms of violence that are still at their doors, ready to break out at any moment. Violent attacks by the rebels and the fierce replies of the army continue. It is like a low intensity war, which constantly demands its dead, but which no one wants to talk about.

Once again it was a real challenge to spend a week in Burundi. The trip had been well prepared with talks with many people at all levels, including ministers and general secretaries, the United Nations and NGOs. But the fragility of the situation is a cause for concern. This boiling pot needs attention. It could break out and engulf the whole region again. Burundi offers every reason to have a certain enlightened, vigilant and prudent optimism. In Burundi, everyone is talking about "dialogue" and arguments. A real division exists in every aspect of society. The Palipehutu (Parti pour la libération du people Hutu—the Hutu opposition political party) is active and determined to take up the struggle. The government is inflexible. Several ministers have been silenced by the appeal of opulence and corruption. It is unbelievable to see a different way of approaching the same problem with more extravert players. In the field, there is violence, attacks, deaths and the complete poverty of isolated and abandoned populations that have been left to their sort since 1993. They are in rags and waiting for foreign help. I was overwhelmed by it all.

7 June 1999: Four marriages and mass

Saturday, I went to the marriage of the daughter of Ephraim, one of our collaborators. I was the only European among 150 Rwandans. I dreamed for just a second of being able to change my colour for half an hour. A crowd of African faces is sometimes very worrying. Nonetheless, I am really at home here and like Africa intensely. In the crowded church, four marriages were being celebrated at the same time and the priest took them two by two in order not to have to repeat. They swore fidelity to each other. The bride, named Hyacinthe, was in white with bows that cascaded off her veil. Life went on, but mixed marriages between Hutu and Tutsi have become very rare.

Sunday, I was invited to dinner at Emmanuel's, the new Rwandan chargé d'affaires who is being sent abroad to a large country. He impressed me by his class, moderation and humour. He is the former head of the FPR in Goma in the 1990s, a brother of Norbert and the uncle of a surgeon, my colleague in the Ministry of Health, whom I met on an airplane. I was slowly beginning to learn about the underground networks that link up all the new people in power. It is like water, which looks for a way under ground to advance taking all detours necessary in order not to bog down. The water drains away with it all the drops that resemble it. The water always succeeds in escaping, but people? The evening was very lively. There were only Rwandans. An extended family of about thirty persons was present. In private, people, just like water fountains, do not stop talking. Emmanuel has been given the task of finding and reconciling all Rwandans living abroad; a risky and big programme. He told me that right now any opportunity has to be seized. He was designated a "volunteer". His wife found this mission already less amusing because they were going to live on the 48th floor in a skyscraper in a European capital.

28 June 1999: School is out

Rwanda cruelly lacks schoolbooks at all levels. I was told that a national policy is still not ready regarding whether schoolbooks should be in English or French, but history books in Kinyarwanda have been distributed with a new historical focus on the genocide. Their authors are English speaking. There is a lot of talk about it. It is difficult to take a global approach to things promoting reconciliation and a new culture of unity in Rwanda. We have seen that the best results have been obtained in all the projects by involving everyone concerned. When people participate in the construction of schools, committees of parents are formed in order to ensure maintenance of the buildings. Officials have the obligation of gathering children in the morning to take them to school, but many adolescents have to go to the fields to farm because a large part of the labour force is in prison. As for the radical passage of the country from French to English, for three quarters of the population it is really another story. A decision becomes very political. How can you ask a poor population without anything to trade English for French in four years, when in our countries we struggle our whole lifetimes to learn a foreign language?

His name is Rafiki (friend) and he works in the Ministry for Education. He described to me the difficulties existing in the schools. Kinyarwanda is the first language, then French and English are taught at the same time. Not at the same time really, but in function of the knowledge of the teacher. There is a great lack of teachers: either they are dead or they have left the country. Rwanda has to make do with the meagre resources that it still has. Others will be trained at the teachers' college, the Kigali Institute of Education. Teachers know either French or English, rarely both, and classes are taught depending on the background of the teacher. The few books that exist are in one of the languages. Rafiki is certain that Rwanda will succeed in one way or another. If they can speak Kinyarwanda, supposedly as difficult as Chinese, it will be easy to learn two other languages later. His optimism is only half convincing, but he is right. They have no other choice. We worked for many hours on pedagogical questions of how to teach several languages and arrived at the conclusion that a bilingual regional approach would give more opportunity for integration of Rwanda into the region, especially with regard to Kenya and Tanzania.

Which education and which history for Rwanda?

The two neighbouring English-speaking countries offer the only two commercial accesses to the sea. I was always interested in questions of bilingual education and a first language. I think it is a unique opportunity to speak two languages well, but in Rwanda the challenge seems overwhelming. A person never has the same voice or the same thoughts in both languages. There are no estimates in Rwanda of the number of people who speak either French or English. Often, Rwandans can communicate only in their national language, which they have learned abroad therefore imperfectly, to communicate. That's an indication of the number of misunderstandings that can take place. The questions of which language and its mastery remain crucial. As a result, reinforced learning of the national language must be promoted. This is one of the urgent and important priorities.

Rafiki warmly thanked me for my ideas. The absence of any real basis for a policy of the Ministry for Education, which hesitating between French and English as second language, makes me angry. A decision and money are urgently needed for the sake of the children. In order to get across my message of priority for education, I went on Rwandan television and argued for a multi-lingual country. Things should slowly evolve by stages with a basic, solid mother tongue, then the gradual addition of another, then, two foreign languages. But here, there is not only a need to rush forward but everything must take place at the same time: English taught to the French-speaking teachers and vice-versa. As if by miracle, books in three languages must be found, schools rehabilitated and parents made aware of the stakes. I strongly insisted on the training of teachers because currently secondary school teachers have often finished only primary school. Classes are overcrowded, and most classes have at least sixty-five pupils. There are no desks, notebooks, chalk or blackboards. Sometimes, there are ballpoint pens that a NGO has distributed to everyone. Means are lacking everywhere. Local mayors complain about not having sufficient qualified staff on the outlying hills. No one wants to go there to teach because most of the time there is no water or electricity. Even worse, Rwandan intellectuals are not even in agreement among themselves about the contents of history books about Rwanda.

18 July 1999: What's the truth?

As for technical assistance activities, programmes are always linked. The right hand cannot ignore what the left hand is doing. Poverty must be reduced among certain categories of the population, and respect for human rights and the right to food, an income, shelter, and health services and to speak freely must be reinforced. Efforts in one domain force choices in the others in a holistic manner. Health, education, decentralization and justice are part of a whole. I am beginning to have a clearer picture of what development should bring in the next three to five years. Something that resembles that magic combination of good governance, efficient justice and respect for human rights. The only obligations are participation in civil society, productive agriculture and promotion of local initiatives. In order to avoid that formulas already repeated a thousand times are not in vain, there should be a component promoting democracy. How can we speak of "just" in Rwanda? Everyone wants to be the leader. Truth as truth does not exist. It's the perspective that counts. It should be unbiased. But how can we fight against distorting ethnic rumours? By taking distance, a Swedish friend who works for the Ministry for Health as an economist told me. He is putting together a system of insurance and mutual aid. He is much more pragmatic than I and asks himself fewer questions. He is really nice and lightens things up for me.

23 July 1999: British crumble

Within the framework of legal exchanges, a European military court was asked to put on trial persons accused of genocide who had sought refuge in Europe. The whole court came to Rwanda with big fanfare. There were a total of fourteen people. It seems that their mission went well. We did everything possible so that they could quickly understand the situation in Rwanda and evaluate what was at stake. They even attended a trial taking place in Gitarama. In an interview with the minister for justice, the local television station sensed that this concerted action marked a turning point in the history of Rwanda. Must host countries hand over perpetrators or try them in Europe? I was able to understand how delicate it is to explain the context of Rwanda to a person who has never been in Africa.

In the car one day on the way to Butare, an important judge looked uncomfortably about him. He was hypnotized and astonished to see how much the country had developed. Traffic lights were working; also there were mail service and telephones. I asked him whether he had expected to hear drums and see cannibals cooking bones in a pot. He confided to me that that was sort of what he had thought. I realized that Africa is poorly known and that people are afraid. Images on television show only horrors, never things that work. Nonetheless, there are 535 million Africans, and there are capitals with tall buildings, automobiles, banks and cinemas. Some judges had never been in Africa and had a very skimpy idea of reality. Africa should make itself better known. The group of fourteen persons had a quick view, which was good. They were honest enough to recognize the complexity of their work.

Many countries are giving money for remodelling the justice system in Rwanda: above all, the United Kingdom. Along with our guests from the judiciary in Europe, I was invited one afternoon to discuss the question of justice over tea. The perfumed tea of Sri Lanka had a slight taste recalling the glory of Queen Victoria. It was a bit out of date. The British legal specialists had prepared some crumble, juicy and reddish like the best pastries of London. What a memory that brought back. All of a sudden, my years spent in England were vivid. It was a trigger that set off memories, like the "madeleines" did for Marcel Proust.

Rwanda causes many people to have flashbacks to their past, like shocks with joy and surprise. During this English teatime, I had a long discussion with the new head of the National Reconciliation Commission, which had finally been named. The commission included university professors and intellectuals in the opposition. The chairman of the commission would have loved to include all Rwandans from

111

abroad. He wanted to convince them to return. Members of the commission frequently organized panels for discussion among many groups of civil society. They announced their real intention to push ahead in order to understand the past better, overcome it and move on. The head of the commission used this lovely phrase, "I would like to have a giant amulet and melt the hatred like bad fat in a frying pan and then throw it into the nettles."

25 July 1999: The Mayi-Bobos' (street children) best friend

This is the story of Nicolas, a head of mission. A tall and good-looking man, he charmed Europeans and Africans, men and women alike. He knew exactly how to make people laugh, how to solve an acute problem when things were going sour with the Rwandans and how to transform pathos into surrealist comedy. His political analyses were sought after by everyone. In the evening after our exhausting days, we frequently met at my house and then went out to eat a chicken brochette at a local bistro. He usually arrived about 7 p.m., out of breath and with about ten stories. I offered him a glass of whisky. Finding a comfortable armchair, he set off right away talking about a woman in a commune who, as a sign of peace and good neighbourliness, took burning coals every morning to the sister of the person who had killed all her family. He admired the force of forgiveness implied in these simple gestures. He simply admired humble people. His stories went on and on endlessly. They were punctuated by the clicking of ice cubes in our whisky glasses. The clock flew by, but he never made a gesture to leave, although I was beginning to feel hungry, and continued to talk about the latest rumours on the hills; for example he told me that men who wanted to get rid of AIDS had consulted primitive healers, who had told them to sleep with little girls. It's terrible. This belief spread like a powder trail throughout Rwanda. Local mayors are at a loss to stop this terrible and devastating practice.

Nicolas usually finishes his stories around midnight, looks at his watch once his bottle of whisky is almost finished and my bottle of Coca Cola is empty, makes a few lame excuses, then admits with a look of remorsefulness that it is a bit late for the brochettes and leaves. After 10 p.m., I don't feel like eating and a few peanuts are enough until the next day. His stories are so fascinating that I would not interrupt him for anything in this world. One bottle of whisky after another was followed by stories about life on the hills. I never succeeded in learning how he gained such deep knowledge about daily life in Rwanda. It was eye-opening for me and made me realize our ignorance. We sit in Kigali discussing the future of a population that is 80 per cent rural. What do we know about life of the Rwandans?

The evenings we spend telling ourselves that we will soon go to eat in a restaurant become frequent. They become almost indispensable for our equilibrium. We often end up changing drinks but never go out for diner. These evenings also act as a safety valve. All day long, we hear about things and every day we meet people who are in such desperate situations in Rwanda that we have to talk to someone who is in the same business. He went chirpily on and on thanking me about midnight for the wonderful meals; a bit heavy though, he said. The diners that we never had had become food for our souls. And that went on for several months. Then one day, he was suddenly transferred back to his country. I was very sad. Ever since then, every time I start to eat a real brochette I think about him. One of his most touching qualities was his discomfort and attitude towards the genocide. A large part of his family died in Auschwitz. He was careful to make comparisons and never stopped saying: "You know, you can't really imagine the survivors of Auschwitz living in the same house as the Goebbels family. Well, that's exactly what we are asking the Rwandans to do as if it were the most natural thing in the world. It's mad, right?"

113

Street children

On Saturdays, I often go with Nicolas to do our "tedious" weekly shopping in the only "large store" in Kigali where everything is displayed in view. Everything is expensive and imported from Dubai. Every time we pass the roundabout near the Ministry for Foreign Affairs, hordes of children suddenly appear as if from nowhere, out of the culverts, the bushes and from behind parked cars. They cry out "Monsieur Nicolas, Monsieur Nicolas, give us some, give us some today." I can't believe it. He knows them all by their first name and calls out to them one by one. He scolds one because he returned to live in the street even though the week before Nicholas had been to speak with his older brothers. He calls out to another because he isn't wearing shoes. He admonishes a third because he has already traded his new shirt for a bit of bread. In Kigali, street children have become a sore of modern society, just like in other developing countries, where the capital city attracts those without work from the rural areas. Often these children are orphans. The government has taken them off the street several times. They are sent to a re-education centre or placed with families who try to send them to school. But nothing happens for very long. After one week, they are again in the streets. Most of them beg. They are real actors. They also prostitute themselves and become aggressive. For some, the street represents the only source of income that they take to their enlarged family sometimes made up of up to twenty persons. Given the high level of unemployment, poor people in Kigali often depend entirely on their children. Nicholas told me that that hurt him. He sees their look harden and grow more and more wild. They become outlaws wearing rags. Their fingernails are always covered in mud and filth.

One Saturday afternoon, I went with Nicolas to his house and discovered the incredible story of the relationship between Nicolas and the Mayi-Bobos. Every Saturday afternoon after his weekly shopping, he goes to the roundabout

114

with a large bus and gathers about thirty children one by one. Then, he takes them to his beautiful house and makes them take a bath together. A Rwandan helper scrubs their backs and brushes their teeth until they are almost white and smiling. It is a real party in the bathroom, with laughter and soap bubbles that never stop. After that, they are assembled in the living room and made to talk about their week: stories about their families, nights spent in alleys behind the Ministry for Foreign Affairs, running from the police, the crows that cried out and the small ones who cried because of the cold.

About 7 p.m., Nicolas prepares them a meal that seems to be a feast for little princes. It is like in a fairy tale. The children become very polite and agree to wipe their nose. They gulp down tons and tons of food. Nicolas has a hard time trying to stop them. Finally about 11 p.m., he gives them a few clothes, and asks them about their family and commune of origin. He later tries to negotiate with a distant aunt or uncle by giving them a bit of money or obtain a status of temporary indigent from communal officials in order to take them off the street. Nicolas explained very pragmatically that some of them go home. Others will spend their whole life in the street, but they will have received a bath for months, every Saturday. It's maybe a way for them to be able to dream about better days.

5 August 1999: The first local elections

Preparation for the election of heads of sections and cells has begun. It is the first step towards democracy. The government announced elections for the whole country for the end of the month. Voters will queue up behind the candidate they want to elect. Everyone in the committees is enthusiastically making preparations, even if the rural population would prefer anonymous elections. The government has promised that elections for local mayors in the communes will be by ballot boxes. Everyone has come to help out and is motivated. When people are asked what they want, of course they turn out: health, blood transfusions, privatization and poverty reduction. I sometimes have the impression of having a head full of glass balls that hit each other and go cling-cling in my brain. You have to move quickly from one thing to another. Rwanda has been calm for the past three months, without an attack reported within the country. This temporary calm gives hope to those who want to build, but where is the real negotiated solution with the outside world?

9 August 1999: Manna from heaven

How can we change the inflexible habit of Rwandans of always waiting for outside help as if it were an obligation? How can we teach them to use their own hands and their own ideas about development when it is the international community that provides the money? The annual report of the World Bank is categorical about this: when consulted, rural populations know best what is helpful for agriculture. Fixing priorities can be guided, but the beneficiaries must be able to express an opinion and decide. The trite word "participation" begins to make me sweat. Examples of the harm of too great a financial dependence are numerous. With this in mind, I gave a forceful talk during a meeting at the national blood collection centre. Because the European Union did not make a payment on time, the blood centre was simply threatening to close. A bit of planning between everyone would not be a bad thing. What can an indebted developing country do not to depend completely on outside help?

13 August 1999: Don't confuse rights and obligations

We left a meeting with a prefect in which we agreed to provide aid to reinforce the management capacity of the local mayors within the framework of decentralization and participation of local citizens. We contributed to the publication of a small pamphlet entitled, "Rights and duties of the Rwandan citizen", written with the help of international legal experts. It is very edifying to be able to give out this little manual in the communes. People are enthusiastic and interested. They have a sort of yearning for democracy. This pamphlet has been published at the right time: elections have just begun. There was no confusion as we expected at the beginning. People queued up behind the candidate of their choice after the candidates had proposed a programme for the commune. People asked about details of the projects for agriculture and justice. They asked for the creation of a commission of human rights and demanded that there be no impunity. "We have to have confidence", a Rwandan journalist said, "the people know what they want, but they first have to have enough to eat." In any programme for reducing poverty, there has to be a balance between projects to raise agricultural production, projects for good governance and reforms of the judicial system. No country can live off justice alone, and no harvest can produce sustainable results if it is not based on an economy that seeks to redistribute wealth equitably.

15 August 1999: Hazard or need?

Nothing is based on chance, there are only needs. Coincidences seem to me to be more and more improbable. Hundreds of chance events make up my daily life. They give me answers that appear after a meeting as keys to the course of a lifetime. Maybe you have to know how to ask the right question in the morning when you get up. After that, opportunities seem to come by themselves.

A professor of applied psychology, John Fitzgerald, who came all the way from California to evaluate the needs of Rwanda for dealing with trauma expressed the idea that it's a real philosophical question to ask one's self in the morning what kind of person you would like to be and then just ask the world questions in order to find the right answers. I told him that I thought that philosophy seemed to be a luxury in a developing country. After my remarks during his talk, he came up to me right away. After listening to me several times, he said "If you would only delete your uncertainties and your fears from your language. They often become excuses for having an opinion or stating an idea. Dare to be certain and to be right when you begin to talk in public. Without that incorrect approach, your ideas will gain enormously in forcefulness." I thanked him warmly for his valuable and wise advice and tried to change. It's true that his little trick, along with the thought about intentions and aims in the morning, gave me a little click and, without a doubt, more clarity.

18 August 1999: The arrest of Bishop Misago

All the international community was excited, upset and worried. The Bishop of Gikongoro, Monsignor Misago, had been arrested. It was a declaration of war against the Church with a strong political message. Bishop Misago was accused of actively collaborating during the genocide. The confrontation between the Church and the Government of Rwanda was intensifying.

21 August 1999: Urgent to wait?

I have just finished reviewing the agricultural programme with our Rwandan partner. He gave me a whole course on various forms of corn shoots. Félicien loves to laugh, and when he showed his certificate in agronomy, it was completely written in Chinese. Does he speak Chinese? No, he said, to study maize it is not necessary to speak Chinese, because the Chinese eat only rice.

This weekend, exhaustion caught up with me. The nurse, Fanny, sent me to bed at 7 p.m. on Friday, and I slept straight through for fourteen hours. Next morning, I fed Walili and Gribouille, my two starving cats with whom I talk a lot. Then, I went for breakfast with my Canadian neighbours. On

Sunday, I worked for ten hours at the office in order to catch up. There are days when I would prefer to be under the sea, because there is too much work. Nonetheless, the programme has been agreed on. I even had time this Sunday to bake a chocolate cake and prepare beef Stroganoff and carrots Vichy for some friends. You have to take a bit of distance, laugh and make fun of yourself and your imagined tragedies. And then, as if by miracle, you realize that the question of something being very important is all relative. Rwanda does not give a desire or many occasions to laugh. Death is everywhere. Everything has to be reconstructed. My Ugandan neighbour told me one day that when you feel completely overwhelmed by insurmountable tasks, it is time to wait.

24 August 1999: The return of witnesses from a trial

The return of Rwandan witnesses who had spent two weeks in Europe testifying at a trial was very moving. They admired all the following without any ranking: escalators, Coca Cola machines that also make ice and clothing stores. It was probably the eighteen different brands of chocolate that astonished them the most. They had a big party with the military police the last evening. They had never seen so many policemen and dogs. Rwandan security services questioned them when they returned. The witnesses passed around chocolates. They were very proud to be able to say that they spoke well and that they remembered everything. One of the women, Eva, was later elected to the development committee for her sector. She is really funny, very debonair. She explained that the trial was well organized and that there were many Rwandans there who live abroad. She had had the courage to address the accused prisoner with the words, "I remember you well, and you were the one who gave the order to have us killed." She was also the one who asked the military judge during a walk in the mountains how the flowers breathed under all that snow. Rwanda is really poetic.

7 September 1999: Lift without rift

I am making great progress in tennis thanks to Forestier, a Rwandan who won the East African Cup in Durban the year before. The tennis club promoted me to the highest category in mixed doubles after we played matches for the ranking and our team now has a total of 130 points. My backhand has gained some lift. My shots have taken on a reassuring mechanical nature; especially when they are repeated hundreds of times. Our team won the doubles match against Firmin and Rudahira, the top-ranked players. I love this sport, and I have to say that it is an interesting way to enter into contact with Rwandans. In addition, tennis is a real teacher. It makes you heart beat steady.

10 September 1999: Sewing together the threads of identity

The FIFA is here. We succeeded in convincing the authorities of the Fédération Internationale de Football Association (FIFA) to invest in Rwanda in order to contribute to reconciliation. Sport brings people together. It's a good slogan and something that is obviously easy. We gave our guarantee that football would allow the re-creation of a national identity because Rwandans want to use this sport as a means of creating unity. In addition, they play football well. The means are lacking, but not the desire. Under the topic of supporting sports, we have just spent a day with several United Nations agencies. The idea is sound, but we have the impression that plans for the future are not clear. A little bit less money for UNHCR, a tab more for UNESCO, a few drops for UNCHR and something for WHO. Where is the unifying overall plan?

I sometimes have the impression that I have become the doyenne of development workers here. The others have all left during the past year: the humanitarian workers and the United Nations officials who arrived just after the genocide in 1994.

The rotation is impressive. It is people who create their post not the other way around. I spent the whole week writing about Rwandan society, demobilization of soldiers and construction of villages. These are texts that will serve, I hope, as the basis for discussion during meetings of the international community. We had a long debate with Bernadette on the role of the National Reconciliation Commission. We also spoke about tension in parliament where fifteen people need to be replaced at the end of the year. It is a question of corruption and stealing of public funds. That's a lot of people implicated in "business" that is not very clear. The media talk about conflict of ethnic interest.

20 September 1999: Erasing the differences?

The new government has to be given a chance to erase the question of ethnic affiliation. But it's not by erasing them that they will no longer exist. What can be done? We have to talk about these differences. I have the impression of having found the proper balance between my duty to remain reserved and my deep convictions. I have built an honest bridge with the Rwandans. The election of sectors and cells seems positive. For the first time, people have chosen leaders and are going to be able to evaluate the results. It seems that the choice was not based exclusively on ethnic identity. Like a woman elected to a communal development committee said, "We are going to be able to tell them to leave if the elected leaders do not represent our real interests, regardless of whether we are Hutu or Tutsi."

An Angolan bomb fell this week on Goma. It was close. Rebels captured the village where Kabila was born: Manono. Quite often, large Bulgarian or Russian airplanes fly over Kigali. How many parties are fighting in the Congo? Is Sudan participating; and Chad and Libya?

4 October 1999: South Africa, crossroads of the Great Lakes Region

I went on a mission to South Africa and had a moving visit to Soweto. I found myself in my favourite film "Cry Freedom", which dealt with the murders in Nashville in 1976. At that time, the film really affected me and made me drop everything. We visited the house of the Mandela family. I am in full admiration before this giant of history, this person who understands, this visionary. I am convinced that he is an inspiration for all of us and for a renaissance of Africa, even if the Burundi peace talks he is leading appear to be stalled. I devoured his book "Long Walk to Freedom". Reality is, however, very hard in South Africa and people are becoming disenchanted. Freedom and money will not be distributed right away to everyone. The motorways are impeccable, but criminality is out of hand. There is a murder every minute, they say, and dissatisfaction is growing in the face of the lack of any real economic change perceptible to the Black South Africans. Often, the Black upper lower class exploits workers. The Indians go about their business of making money, and the Europeans try to make some sense out of all this. The current president of South Africa, Thabo Mbeki, now has to fulfil his electoral promises for the Black majority, which is itself divided. The annual GNP is close to two thousand dollars per person. South Africa has the most powerful army on the continent and so many mineral resources. Nonetheless, few people seem to be benefiting from this. These are serious questions that cannot simply be swept casually under the carpet. In contrast to South Africa, Rwanda is in 154th position out of 157 on the poverty scale of the World Bank, which is another challenge. In Rwanda, sixty per cent of the rural population earns no more than two dollars a day. I am leaving South Africa overwhelmed by the beauty of the landscape and the advanced development of the large cities. I am leaving without having had a chance to visit Cape Town, which I have always dreamt about.

7 October 1999: The merry-go-round of meetings

Through my participation in a seminar on corruption, I met the new head of the World Food Programme (WFP). He seems to know how to distribute tonnes and tonnes of food. He is most at ease with large distributions and is obsessed with details, he told me. He is Dutch. Then I met Serge while clearing shipments through Customs at Magerwa, the government's Customs warehouse. Then I dropped by the papal nuncio's residence to coordinate the question of the thirty-per-cent tax that the government wants to charge our Rwandan employees retroactively. Then, I went to talk to the head of the blood transfusion service, contacted Jean about the farm associations and Maurice about human rights. I have been running about all morning. I had lunch with a representative of the Foreign Office of the United Kingdom who wanted to talk about the Congo. I then rushed to the Jali Club, a restaurant in the centre of Kigali, to contact Julien and discuss the economic indicators for Rwanda and talk about the resignation of the public prosecutor of the Rwandan Supreme Court. I then ended up going by the American embassy to talk about projects in the North. It's difficult to be present and attentive for everyone when these meetings follow one another the whole day long like a merry-go-round. It's very exhausting and the topics are too numerous. Because of this reality, it is difficult to discuss anything deeply. And yet, that is just what we have to do. I rush from one meeting to another. The country is really crippled by endless and impossible internal dissensions, and I have decided to take a break.

19 October 1999: Escape to Robinson Crusoe's island

I spent the weekend on Bushara Island in Uganda for a break. We left in a small group and spent our time in a boat, diving, barbecuing fish and laughing late into the night. Bushara is like Robinson Crusoe's island: you can walk completely around the island in half an hour and you can imagine with real pleasure that everyone is going to forget about you. I thought about my schedule last week. I have to slow down and take more time to think. I'm going to stick to my principles about being firm. At the same time, I don't find these stories of power and the struggle for influence pleasant. Once again, I'm up and ready for the next week.

23 October 1999: Driving a project like a Formula One car

Our group tested an exercise called the "Titanic". It tests the survival of projects using mechanisms for controlling and monitoring that begins with the setting of objectives, project review, monitoring of indicators, aims and results and any correction that can be made. Even the field of observation of the process, the impact of roles and the project's context are questioned. It's a fascinating process that always takes place with the participation of the project's partners. Above all, it's an instrument, like a thermometer that has to be mastered applying the user's good eyesight and acute hearing, making it possible to know the true temperature of a project. In Rwanda, however, despite many efforts by all parties I have the impression that things have broken down a bit. As if we had to make development plans by integrating both supply and demand. Our partners give me the impression of knowing without really knowing. All the time, we have to renew their courage and understand their circumstances.

We have to place things back in their context. Are the results sustainable in a country so torn apart? That evening we went to a reception to mark the end of Germany's six-month European Union presidency. Germany passed the presidency to France offering a symbolic twenty-four flowers representing a twenty-four-hour day. The end of the German presidency was accompanied by a beautiful speech of rather unconditional support for Rwanda. All the ministers were there. P. brought me chocolates, which soothed me because I was a bit shaken up.

Right now there is a wonderful exhibit of products from Egypt in a large hotel in Kigali. Rwanda lays claim to being the source of the Nile, and the two countries have close relations. There was blaring music, and goods were sold directly: mainly carpets and household articles. There really is a market here for something other than rolls of toilet paper at two dollars a roll. The evening with the Egyptians ended at the Cactus with a giant plate of spaghetti and laughs with Sudanese refugees who had no idea how to eat spaghetti. Altogether, there were about ten of us. I was so hungry that I cried, and I was served first to the disappointment of the others.

25 October 1999: The little cat is dead

Rwanda: violence and more violence. My cat was killed by mistake. Walili died on the operating table after having been taken by force—in my absence—by a veterinarian for the sum of 65,000 Rwandan francs (about 230 dollars). The misled veterinarian thought he was supposed to sterilize it, while all I asked for was an anti-rabies vaccination. On the telephone, the veterinary assistant announced, laughing, that the cat had woken up in the middle of the operation and he had to add a second dose of anaesthetic and the cat's heart gave out. What is the life of a cat worth in this country among so many others? I told myself to calm down. You have the impression here that people will kill each other over a television set. Everything is set up so that no one succeeds in finding his or her true values. Why is there permanent defiance and so little regard for life or death? How was it before? There is no excuse in Rwanda for shilly-shallying and pity. Death is everywhere, constantly present, giving people sad souls. It's difficult to see the end of the tunnel, and yet Rwandans are very religious.

In Rwanda, orders from above make things go forwards or move backwards. Decrees are issued all the time. The authority remains incredibly strong. Where is the solidarity; hidden on the hills? There are many grey days for expatriates in Rwanda. We ask ourselves whether we can still provide concrete assistance. Nonetheless, at other times, we are again filled with enthusiasm. It's a bit like the hills: "They go up, and they go down."

3 November 1999: The Colonel prefers the knight's opening

A very successful evening at the American ambassador's residence. The embassy residence has well-groomed flowering gardens worthy of the Tuileries. That evening, we were celebrating Thanksgiving Day. I met a retired Rwandan colonel there in uniform and with great dignity. He insisted on telling me his life story after we had talked at length about the slowness of the justice system and the ICTR. He is the head of the Rwandan Chess Federation and owes his survival to chess—like in Stefan Zweig's novel—following long years of internment and torture. He explained to me how he had spent weeks playing with the white pieces and then with the black pieces. He almost went crazy because it was a mental exercise close to schizophrenia. In his damp cell, he went from one side of the chessboard to the other playing openings. The opening with two knights first was his favourite. What struck me was that he resembles "the tall and thin ones". But no, wrong, he told me that he was not Tutsi. I'm always glad to learn that the use of criteria of ethnic morphology is inapplicable. Another time, I had the same experience with a minister. We had talked for a long time about Rwandan refugees who had come back from refugee camps and about the question of compensation for survivors. I was sure that he was a Tutsi survivor but he was a Hutu. That's another example that proves that I have to continue avoiding using any ethnic criteria in my relations with Rwandans. I have to use cultural and linguistic information based on a life story or competence as parameters in the infernal cycle of the simplistic guessing game to learn who is who and what he might have done. But I am still unable to explain what I feel is intrinsically false in using an ethnic approach.

8 November 1999: In the muddy fields of Byumba

National Heroes Day took place this year in the rain at Byumba in northern Rwanda near the border with Uganda. Every year, this day represents an important commemoration for the Armée patriotic rwandaise (APR), which first entered Rwanda in 1990 and then again in 1994 to conquer Kigali from the north. The soldiers had camped on the hills and in the bush. This commemoration is impressive, but also restrictive. Like other commemorations, it represents a founding myth: that of the hardened revolutionary combatant and a principled fighter, like Che Guevara. During the ceremony, the band and the military marching exercises were disciplined and concentrated. The soldiers believe in it, and we are led to believe that the refugees were originally guerrillas. The military parade and music lasted for three hours. Near me, an ambassador bounced up and down on his chair because he had to go to the toilet but could not because of the crowd; we were in the middle of a field. The population of the region of Byumba was gathered around on the hills. The most applauded group was the brand new "local defence force", dressed in dark red uniforms. The president gave a speech frequently using words such as "transparency", "democracy" and "development". We waited and waited hoping for a translation. At the end of the event, cars could not turn around because their wheels sank into the clay like into butter. A heavy rain began to fall, and we remained stuck for three hours. The international community's whole convoy of twenty-eight cars was stuck. The rain poured down, and the four-wheel-drive vehicles spun their wheels. We had to wait patiently for the ground to absorb the water and dry out a bit. It was a good opportunity to start a chat with the soldiers and our colleagues. There were about one hundred persons that had to make do and share bananas and Rwandan biscuits with pink filling, which normally would have caused even a starving army to flee. Out of our cars and hanging on to umbrellas, we watched the rain fall in the forest. No one was angry, merely resigned. One of the APR officers said, "This is all very well. It will give the international community a taste of what it is like in the bush." Ah, Rwanda. You have to love the vindictive and abrupt nature of its leaders. Very politely, they asked us to show our patience. I had already spent time trying to understand the events of between 1986 and 1997 (economic difficulties), and then those from 1992 to 1994 (preparation of the genocide). And now we are in 1999. It wasn't the books I read that helped me, but the people I met. Here and there, I was able to put together an idea of the chronology. Nonetheless, opinions are fundamentally divergent about responsibilities. The reassuring speeches didn't make me forget my concern about the meagre economic progress and the Rwandans' absence of transparency. They have a hard time sticking to a budget, and their presence in the Congo does not stand them well with the international community. A small two-room house costs, for example, about RWF 50,000 (about 200 dollars) per month. When a Rwandan has the good fortune to find a job, he earns an average of RWF 60,000 per month. In order to get around the lack of liquidity in the government's budget, taxes are going to be collected because the law obliges everyone to pay taxes retroactively. These are the IMF proposals for structural readjustment so that the government can collect money. The rumour is that people and money are fleeing to the Congo.

12 November 1999: A weekend on the road

Rwanda is really a beautiful country. We went for a visit to Cyangugu in the south-western corner of the country and walked during more than four hours to see monkeys, lit colobus monkeys that shout in your ears and steal your food. We admired the waterfalls at the heart of the Nyungwe rain forest. This landscape is magnificent and should help people to reconcile themselves with nature and themselves. Or is that just wishful thinking? It's tourism based on hiking that should be started up.

14 November 1999: Shameful pay

My rural development project is going well. Firmin is doing his job, dominating a bit too much the others, but that's what a boss is for. He quickly understands how to run project activities. Thanks to him, I can finally deal with the project's paperwork, a useful tool that gives me a weekly summary and a framework for everything. I am pleased. Several projects are being implemented directly. We are beginning to establish contact with the local population that is building confidence, but everyone is wondering about the building of houses and villages. How can we make people participate without coercion? How can we convince small farmers to leave their land and banana groves to live next to each other along the roads? Exclusion is only a time bomb. History has proven that to us. The question of salaries is often raised in forums. How much should Rwandan intellectuals who are trained abroad be paid when they return to Rwanda? Why is there so much disparity? I had a long talk with a Rwandan who returned after thirty years of exile. He has a doctorate from a European university but doesn't know a lot about his country. What kind of a salary can he hope for with his university degrees? He is wondering who earns what in this country and why and is very shocked because aside from the government and the international agencies he finds no way to make his knowledge pay him a decent salary.

This is, in fact, a common phenomenon in Africa. The payment of high salaries for Europeans in the new African

led to an extraordinarily violent struggle for
anda is no exception. Formerly poor and
w government officials occupy important posts
ey to spend. A new bureaucratic governing class
is appearing. It produces nothing, but manages the profits of its
privileges. Nonetheless, a nouveau rich cannot forget the old
traditions of his clan, which call for sharing with brothers and
cousins who come down from the hills like rain on roses:
softly. Whoever does not respect these principles of "helping
the family" is condemned to ostracism, exclusion and solitude.

In Africa, solitude is a horror. There are several words
in Kinyarwanda to indicate poverty. A poor person with family
is saved, but the poor person who is all alone without a family
is lost. He is condemned and shamed; rejected by society. If
individualism is valued in Europe, in the South it is a synonym
of a curse, and the infernal cycle is difficult to break. In order
to be valued, you have to work for the government. "When you
work for the government", a chief of staff explained to me,
"you have to share more and more with cousins from all
corners of the country. You have to borrow and steal money in
order to meet your family's demands correctly, and then you are
caught in the mechanism and everyone covers for everyone
else."

The Rwandan "returnee" was bitter. He had thought he
was returning to an eldorado and would be welcomed like a
pope. Unfortunately, he didn't understand at all to where he
was returning. He had become an out-of-phase intellectual
caught up in his opaque and closed jargon. I advised him to
look for his African and Rwandan roots and to try to abandon
the fear of talking about what he was feeling. A thick haze
seemed to have covered his real identity. It's a real drama and
an impossibility to relate that he shares with many other
Rwandans who have returned home. It takes them months to
adapt. He finally chose to work for an international
organization. Some cynical theoreticians sometimes define
development as an industry at the service of African

governments and not sufficiently serving the people. They speak of aid that leads nowhere. In the shadows in the background, like in Plato's Republic, there are the small farmers who become passive actors of a system that is beyond them. They grow poorer and poorer. That's not the whole truth. Things are much more complex and development is often successful there where it is least expected. In reality, there are strong partnerships, and these are not stressed enough. This is also the analysis that the international development specialist, Peter Uvin, makes. He knows this region and is going to come back soon to Rwanda. I am pleased because there is no one like him to raise embarrassing questions. But he is an optimist. He is going to present his book "Aiding Violence" and explain his vision of social development by insisting on respect for human rights and talk about accompanying measures to decrease the number of government officials. He is going to make it possible for us to discuss our knowledge about the concept of "participation". Strangely, our current vocabulary seems to date from the beginning of the 1990s, but it hides another reality. It's up to us to prove it.

15 November 1999: The papal nuncio's gnocchi

Delegates from an international agency explained to me their point of view why the international community should help Rwanda. It was a question of habitat and the cost of the war. The representative of the agency was, nonetheless, optimistic because even if part of the population seemed to monopolize more and more goods than others that was just one stage in the process of democratization. Given the level of corruption in other African countries, Rwanda would still have a margin. At any rate, that's the opinion of the Bretton Woods institutions.

The papal nuncio had prepared gnocchi at his residence for the departure of the representative of the World Bank. I think that I should learn to be a bit more frivolous. I envy the vapidity of some diplomats, something I could have become in another, less serious life. The Monsignor wished me goodbye and said offhandedly, "It's not easy, right?"

I had dinner, one of the last, with my friend Nicolas, the head of mission and the good friend of the *Mayi-Bobos*, who is always nostalgic and sometimes so funny. One of the difficult aspects of this profession is to have to say goodbye all the time to people that you like. He was very devoted and in favour of the "new Rwanda". At the end of his mission, Nicolas began to become a bit sour. His doubts had sometimes become so strong that he asked himself if his allegiance was still authentic. He was leaving Rwanda against his will, a country so radical and demanding, so black and white. The landscapes are so peacefully beautiful, but jealousy and hatred are everywhere. He will probably be asked to work in Eastern Europe, in Frunze (Kirgizstan) or in Kiev.

This Monday, I participated in a meeting that renewed my hope about the relocations and the *imidugudu* (new villages). The minister himself came to present the participatory habitat project and ask us for support. It's a revolution that this country is asking us for our opinion. I am joking a bit but even if Rwanda needs money for development it is obliged to enter an era of consultation and dialogue, which is positive. We are slowly advancing towards democracy, although the inner circle does not seem to be expanding rapidly.

18 November 1999: What do we know about what happens at night?

We had tense intellectual conversations with Peter Uvin, who finally arrived. His book, "Aiding Violence", has made him well known here. There are endless evenings of discussion. What is structural violence? What does it mean to reinforce civil society? Talks are going well. I am delighted by the evening organized with the United Nations, Rwandan partners and this academic specialist around these topics. The discussion of genocide was controversial. Uvin recalled that support of the structure of violence and thoughts about strictly unilateral assistance to a small number of non-representative persons among the small farmers for over thirty years had contributed to preparation of the genocide. He gave us hope. Are we doing something differently now? Peter Uvin concluded that in 1992 no one had a clue as to what was being prepared on the hills and in the banana groves at night, we knew nothing about the daily life of the Rwandans. We had contact only with the big shots. In 1999, we still don't know what is going on at night on the hills, but at least we know that we do not know.

21 November 1999: The exquisite woman in her eighties

On the road to the North, we are going to Gisenyi, the town in the North that is just a stone's throw from the Congo. We are going for a weekend visit with Rosamond Halsey Carr, an American, originally from high society in New Jersey, well known and respected at the age of 87. She has lived in this area for the past fifty years. Her husband owned a coffee plantation in the Congo in 1950. Then, after independence, she returned alone to Rwanda where she began a flower business that ran well. In 1994, she lost everything and left. Then, she came back to open an orphanage. She has just written an inoffensive and harmless biography called "Land of a Thousand Hills", describing her life in Rwanda mainly in the 1960s and 1970s. What is a bit upsetting is her romantic descriptions of "the wonderful small farmers". She writes that she had no idea what was going to happen. This book was not well received by everyone here. We all wondered how a woman could so delicately live through so much drama and come out unhurt like a flower. Roz Carr was a friend of Dian Fossey, the gorilla specialist. Then, after the events of 1994, she was the last to leave. Everything was plundered at her farm. What she regrets the most are her diaries, her papers and her photographs. She misses them, she whispers conspiratorially, but she found almost all of them and bought them back at the central market.

She returned in 1996 and was attacked again by the Interhamwe in 1997 and 1998. Patiently like an ant, she again went to the market to find her things. She is now back at 87, straight as an arrow. When we asked her about events in Rwanda that morning she said that the country was going forward but she still didn't see any real guaranty of reconciliation. She thinks we are asking them for something that is impossible; we are asking for too much. She's right, although it hurts. She reflects a sadness that we all feel. We want to give hope, but so many things still shock us in our relations with Rwandans. They are ruthless towards each other. It's a shame. Roz is wonderful with her blue eyes, her neat dress, her love for fellow people and her Swahili with a touch of American accent. We spent a wonderful day with her. She is a person who fills you with joy. Back in Kigali that evening, I talked with a minister who knew about the book published in English and written by Roz and her niece. He said that he knew her well and that she had told him about her fears that the book had too many positive thoughts about the past. The minister smiled then with a sigh he finally admitted that earlier many things were positive.

25 November 1999: Let's get married!

This Saturday, I was invited to the marriage of Vestine. She was glorious dressed in a long muslin dress with pink-white lace. She was wearing pearls around her neck, which is discouraged in Europe because white pearls bring bad luck on the day of a marriage. But apparently in Rwanda, a pearl necklace does not have the same meaning. In Rwanda, there is a superstition about rain on the day of a marriage. That day, it drizzled. The best part of Rwandan traditional dress is the folds of muslin cloth worn like a toga over the shoulder. Vestine baptized her three children and was married at the same time. She was to have married on 19 April 1994 but at that time the young couple had to concentrate on saving their lives and remaining in hiding. This country is filled everywhere by the tragedy that interrupted everything during three months. The fact that there are many marriages in groups is a reflection of the willingness of people to move on beyond events. Their acts are courageous although it takes years to forget the nightmare. I feel close to those people who are trying to get on with their lives although they are not at all naïve about the difficulty of starting out again.

26 November 1999: Look out for the gorillas!

This Saturday, I spent a wonderful day with journalists from Reuters, the National Geographic Magazine, the Rwandan Office for Tourism and the information team of UNDP. We finally went to see the famous gorillas on the volcanoes in northern Rwanda. This excursion is a real programme and the rebirth of the whole past glory for Rwanda. Is it a sign of a slight taking-off of tourism again? For those who know Rwanda, the symbolic meaning is even stronger. Gorillas represent a unique attraction in the world that could attract tourists to Rwanda like before. Of course it is too early to make any predictions. It is still not at all one hundred per cent certain, but it is an encouraging sign. We hiked for five hours climbing into the rain forest where we had to hack our way through lianas with machetes (a terrible object). We were on the slopes of Sabinyo with an escort of thirty-five soldiers. We were hoping to inaugurate a new era in peaceful Rwanda, but there was danger all around us. Nature here is all around you and absolutely unique. The gorillas are amazing. They so closely resemble us that it is a bit disturbing, and they behave like they were imitating our casual manners. They are our reflection in a mirror.

Several Rwandans who worked earlier with Dian Fossey, the gorilla expert, still know how to speak with the gorillas. Early in the morning, they left to scout for gorilla groups in the forest. They set off to announce our visit. They talk with the gorillas through onomatopoeia and grunts from the throat. The gorillas responded through the patriarch and calmly waited for us. We arrived quietly one after the other and then waited patiently five metres from the group during at least two hours. During all that time, the oldest gorilla, the patriarch of the group, carefully watched us out of the corner of his eye and followed all our movements while several of the females played with the young ones. I could have stayed there and watched them for centuries. The gorillas looked at us as though we were from outer space. As if by ricochet, we were the ones who had become special, not them. What a hilarious scene. Finally, the patriarch stared a long time at us then turned his back and calmly walked into the bushes.

2 December 1999: Donors for Africa

The whole international community is saying the same thing: everything is for Kosovo. Money from donors is no longer going to Africa. The Africans are protesting loud and clear about the injustice and lack of interest in Africa. A representative of the Rwandan government, however, is not discouraged and declares that what is important is to make people come to Africa so that they can see for themselves the progress that has been made.

Linked to the question of democracy is the question of the place of majority and minorities that comes up often in conversations. This question is important but has several traps. Habyiarimana, wasn't he a representative of the majority? Even at the end of his reign, he represented his own privileges almost exclusively. The question of an ethnic majority or minority does not necessarily resolve that of representatives. You have to judge by political parties and abilities. In this field, the new minister for land brought a bit of fresh air: that of an opening. The minister for territorial administration raised good questions linked to sustainable development. Priorities within the framework of development create a big problem in Rwanda: what should be developed? With which focus and with which type of coordination should it be led by the donors? Is the coherence of the donors a guarantee of freedom for the beneficiaries? The rather weak previous minister will probably be transferred somewhere. He didn't adopt the right procedures fast enough. It has to be admitted that his character, very intellectual and not sufficiently active, worked considerably to his disadvantage. His transfer was decided immediately. Damn it! How things change so quickly here. The first one hundred days have to be used with skill and members of the government are replaced quickly.

3 December 1999: Language access codes

Something that we still don't understand, we the "little white people" (that's the way they call us) is that Rwandans seem to be capable of killing each other on Friday and then going together on Sunday to a baptism or to mass as if nothing had happened. They don't see any contradiction in it. Relationships of solidarity or intimacy are very difficult to understand. Their way of behaving is partially due to their oral tradition but also to an ambiguous, abstruse literary language, for which multiple meanings have been developed to an extreme, like foils in fencing. Oral exchanges occur in a veiled polyvalent sense, riddled with taboo and requiring deduction. For example, *imbabazi* means pity, but also maternal love, confidence and compassion and sometimes contempt.

Depending on the context, a word can be understood positively or negatively, as condescension or praise. This very refined language, Kinyarwanda, allows Rwandans to play with meanings and not to reveal intentions. But it is above all a trap for their own communication. Confronted with my astonishment and irritation, a friend told me one day that they were simply other codes and in diplomacy Europeans also lie. "But at least, we try to let the truth come out between the florid speech", I replied.

4 December 1999: The court: a source of anger

Attorneys from Mali, Cote d'Ivoire, Cameroon and Nigeria who work for the International Criminal Tribunal for Rwanda (ICTR) have a hard and difficult time. They have to find the guilty parties, listen to witnesses that they have to protect and render justice in a complicated society where an unimaginable genocide (at least for an African) was able to occur. African solidarities are sacred. How did we reach there? they are asking. But if you listen to them more closely, African brothers have terrible rows among themselves. They won't admit that Rwanda broke their most sacred law.

During a press conference, Louise Arbour, the Canadian prosecutor for the International Criminal Tribunal, came to say goodbye because she had completed her mandate with the ICTR. In her farewell speech, she emphasized the difficulty of setting up any system of inquiry and filing charges. In the future, ICTR will emphasize closer ties between the tribunal in Arusha and that based in Kigali. The tribunal hopes to encourage better "appropriation" by Rwandans of their past. One of her main duties has been to find the right tone in relations with the Rwandan government, which is very biased and necessarily partial in the process of enquiries. This makes independent justice very difficult to render. The tribunal is faced with a big contradiction: it must be especially discrete even though the ICTR, according to her, has a public cathartic and undeniable quality and at the same time must be publicly accountable for progress made. Ms Arbour announced that 2000 would be the year of the real trial of Bagosora, the former minister of defence under Habyarimana, and twenty-eight of his henchmen. The tribunal wants to bring to trial only the architects of the genocide in order to show the mechanism that led to the extremism and give an example of manipulation by the decision-makers. She thinks that symbolically the trial of Kambanda, the first high-level person to be accused of genocide whose trial was broadcast live on national radio, has had a very positive effect on Rwandans, even if the accused did not admit even the slightest regret. At any rate, it is not part of the mandate of the tribunal to force him to confess. Justice must establish the truth. It is not there to teach morality.

7 December 1999: The court machinery

Several days later, the news came out: the attractive Carla Del Ponte will be the new general prosecutor and will spend time between The Hague, Arusha and Kigali. Protection of witnesses is still a hot topic, and this news is well received. In the meantime, the Rwandan government feels that the trials are not moving forward at the ICTR. A budget of sixty million dollars for the ICTR in Arusha and Kigali is a lot. The government has publicly expressed its disappointment.

For the time being, only three convictions have been pronounced in four years. It must be admitted that it is very difficult to find tangible proof and encourage those who take the risk of admitting anything at all. The process of investigation is necessarily very long, requiring skill and patience. The laws of silence, fear and time often take precedence. To make people tell the truth is not always easy without putting them in danger. In fact, many of the witnesses have simply died. The ICTR is looking for only the "big shots", those who organized the genocide. Apart from Mali, Cameroon and Kenya, who have agreed to extradite any person accused on the list of perpetrators, most countries have made no real effort to hand over the guilty who have found refuge. The ICTR cannot apply capital punishment. A convicted killer can receive a maximum sentence of life in prison. On the other hand, if an accused killer is handed over to Rwandan justice, a country that applies the death penalty, he risks losing his head. Contact with the ICTR is always very interesting. Seeing the same persons often creates a relationship of confidence and facilitates an exchange of information and maintains continuity. There are receptions, speeches, but also rumours. Rumours are unfortunately one of the main sore points of Rwanda.

That evening, I was delighted to be able to speak calmly during a meeting with the minister of justice and the ICTR, during which I met an important official who is a judge. He is extremely cultivated and distinguished. At the end of the dinner, I realize that I had just finished telling him what I thought about the Rwanda of today and the Rwanda of tomorrow. I had a lot to say. Remaining very prudent, he said almost nothing. In his speech, he did let it be known that he was very worried about the future of his country. He told me that he hoped for the best under such difficult circumstances and remarked that very few detainees wanted to confess the crimes they committed during the genocide. When you live in Rwanda, perhaps you learn better how to understand the opposite side of the coin. The government is constantly fighting with many problems at the same time. Among them are some of the most unimaginable problems in the world: a justice system that has broken down, the detention of 120,000 prisoners, a ruined agricultural sector, deficient health care services, dispersed villages under construction, the difficult modernization of agriculture, a lack of space, the coffee and tea sectors in decline and the war in the Congo. How do they get out of bed in the morning? Daily life in Rwanda is really tough. How does the small farmer with ten to twelve people depending on him do it? How do you deal with unemployment, demobilized and helpless soldiers; exorbitant school fees for the children, the need to take care of an ailing mother, and having to go to feed a brother who is a prisoner in the central prison but against whom no charges have yet been brought? How can you live with tears of anger in your eyes? The limits of patience are often over run, and yet, people complain so rarely.

10 December 1999: Giving hope

By chance, I met a journalist called Alphonse. He felt that the speech about Rwanda I gave on the occasion of the national holiday was a bit too strong. I had talked about the lack of transparency and the difficulty of providing assistance to a country that never clearly declares its intentions. He was pleased by my way of identifying with the people and with the great simplicity and interest for the little guy. He told me that earlier he had gone to a seminary to become a priest. Then, because of the events he had to abandon that idea. We talked for a long time about the question of the lack of initiative of some Rwandans. That lack is perhaps the result of the thirty years that Rwanda has just spent under a closed regime, perhaps also because of the religious teachings that were taken literally because of the fear of the authorities. Does the press feel free in Rwanda? He replied that if a journalist knows how to act, everything is all right. But many journalist practice self-censure out of fear. I often think about that African poet who spoke about "giving back dreams of dignity to the people of Africa, torn by imaginary borders".

I am always very shocked when I hear people say that Rwanda has used the genocide "as a business". What a sad thought. Reality shows that for survivors to live after the genocide is above all a personal struggle and depends on an enormous willingness to be able to continue in poverty. Everyone agrees that at least a generation is needed to heal the wounds. Even if the genocide is referred to in every speech, in every conversation, it shows first of all a reality that cannot be done away with easily. How not to exploit it without completely forgetting it? A member of the National Commission for Human Rights in Rwanda explained to me one day that the massacres began a long time ago. Killings led to more killings and created cycles of revenge on both sides. In fact, the killings have never ceased. Where did the genocide begin? Were does the deep hatred come from? Where are the traditions? I am reading the remarkable book of the American journalist Philip Gourevitch: "We Wish to Inform You that Tomorrow We Will Be Killed with Our Families". It's the story of a Rwandan family that knew the day and the exact time of their death and asked the local mayor of their commune for help. The story tells an experience lived from day to day at the beginning of April 1994 in a hyperrealist style. The story is told in turn by all the members of a middle-class Tutsi family that will be assassinated. No members of the family can understand why they are going to be killed. Then, when the Interhamwe militia arrives, they let themselves be killed with resignation. Today, it is the survivors who do not understand anything about what happened. They feel guilty for everything.

12 December 1999: Accounts and letters

I spent an infinite number of hours trying to analyse figures on Rwanda's economic growth estimated by the International Monetary Fund. Five persons have just arrived from Washington, D.C. to explain that the government's budget is not strict enough. There are too many civil servants, and it's true. The growth rate is projected at about 5 per cent instead of the 8 per cent previously announced. The budget is finally adopted, and Rwanda will be on track. I have the impression that we have to play with the figures, like jugglers juggling plates in the air. While we do everything to keep one plate in the air on the right, we have to rush to the left to give a spin to the plate on the left that risks falling. The Rwandan government has decided to reinforce the collection of taxes even more. When we express doubts and offer the opinion that more taxes will kill the small businesses that are just being set up, the authorities answer that you have to find the money somewhere. It's clear for the government, but incomprehensible for the small businessman. Furthermore, the confidence of foreign investors is not very high. It didn't help that this week was marked by the exhausting conflict between the Ugandans and Rwandans. The minister for foreign affairs gave us an explanation during a press conference, but we have still not understood why former brothers have become enemies. This week ended with National Culture Day at the University of Butare. The only people staying in Rwanda are Gerard and a few tough ones who are meeting in the south in the heat of the summer. Everyone else has left on holiday. It is very hot in Rwanda in December. The Germans, UNICEF and a few other donors have put on hats because we are seated on the grass under a burning sun. Drums and folk dances brighten up the day, but the feeling is a bit low. The drive for culture seems to be blocked, but the performers try to find a way to express joy. There is always a certain nostalgia and a sense of death hanging about us. This Rwanda is really difficult.

16 December 1999: The poisoned cook

One day, Paulette, my cook, became ill. Her brother broke the news to me and then came back to confirm it the next day. Paulette had left the house on Monday about ten in the morning and was admitted to the hospital for suspected acute malaria. I paid for the medication and told her brother, who was our intermediary, that I wanted to talk with the physician before paying for more medication. She died in the hospital the next day. It was a mistaken diagnosis: typhoid fever instead of cerebral malaria. There was chaos in the whole house. The cleaning women talked about poisoning and jealousy.

Dorothée, the cleaning woman who had accused Paulette of stealing things from the house was accused of having poisoned Paulette. What a mess! Paulette wanted to take care of the whole house by herself and didn't like Dorothée. It seems that she wanted to receive two salaries. I called everyone together. I am left with a real puzzle of cleaning women, kitchen arguments, truth and the opposite version. The gardener, the night watchman, everyone got involved. Both women had survived the genocide. It was said that one was poisoned and the other was being directly accused of a poisoning but denied all the facts. In the meantime, Paulette had died. And even if I succeed in avoiding becoming involved in this mess, I am stuck with all the accusations. In the end, I called in the police. Paulette's brother came back several times. He asked me to pay for the burial and the cost of the whole family coming from Kibuye, which I did but still wondered what had really happened in the house. To be unable to speak the language of the country is an enormous handicap in Rwanda because three quarters of the reality probably escapes us. Poisoning is commonplace between families on the hills.

I had hired Paulette and Dorothée out of a desire to help. Paulette, very needy herself, was a survivor who was incapable of speaking. Everything frightened her; every ring of the doorbell was a reminder of the arrival of the Interhamwe. One day, workers came to repair the roof of the house. She recognized a killer among them, and she locked herself in the bathroom. We had a real problem in calming her down. Every other day, she collapsed or fainted. Now, the death of Paulette was attributed to Dorothée and indirectly to me: either through charms or by poisoning. And then she had not been taken to the hospital in time, and I did not visit her. This death worried me for many nights because I thought I had not done enough to help a person who was in danger. Living through this sad episode, I felt to which point daily life in Rwanda can be criss-crossed by obscure beliefs and uncontrollable fears. Dorothée, the survivor or the person who poisoned, depending on your interpretation, did not know what to do and hung around all day pathetically. She finally left. We found work for her with orphaned children. I started again from zero, hiring another cleaning woman and another cook. It's so often the case in this country of having to begin again from the beginning. But at the bottom of it all, nothing is lost; you simply go on.

17 December 1999: For meditation: the little pieces

What is the present? It's eternity lived now, entirely, completely, according to the Tibetans. I like that idea. Martin rented a house on the shores of Lake Mohazi, and we sometimes go there on weekends. I met the former president of Mali at the Mille Collines Hall, and we talked a lot about Rwanda. He recognized me in a meeting and asked what I was doing in this very sad country. He is a member of an OAU mission of enquiry. There is continuity in life. You often find the same people on a given circuit. Life is a puzzle, but we have to pay attention to all the little pieces because they fit into one another suddenly, very clearly.

18 December 1999: Zanzibar

The Tanzanian shores on the Indian Ocean are simply superb. It is wonderful to be next to the open sea after having been boxed in by the hills. We are a wonderful team taking advantage of a few days of rest and recuperation, a moment that we have needed for a long time. Everyday life in Rwanda is a heavy stone to bear. We read, lie in the sun around the swimming pool and swim in the Indian Ocean. It's a privileged time to think and question my experiences during the past few months. It's a time to think frustrating or affectionate thoughts for my Rwandan friends associated with daily events in Rwanda. This long inward journey and search for coherence is beginning to bear fruit. I am making sense out of this mission that suits me more and more. Zanzibar in Tanzania is a famous and magical island. It is the rallying point for all sorts of eccentric and alternative Europeans that have landed on the beaches of the Indian Ocean. It is also an ancient Arab sultanate where African slaves were captured and transported in ships' holds; part of the heavy past of Europeans and Africans.

I am reading the book "The Catastrophist" by Ronan Bennett, an American novelist, which takes place on the eve of independence in the Congo during the episodes in Lubumbashi. It knocked me over. It is an edifying story about the Congo in the 1960s with all sorts of ruthlessness linked to the mineral wealth.

In Tanzania, sunrise over the Indian Ocean makes me float with joy. I almost don't want to return to Rwanda. I take time to find my bearings a little, to say nothing, to observe closely and to listen. Then, here I am back in Kigali to deal with all the problems at once: the health sector, agriculture and discussions with other donors such as Canada, the Netherlands, Belgium and all the others. Upon arrival at the airport, I met one of the heads of the Rwandan military intelligence. He told me that he had attended a training course in Lusaka and did not agree with the presence of Rwandan troops in the Congo.

20 December 1999: China out loud

This week was marked by the difficult task of moving on. I had to deal with incredible administrative paperwork. Then, I began serious discussions about human rights with a representative of the United Nations. He is very perplexed about what is happening in Rwanda, but remains optimistic. Everyone who has just arrived in Rwanda says the same thing: "It's really complicated and confused here." The highlight of the week was a cocktail organized by the embassy of the People's Republic of China in commemoration of fifty years of the Chinese Revolution. Harsh harp music was being broadcast, and a film recalling the history of China was projected again and again on a giant screen. The ambassador of China announced his imminent departure. We had very interesting discussions about the "friendship between the people of Rwanda and the people of China" (those were his terms). The ambassador recited a beautiful poem about the Great Lakes and the majestic flight of the birds there. The ambassador's poem on the beauty and calm of Lake Kivu at Kibuye made a big impression on everyone. His final words were an excellent joke, like in a Peking opera. He said, "Rwanda is wonderful because there is no...pollution." Those words reminded me that the Chinese also love Kibuye and Lake Kivu.

As for myself, I am having trouble starting up again. All the staff that came here between 1995 and 1999 is going to leave, but I shall be staying on. I have to think about our progress and make new friends. Another generation is beginning, and thoughts about genocide are more and more distant.

21 December 1999: The miraculous recipe

There are days when it is more difficult than others to manage conflict. When I am really annoyed and under stress, like on Thursday, I use a remedy to deal with problems. I drive away in my four-wheel drive vehicle, which is high off the ground and gives me a raised position above people. In the car with the windows closed, I swear at everyone by name, shouting and letting off my anger. I am on the road all alone and try to explain to an imagined public, namely the trees, shrubs and houses along the road, that nothing works here, that I'm fed up with this Rwanda, that no progress is being made and that all I do is solve other people's problems. And then, I explain to the trees that I can't do anything about their having killed each other. First of all, I wasn't there at that time. It's not my problem. This whole story is just too much. And then, like in the case of babies, everything calms down thanks to the swaying of the car. The curves are smoother; my pulse slows down. I put on classical music and drive around the outskirts of Kigali from one hill to another. My stress evaporates as if by magic. The next day, I can go back to my yoga exercises with a smile and get on with my work. That's my safeguard; all the trees in Kigali have heard about it from me. After that I can focus all my energy in perfect alignment: we will do what we can with the means we have.

22 December 1999: False condolences

Once again, I am overworked to the point that I am obliged to pinch myself in order to take things one after another. It's as if I were trying carefully to string pearls that are not all the same size on a necklace. As a result, I made a big diplomatic gaffe at a party on a poorly lit terrace. One evening, there was a party at the residence of the ambassador of Germany on the occasion of the visit of members of the German government. I was wondering how to leave the party quickly when I thought I recognized someone. I approached a Rwandan who was sitting in the dark. With a drink in my hand, I moved closer to the person I thought was the minister of the interior and began a sober greeting and then immediately offered my condolences. I had heard that the father of that person had died. In fact, once I was close, I recognized my error. The person in front of me was the chairman of the Rwandan National Human Rights Commission. Because he was sitting in the dark against the light, he is an African and it's pitch black out, I can't make out his features. There was every possible reason for me to make that mistake. And, that's exactly what happened. The Rwandan jumped up obviously worried. It's rare that Rwandans express their feelings like that but I must have touched him. He told me that his father had been dead for the past twenty-five years. Then he caught hold of himself and told me that the Human Rights Commission had difficulty in beginning its work. They could not obtain reliable information, didn't know how the country was going to evolve and how the war in the Congo was going to end. The atmosphere was unstable. It was difficult under those circumstances to report on violations of human rights.

Murder in Burundi

Nothing is going right in Burundi. There is one catastrophe after another. The international community has decided to provide again humanitarian aid to 300,000 forcibly displaced persons abound rural Bujumbura. Is the government in a weak position? Rumours are spreading, and there are many violations of human rights. While we are focusing on human rights, Burundi is going through one of its biggest moments of horror. Four persons from the United Nations were killed in cold blood; the representative escaped by running for an hour, and the security officer was wounded. This tragedy gave me nightmares. I sent messages of solidarity and sympathy to the representative in order to help her. This kind of event should be taken seriously. She has to be careful because it can leave traces that mark you for life. A whole battalion is stationed near the Bujumbura airport but cannot stop the fighting. Artillery fire continues to kill civilians on the hills around Bujumbura. It's terrible.

23 December 1999: Macroeconomics; when will you make it clear?

I spent a good part of the week studying macroeconomic indicators with an attractive Belgian economist named Jean-Yves, who is a specialist in macroeconomics. The figures are interesting but also circumstantial. The World Bank and the International Monetary Fund lend money at favourable conditions to Rwanda, but the Rwandans continue to grow poorer. How should the problem be approached? The study of economic problems encourages me to regain a bit of hope. There is a feeling that there is a willingness to manage the economy well, to adopt liberal economic measures but neither investments nor the private sector are following. The laws in Rwanda are no longer adequate for the situation. A culture of entrepreneurship is not taking off. Banking facilities are no longer functioning. In addition, respect for human rights is very flexible. Once a Rwandan is arrested, it is difficult to have him released. If he is innocent, it is difficult to move his case forward. The judicial system is saturated, overloaded. It is enough to have two eyewitnesses to order an arrest. Fear of being arrested is still very widespread because unfortunately informants still exist. Rwanda has made many enemies during the past few years both inside and outside Rwanda, even in Uganda, and there is nothing but problems everywhere. Nonetheless, given the figures and studies, the international community has been able to explain its point of view coherently. We were able to coordinate things among ourselves and submit our conclusions to the interested parties. We even proposed studies that have a sort of common denominator: yes, the parliament is named; no, it is not elected; yes, the elections at the level of sectors were organized too early and people were not trained; no, Rwanda is not like other countries where people have the habit of obeying orders given too brutally by the authorities; yes, there really was a genocide; and so forth. And we spoke about Rwandan society, which needs support, a presence, patience and understanding. Not just a little bit, but enough to liberate its conscience. Yes, the authorities in place are omnipotent and their domination strangely resembles a dictatorship.

24 December 1999: Christmas Eve: Work of God and the devil

We are aware of many impasses in efforts to promote development, especially in reconstructing the social fabric. However, we are not blind even if sometimes we are accused of being blind and the accusation comes from those who used to know Rwanda well. God does not perpetuate acts of murder, and it is men who know how to use their sovereign liberty for good purposes. An Italian priest told us one day: "The part of God is the freedom to choose Him or not. The part of the devil is what men do with that freedom." I could verify the accuracy of his observation in the eyes of the ministers and most of the educated persons that I know in Rwanda. In answer to the question of why the genocide occurred, everyone closes up. As soon as you raise the question of ethnic affiliation of the Tutsis and Hutus and their options, there is a stiffening and a fear deep inside that surprises you. Curtain, the end. Their look becomes fixed without any recourse. But if we don't have anything to do any more with the question of ethnic affiliation, we will have to talk about it one day, right?

27 December 1999: Soldiers, on your marks

The creation of a traditional legal institution called Gacaca (pronounced "gatchatcha") has been announced. These are tribunals formed by the local population to judge crimes in groups. It is a risky bet. But how else can we accelerate the trials of 120,000 prisoners? Is there an alternative for this country other than that which has been proposed? Not really.

We all agree that many positive things have been accomplished in Rwanda since 1994. The country has integrated ex-FAR soldiers (from the former army) into the new army. They have repatriated Rwandan refugees from Bukavu and Goma. They have re-started the economy, built schools and rehabilitated many administrative buildings. The postal system, banks, traffic lights and road traffic in general have become operational. They have repaired the roads. We do not sufficiently emphasize the successes. Too few compliments are addressed to the new Rwanda, but on the other hand it does receive a lot of criticism. It is perhaps a question of attitude. Paradoxically, this negative climate comforts the government in its determination to be able to advance in its own way. But the problem is not located only there. The Congo, Burundi and Tanzania must be included in a regional solution for the equilibrium of the Great Lakes Region. One day a Belgian complained about the unfavourable reputation of

Rwanda abroad. He said, "How can we tell others that their opinions are one hundred times more critical than normal for this country that we all love so much? How can we plead the case of Rwanda when everyone smiles as soon as you begin to talk about the new Rwanda?

28 December 1999: Rwanda through the small end of the telescope

What will be Rwanda's future in the next century: war, occupation of the Congo, isolation of Rwanda on the international scene and the difficulty of defending their authoritarian and exclusive regime? The budget is a bit distorted. The amount of 28 per cent for military expenses is too high. These are factors that make you think about the future. Nonetheless, there is a sort of security in Rwanda that should not be forgotten. The dynamics of development is weak despite everything as soon as you leave Kigali. You can see some progress in the hospitals and the public administrations, but reconstruction and making the economy more dynamic will require time. Africa and the Great Lakes Region, there where there are no surveillance cameras. It's only a regional war that is breaking out in the Congo. The media ask who are the villains. It seems that everyone is exploiting the mineral resources of the Congo. What can we deduce from that?

Traditional healers

This has been a full week of new events. I thought I had a bit of time for filing but finally there was no time available. On the other hand, I met Rwandan healers who work wonders. There was an extraordinary day of exchanges with the traditional practitioners who heal sick people with plants and herbs. They came from all corners of Rwanda to participate in a forum in Kigali and discuss physical and psychological trauma linked to the genocide. These healers are also real poets. They give names and explanations to illnesses, poetically and lyrically evoking occult forces, ancient presences and strange travellers in the body.   They hold an ancient knowledge that was transmitted to them by knowledgeable people. They diagnose illnesses by giving names of animals or spirits that come to upset the body, closing their eyes, murmuring a prayer and explaining the situation they feel. Their hands are warm and energetic. Often, they do not know how to read and write, but use extraordinary therapeutic capacities. We had long talks about traditions, the power of healing that several have possessed from their infancy. Sometimes, certain women have attributes for specific illnesses, while others give calming herbs for those who have nightmares at night. There are many of them. They agree that illnesses were also the reflection of all the hatred that eats away at the livers of people. Will they be able to overcome all the problems of hatred in the world by treating with herbs and words the illnesses that are above all illnesses of the soul?

30 December 1999: Along the lake

I had to go to northern and western Rwanda to monitor several projects. This time, the trip from Gisenyi to Kibuye was made by boat on Lake Kivu. The lake produces a strange sound. It has a metallic consistency because of the methane that it releases. The ride was thrilling. Later, I visited a site of resistance on the hills at Kibuye. On Kishina Hill near Bisesero there are still traces of the massacre. We were making a solemn pilgrimage. It was a lesson in humility that made any attempt to express thoughts vain. All of a sudden, we were all very close, conscience of our differences but also of what joined us; each in our own way in quest for reparation and empathy. The visit to the Saint-Jean Church in Kibuye, which has become a memorial, allowed us to join our thoughts for a few moments with the victims. We do not have the right to forget but we have very few means for remedying the past.

Time is the only factor that will allow repair. The present sometimes gives us a feeling of impunity. We want to build better bases for the future. Seeking a better world is that utopian? How did God feel about the massacres in his place of worship?

Within the framework of projects linked to health, we worked straight through until late at night with Nathanaël, a Rwandan psychiatrist in order to better understand how Western approaches could be better used in the case of survivors' trauma and with patients in the Rwandan psychiatric hospitals.

Graduation

We spent a very amusing evening this week "with the girls". Eight women at the British residence. Gathered together, all nations together, we had fun thinking that over apple crumble and jelly dessert we would have enough to tell hilarious stories about Rwanda. It's a good change to laugh a bit. It was surrealist: we played charades to relax as if we were on television. It did us all a lot of good to release a bit of tension. We recalled in comprehensible episodes such as when we all had to queue up for the visit of Timberland, the United States representative to the United Nations. We had waited for almost two hours in front of a closed door without moving. Finally, he came out of the conference room and told us nonchalantly: "We have reached agreement on peace in the Congo." At that same time, a group of Congolese came out of the same room and stood in front of the television cameras, and then loud and clear they affirmed just the opposite. There was a moment of indecision. Then, they all went back into the room and locked the door.

This Sunday, we returned to southern Rwanda to Butare to attend a solemn but beautiful ceremony. For the first time since 1994, medical diplomas were being awarded. The students, all very proud, were wearing coal black suits , a belt with the colours of Rwanda—red, green and yellow and triangular caps. They looked like they had come out of Rabelais. The rector's voice trembled when he gave his speech. He handed out 180 diplomas, the first since 1994 out of 2500 students of the National University of Rwanda. It was a moving moment, above all the heads of the future physicians. A touch of hope for this end of the year.

Chapter 6

Nathanaël and the Hills of Rwamatamu

Nathanaël, a physician, is a returnee. He is one of those who came back after the genocide and who feel very guilty about not having been able to give a hand to their families during the massacres. This group of Rwandans does not have an easier life than the others. Endlessly ghosts chase them in their dreams. Why were they not there, how could they have helped their families, perhaps they should have returned, why had they left? Nathanaël was born into a family of Protestant pastors. The first sentence that he said when we began to talk about 1994 was his shame at not having been with his family in Rwanda and having stayed in Belgium as head of a clinic in a hospital. All the time during the terrible events, he wanted to take the airplane and a gun. But he returned later. The 19 members of his family were killed. He did not want to go to Kibuye, his home prefecture. He has stayed in Kigali for more than two years, hiding and frightened but with a single idea of helping his people to try to recover reason and not to drift into madness or denial and to stand up to what had happened. He thinks Rwanda must begin a process of mourning and reflection about what could have led people to want to eliminate others. He wants to take care of those considered crazy, in a single word, he wanted to become a physician of the soul. Nathanaël became a psychiatrist. He wasn't able to return to Kibuye and the destroyed house of his happy past. It was way beyond his possibilities. Nonetheless, one day he returned almost against his will, and it was with me. A poet and idealist at the same time, Nathanaël is an epical character; a scientist by necessity and a storyteller by nature. When he gives his full name, there are about three metres of words pronounced in one breath, which in Kinyarwanda mean something like this: "he who is not afraid and faces danger, who was born in a field in the sun among cows and prosperity and whose mother saw the first sign of his existence as unequalled happiness and a promise of courage."

Nathanaël always thought that at least his mother would not be harmed because everyone loved her; because everyone came to visit her; because she, in addition, had received the gift of knowing how to comfort, say a gentle word or give someone advice that did away with problems. She knew how to heal. His mother was a traditional healer and source of advice. She was a wise woman: a born psychologist who had never studied. Everything she knew was by intuition. She had given birth to seven children, two of whom had survived. Nathanaël remembered since a very young age that his mother represented a point of attraction for the whole hill, for the whole commune.

From the end of the 1980s until the beginning of the 1990s, she was extremely surprise that it was possible to burn houses, kill "cockroaches" (the name that had been given to the Tutsis) and then go to mass on Sunday as if nothing had happened. She neither wanted to nor would believe it. Even though already at that time, everyone knew quite well who were the authors of the crimes, everyone remained silent. Nathanaël's mother concluded that people just had to have seen evil. She could not imagine that during a raid the next day the same persons would come to ask her for a light for their cooking fires, a herbal remedy for an allergy or advice about a child with malaria.

When Nathanaël's mother was killed, the world was lost for him. There was no longer any rhyme or reason. While he was travelling some 5000 kilometres from Rwanda, friends rang him to tell him that a group of persons was resisting on a hill. His family was part of that group, and his father was leading the group, calling people to resist, tolerant and encouraging. Then on April 24th, the militia attacked the hill with dynamite and finished the job with machetes. His mother was alongside her husband. When her death was announced to him on the telephone, Nathanaël was speechless; nothing no longer had any meaning. He himself had nothing left but to die, he told himself. He entered an almost cataleptic state. It was his wife who was able to find the right words to comfort him and shake him out of his paralysis, to bring him back to life and give him courage to return; she who had lived the same experience. She had also seen her whole family killed. It's on the basis of connivance and sharing of the same reality that Nathanaël has lived. Who else could understand what he was experiencing? Of course, only someone who had lived the same reality under the same circumstances. He began to work earnestly on his doctoral thesis in university hospitals in Europe. He thought about his country and already imagined how he was going to transform the theory that he had learned on the Old Continent into a practice in Africa. Through the psychiatric medicine of the Europeans, he would become a doctor of the soul and would use that training to deal with his personal experience and the shameful history of Rwanda.

Nathanaël began to study the psychiatry of White people (*muzungus*). How could it really be useful for the Rwandans? Was there a tie between post-Freudian approaches, behavioural studies, active listening, medication for societies suffering from interior solitude and the healing of a devastated country, torn by a huge scar slashed across the whole country? Little by little, he was becoming known in Europe. Everyone began to come to him to talk about their problems. It's not easy to be an African psychiatrist and treat the illnesses of Europeans. He wanted to make all those hospitals with the grey, aseptic walls more colourful and warmer. Many patients talked to him and he became a bit everyone's refuge. He loved to talk about the visit of one of his first patients who wanted to see a physician. He remembers her with affection. A lady came to visit him, one day with a problem of not being able to sleep and fear at night. Nathanaël received her. Of course, she looked around and asked to see the real physician. He assured her that he was the physician. He could see the look of panic in the patient's eyes, and the impossibility for her out of politeness to leave the room. Then, with a long sigh she sat down, looked him up and down and blurted out "I want to see a real doctor, but in the meantime could you give me an amulet for my headache?"

This lady finally underwent therapy with Nathanaël for several years. Through patience and an overturning of all her prejudices she became a fervent adept of his theses. The doctor of the soul began to become interested in all forms for treating trauma. He treated difficult cases. His life in Europe was not always easy. Integration, even for an intellectual, is often an obstacle course. Even if he reaches the end, it is like taking a very cold shower. In addition, Rwandans in Europe are very divided among themselves. They don't limit themselves to flattery. They don't always speak kindly to each other. Where should reconciliation begin? Despite his success and integration into scientific circles, Nathanaël wanted to go back to Rwanda. It was there that he could do something important. He wanted to return to Rwanda to be with the 300,000 surviving children, without families, traumatized. He wants to work with the women who have become heads of families after having suffered all sorts of corporal indignities. He also wants to meet the 120,000 detainees and all those that the fact of having killed must haunt and follow them in their dreams. He decided that his aid would take the form of support for reconciliation through care for treating the sequels of the genocide: "*Nutanga imbabazi uzabona amahoro*" (you must forgive, if you want peace) states the Rwandan proverb. It's easily said, but there is reality and heavy hearts. Nathanaël left Europe and moved to Rwanda with all his family. His oldest son was enrolled in a boarding school in Butare. He re-learned his own culture. Back in Rwanda like many exiles, he was filled with hope. All his family was determined to set to work. The shock was enormous. The promised land would have to wait. Rwanda belongs to all sorts of different people. Was that the case after so many years? Returns are always painful. This one was especially painful. The country was in ruins, especially in the field of human psychology. One question came immediately to mind: what does it mean to be Rwandan? Should you speak of the past or forget it? That is a difficult question to answer. People no longer laugh as before. Vocal cords are disturbed, off key. Nathanaël discovers that if the patient does not express his pain, it becomes even stronger. The only way to gain control and decrease the pain is to speak out, shout, make it understood, have someone listen and share it.

But how can it be done while maintaining respect for one's culture and retaining dignity? The extrovert practice of complaining is the complete opposite of everything that Rwandans have always known. To speak out is so very distant from the ancestral culture. His mother always told him: hide what you feel, be a man, don't show any hatred or enthusiasm. Be polite, especially with people that you totally despise. In that way they cannot reproach you." But Nathanaël did not want to play that game of hide-and-seek and risk giving ambiguous messages, even though he was a Rwandan. That's when the inner struggle began that is the case of those impregnated with several cultures. The return to Rwanda became a real challenge for him. He asked himself how to find an old identity in new clothes? How could he remain himself and understand others around him. Should he bring new perspectives to bear? Quickly, he realized that he was not alone. His return and reintegration into his own country was one of the dramas that touched all those who have returned. There are more than two million of them. To know how to behave after so many long years of absence is a real challenge. Who represents the real Rwandan values? Those from before? Absolutely not. Those who have returned from the Congo, Canada or Tanzania? Maybe; but who will determine the real face of Rwanda?

It seemed to Nathanaël that all efforts at reconciliation must begin by the recognition of a common identity, which no longer exists. You have to reconstitute it, look for it at the very beginning of time, before the hatred and division at the time of the Tutsi kings or even before that. Where is the quality of being African, where are the roots, where has solidarity gone? When was the basic unity of a whole continent lost? Nathanaël sadly realizes that the roots will slowly return. He is already working for the following generation; for those who will be born after the war. In the meantime, he has to perform a surgery that is just a placebo. He had already asked his mother in the garden of their house on the hills around Kibuye what it meant to be different? When he was little, he had already understood that he was surely not big enough, that he was too big or that he did not have the right head. Always first in his class, he had to repeat the last year of primary school five times. The reasons given were that his race was not right. His teachers had told his parents that they had to bring those arrogant people who think they are always the best down a notch. That's probably why they become that way, he realized later. He meant becoming arrogant.

Our collaboration did not begin at all under propitious circumstances. The first time I met Nathanaël was like when two cocker spaniels meet, sniffing each other and looking distrustfully at each other. He was presented as a physician, psychiatrist, a Rwandan who had studied in Europe. Suddenly it's I who finds myself in his country talking about health and traumas. What kind of a partnership would we have?

Psychiatrists are always feared because, it is said, they know how to look behind appearances. I had no desire for him to look behind my curtain. In a short time, he proved himself in his own country. He quickly showed through therapy sessions that he is a great person. At the psychiatric hospital in Kigali, so over worked during the period of genocide because unfortunately it was placed under the protection of the peacekeepers, Nathanaël introduced a wonderful programme of care for the bipolar troubles of his patients. This new approach made it possible for a group of persons who had suffered violent trauma to undergo group therapy. He began with the principle that no one wanted to speak about these things except to persons who had suffered the same trauma. He was well placed to feel it himself. That's how self-help groups began. I attended several group therapy sessions in which men and women talk and other help them to tell their story because the same thing happened to them. They explain what they did to survive, move on and try to continue to live normally. Suddenly, they feel less alone with their problems. Sometimes they even agree to help others. Nathanaël is very attentive. He heals with his head and his heart.

The patients have confidence in him. From the moment he begins to speak, everyone stops, sits down and listens. He has a lot of charisma. I don't know how he does it, but probably the intense pain with which he had to deal gave him a pleasant soft voice and very precise words filled with empathy. Useless words are done away with. Furthermore, his smile shines, and his eyes say everything. Nathanaël knows how to keep a secret. He began working at the hospital where I had the privilege of being able to listen and understand. I listened to the patients' stories that tell the tale of a real nightmare. But because someone was dealing with their suffering, some patients were able to begin to laugh again. Men and women began to have a desire to live. They began to walk in the gardens and greet each other. The many staff training sessions are models of patience. The stories that they heard are the echoes of their own pain. Little by little, the team introduced new and gentler methods, without force or hallucinogenic medication, straightjacket or disrespect. An attentive ear and respect for individual pain specifically linked with that of others represented for the whole group of nurses a real revelation. The stories are touching, always very dignified. The patients recall everything, with full details and an impressive fatality.

A shrivelled-up woman called Monique told me one day in a dried-up voice that the devil had chosen the Hutus for this horrible job because there were more of them, but they could have been someone else. I continue to go frequently to mass and ask myself why God is so often absent from Rwanda. I pray that the souls of the Africans who died and those of all the people who suffered under the genocide can go to heaven. That's all I want from him.

Sitting in a circle, the patients listened. They agreed. They understood that there were several different truths, not just one, but they still wanted to understand why. A neighbour of Monique named Claire-Chantal answered her, "Yes, God, I ended up accepting him. We Tutsis have always been compared to the Jews. But I don't think that is right. We were never given an Israel. We are not at all the elected people. I think that I have to thank God who is in heaven for having let me live. And now, because I have lost confidence in the whole world, my colleagues, neighbours all the others, he is the only thing that I have. It's as though I had met him for the truth because I am a survivor."

References to religion come up often. Not only have Rwandans never had among them the possibility of saying certain things but, in addition, at the hospital, Nathanaël asked them to speak kindly to each other, not to impose their personal suffering, to listen to others and to question themselves about the way in which they speak to each other.

The cultural revolution began over there. After having succeeded in advancing a bit on the road towards healing, groups of survivors became themselves in turn helpers in the group therapy. Some were able to begin to come out of it and become outpatients. Others stayed locked in their refusal to speak. Then, whole families were recomposed, monitored and helped. They were able to take over. After several months of practice, Nathanaël thought that it was possible to advance a bit. After having helped the surviving Tutsis, he was going to look for Hutus that had committed crimes during the genocide.

Even former soldiers who killed during the genocide came forward. They also had sometimes madness at night about which they were not aware or autism. For some of them, the walls still reflect the cries of the dying and are covered with blood. One day I was able to attend the telling of a story of one of Nathanaël's patients, Bastien. A former teacher, he was trying to explain the origin of the conflict. "I think that everything began in 1991, when the multiparty system was authorized. The Interhamwe started saying in public that we were "cockroaches". I saw that the Hutu politicians were increasingly afraid of an invasion from abroad. They thought that the vengeance for 1959 would be terrifying. From then on, they began to prepare the genocide. When the war began, we were already used to the killing. We were not at all surprised. We should have prepared ourselves and defended ourselves, but we were so used to hearing that we were worth less than nothing that we ended up believing it and were waiting to be killed without resisting." Sitting in front of him, another woman, Immaculée, answered, "Since 1991, the government had been afraid of being chased out by the FPR and the Ugandan." Tutsis who had sought refugee in Uganda and who had tried to attack from the north in 1991. But that does not explain why the Hutus, who first of all wanted our fields and our houses, thought that extermination was a means of living happily and prosperously. I think that all the explanations based on history and handed to us by the colonizers are false. They say that the Twa pygmies, with bows and arrows came first. Then the Hutus with their farming tools and then last of all the Tutsis with their cows taking over the land. These are stories to make us fight each other and not live in peace. I think that we arrived all at the same time." It's exchanges like that that allow the traumatized to express their disarray and doubts to others. These dialogues are essential for healing. The word reconciliation takes on its full meaning.

In therapy groups at the hospital, several women were able to shout symbolically and even to fight with former soldiers physically. At the same time, the soldiers were able to try to be more aware (the rare times that was possible) of what they had committed. It's not easy. Denial is strong when events go beyond all interdictions and taboos. The reality of the massacres becomes intolerable, even for the soldiers. It's unbearable, even for them, when they realize it. Others adopt an attitude of having done nothing or almost nothing. Those there are also accepted as they are, without being judged, with only their physical presence, coming from the other side. It is only from then on that forgiveness can take form. There are some horrible stories during which no one speaks. We simply hear the sound of breathing.

I remember the story of a nurse. "My name is Charles-Gratien", he said sitting in the middle of the circle of the therapy group at the hospital. "I don't know how to live. I am from Cyangugu where I was the head nurse at the university hospital since 1992. I knew I was on the list. Every day for months, the physicians repeated that it would soon be our turn. They laughed as if it were a joke. We were afraid, but we also thought that it was impossible to kill all of us. When they came to look for me with a lorry on April 17th to take me and about ten other nurses to an empty factory outside the town, we did not resist. Everything was planned. How could I say anything? I thought that stories of ethnic group were like AIDS, no one ever spoke about it. We pretended as though everything was normal, but we knew we would all be killed. They pushed us in with about 2500 other persons who were already there and then began to shoot at us and cut people up with machetes. I don't know how but I fell into the pile onto dead bodies. I didn't move. They forgot about me. They were drunk and laughing. And then they left, shouting that they would come back the next day to see whether their work had been finished. I waited for darkness and then left the factory, stepping on corpses and moaning bodies. I couldn't help the others. I would have liked to have carried away all of them, but I had to think about saving my skin. It wasn't a good idea, and then I ran away. I spent three months hiding in ditches, woods and marshes. I don't know how I survived, I'm embarrassed. All my family in the commune was killed. I never saw them again. I can't even bury their bodies, and my family's house is now occupied by other people. Even though I escaped, I live like a mommy and think about it every day."

We didn't move. Nathanaël put his hand over his face to wipe away a tear. We could hear others breathing. "You know", said Charles-Gratien, "those responsible for the genocide are not the poor small farmers and the uneducated but really the Interhamwe (those who fight together), even if they were mad and vicious. It was the educated people: the teachers, politicians, journalists, all those who studied social sciences, physicians, the mother superiors. The intellectuals did not dirty their hands; they sent others to do the dirty work in their place, the work on the hills. And now they are living in Europe, and we are here. We have to begin again to rebuild. This hospital is incredible. There are not enough beds, not enough medication and people are dying all the time, even those who succeeded in saving themselves."

After these difficult sessions, they sometimes played volleyball outside. The nurses stared. Is this a true story or is he pretending because Nathanaël asked for his opinion about forgiving the murderers? He gave very clear instructions to all the staff. He said that there had to be a forgiving. It was an order. Like orders in the past? Everything is possible in Rwanda, even orders to be nice. One of the greatest difficulties for patients is that without having been able to bury the dead, they cannot properly morn the dead. Some of them still tell themselves that as long as no corpse is produced the person might have also succeeded in escaping. Having to live with a false hope is very trying. This situation does not make it possible to solve the problem. Often, some people think they recognize someone from their family at the market, in a passing hope. The genocide has not allowed people to identify the dead and pay their last respects. On the other hand, a survivor often recognizes one of the perpetrators from his commune with certainty at the market. That person usually panics and runs away not daring to accuse the person. And then all the fear from before comes back unacceptably.

Nathanaël does not want to play politics. He wants to heal, but here you have to struggle just to be recognized as a person. The various currents in society are too strong. He tries to promote reunion with his stories, with images of comparisons, his gentle manner of speaking and his interest in each life story. He has to confront Rwandans who, like him, were outside the country at the time of the genocide. Every time he defends one of his traumatized patients and talks about his slow work of reconciliation, some of his colleagues think that he is exaggerating a bit. Those who were not there want life to go on. They tell him that it is a good idea to listen to the survivors, but you also have to listen to others, for example the Tutsis from outside Rwanda, those who lived in Bujumbura, Kampala, Kinshasa or someplace else. They don't really understand all the ceremonies of commemoration and mourning. They don't want always to see life in black and white. They ask him to suggest to his patients to stop thinking about it. Nathanaël feels caught in the crossfire. He also comes from abroad, but he sees the results of the genocide. He explains that as long as the survivors' questions are not dealt with, there can be no true reconciliation. It is not a question of numbers, he thinks, but of the precariousness of the social tissue. Since it has torn, it has to be repaired. A survivor cannot and does not want to forget. Despite all the difficulties, Nathanaël doesn't back down. There is no reason, he says, that we are unable to heal this society of its artificial and historical disease, that of ethnic affiliation. You can see that there is no common trait among those who are designated as Tutsis. Often, they are mixed. Some time ago, Hutus bought many cows and became Tutsis. They don't always agree about their origin. Does ethnic affiliation make any sense? No and no, he repeated. Let's stop the nonsense. For Nathanaël, these ethnic categories had become the equivalent of the words "plague, malaria, infection, bubonic plague and excrescence". He does everything he can to find the right vaccine.

We spent many hours together talking about the usefulness of nurses learning new methods, assuming responsibilities and a sense of initiative. I always thought that Rwandans' problems should be tackled first by the Rwandans. We did not always agree about the question of outside help. Africa, especially Rwanda, has gone through terrible human suffering. For years, Rwanda expected to receive outside assistance as a right. Today, the country cannot understand that providing foreign assistance is not an obligation. One day, it has to decrease. Africa has to deal with its own problems. There has to be equitable partnerships, and there has to be a decision to find a solution themselves. Our talks sometimes went on late into the night, and we rebuilt the world.

One day, we worked on an especially difficult case, and I again made one of my typically impatient and quick *muzungu* statements. The results of a project are not only bad and, in addition, everyone seems to be little concerned. Nathanaël got up angry and incensed and all red (not easy to see on an African's face) and began to scream at me, defending his people. It was a first time for me in Rwanda. I was paralysed. He was too. After a few seconds, he sat back down and told me that it was the first time that he had lost his temper. Quite ashamed, he realized that it was with a European. There was a pause. Finally, we looked at each other and began to laugh. It was the greatest proof of friendship that a Rwandan can give to a European woman, that of no longer being able to control himself and say what he really feels. I sincerely thanked him even though I was flabbergasted. I don't think I really liked the argument, but I did appreciate his candour. We laughed a lot about this incident that was the keystone of our relationship and touched on the core of our intercultural differences. It's also the typical stumbling block between an outsider who wants to do things the way he wants and a local who wants to do the opposite. Quite often, when he is really consulted, an African explains that it is not at all what he wants and that his way of doing things may be twisted but it is much more sustainable.

Shortly after this incident, we went together to Kibuye. Two physicians working with Nathanaël also went with us. It was the first time that he had accepted to return to his home commune. Nathanaël bundled himself into the back of the car, whistling in order not to reveal his nervousness. A tape by Youssou N'Dour set the mood, as if everything were normal. In order to hide the real purpose of our visit, we visited the hospital at Kibuye. But our real destination was Rwamatamu in the prefecture of Kibuye.

The weather was hot, and we stopped several times as we climbed the hills. At every curve, Nathanaël recognized places; he had been to school here and his friends lived over there. His nervousness was gradually increasing. How would he react when he saw his destroyed house? What would be the effect of all his memories? Finally, we arrived at the bottom of his family's hill. We climbed on foot for more than half an hour through sorghum fields and green banana patches. Nathanaël was ahead, and we were following a bit behind. We couldn't see his face but we could sense the tension created by his memories. Once at the top, we discovered the remains of his ruined house. There was grass growing out of the joints among the bricks and nothing else but silence. Birds were chirping on the fallen-in roof. We waited several minutes for him to deal with his past. Nathanaël quite calmly began to explain where the kitchen was, his brothers' room and his uncle's place. He was calm and controlled, and we kept quiet. We let him speak for a long time. Then, we sat down on the grass for almost an hour without talking, trying to recall the past. Mentally, we said everything. That was probably one of the most intense moments of communication in my life. In silence, we went through all the stages of the slow agony that Nathanaël's family had gone through. The hill where the resistance took place was just across the valley. It was there that they had all died. Finally, Nathanaël got up and very calmly pointed. On this hill, his whole commune had succeeded in resisting for ten days. He was proud of them. We went back down to the fields, running down the hill. In the car, Nathanaël asked me to play the tape of Youssour N'Dour again. There was absolutely no need for words. All of us were with him, off in our thoughts. My future was now tied to that of Nathanaël. He had given me a key to understanding his people. As for me, I had been with him at a very painful time in his life. I had the possibility of seeing and understanding his past and going to his home or what was left of it. It was the first visit that he was making to his commune and to his family's home since the genocide. It was a step that took a lot of courage. Everything had been destroyed. The only thing left was memories; memories of a happy family in the area of Mirorowe, commune of Rwamatamu, in the Kibuye prefecture. There was no member of his family left. That was one of the reasons why Kibuye had become a pole of attraction for me. Often during my visits to western Rwanda, I was drawn to the end of the lake, under the volcanoes and hills around Kibuye. That day is forever engraved in my memory. There, the lake stares hard, metallically and calmly. The friendship between Nathanaël and me is unique and deep, even if our lives seem different. His four children and his wife are for him the basis for a renaissance. He is struggling and mending his wounds and those of his family and others.

I left Rwanda, but this country has not left me, nor has Nathanaël left me. The silent sharing of what cannot be said and the confidence we have in each other are a precious gift for both of us that nothing can erase.

Part III   Justice, A Small Grain of Hope

Chapter 7

Diary (2000)

Supporting the Process

4 January 2000: The beauty of nature

The New Year began for me in Kibuye with bronchial-
pneumonia, as if my body was saying that it needed looking
after it first and that I needed to re-adapt to the 1500-metre
altitude of Rwanda. My body was telling me that I needed to
begin to look at the hills more calmly. I tried to step back a bit
by coughing. It is the rainy season. Outside my window, the
Bougainvillea, lilac and yellow frangipani are growing up in
order to be the first plants to be watered. My garden is
waterlogged green, drowned by noisy and frequent storms. I
have spread out a net under the avocado trees because the fruit,
which is very hard and heavy when it falls, falls on a light
fixture and frequently breaks the bulb.

My cat, Gribouille, has once again given birth in a
drawer in a cupboard in the attic. I am going to have to find a
new home for them. My house is really beautiful. I'm like a
pearl in an oyster. I'm determined to get off to a big rousing
start in this new century, even if it is a sniffle and a common
cold that have gotten hold of me for the past 72 hours. I am
suffering under the effects of a cough, 41 degrees of fever fit
for a horse and an avalanche of telephone calls asking me to
follow this or that case. I have begun to laugh at it all because
everything seems so distant. It is probably the very heavy
medication that causes a vaporous and giddy effect. The ICTR
prosecutor is arriving at full speed in a few days. I have not yet
officially presented my wishes to the new president. Piled on

171

my desk is a two-metre-high stack of files to deal with. I'm going to cough my way slowly through them in stages.

9 January 2000: Nostradamus was wrong

I began the new millennium as if on a toboggan. After a bit of worrying at the office, we even made it through the millennium bug that, as it turned out, did not affect the computers. Prophets and astrologers like Nostradamus were wrong: we survived the twelve strokes of midnight. The Earth did not fall, and Belpheghor, the phantom of the Louvre, showed his true face: transparent and that evaporates in a wisp. Why do we keep diaries? Probably because the act of writing allows us to recall better, to understand certain ideas better and to let go of others forever. It's a bit like compressing a hard drive in order to make space, gain time and think, sharpen thoughts and spread a bit of calm.

It has been more than one month since the most recent entry in my diary. That's a lot. I just had the thought that I have never read Amiel's book. Everyone says that it is a wonderful little book. It will have to wait with the rest that have been there for several years for the next vacation. Not to write is like committing an infidelity that has to be made up for right away. It is the expectation for both an imaginary reader and for the person who is writing and refers back to a diary. The writer creates a relationship with time. For whom do we write? For an answer, we have to turn to *Les Nourritures Terrestres* by André Gide. He explains that the sight of a glass of water in the middle of the desert is worth more than its real absorption. To be pleased with writing has perhaps as much value as that of being there.

17 January 2000: Disappointment

Ephrem came to see me one evening at the house, completely hopeless. Ephrem is a Rwandan who returned in

1995 with a doctorate in economics in his pocket. He went into exile in 1982 and had met his Rwandan wife in Canada. She is from the hill in front of Gitarama. They have four children and through mutual friends in Mali and Switzerland, they became my close friends. That evening, Ephrem was all worked up and could hardly speak. "You can't imagine", he told me, "what has happened. "Me, the director general, I have just been fired by the Machines Agricoles company because they accused me of being too curious about the accounts and too haughty in my asking for results from the investments that we make. In addition, the board of directors made me understand that I was too friendly with former Hutu employees. But I was only trying to bring about some form of reconciliation. I lost everything during the genocide, all my family and that of my wife. Am I dreaming? Do you think that I have become too European? Do you think that I am incapable of running a business? Absolutely no one is behind me. The verdict is there, I don't really know from where. I am a persona non grata. What am I going to do?" First I gave Ephrem some chocolate biscuits, and we went to sit in the garden, then we phoned his wife. I promised him my help and helped him find a new job.

20 January 2000: Brochettes and tennis balls

I had one of those memorable weekends when everything seems to go just right. In the end, it is not so difficult to make an effort at integration. One day, the president of the Tennis Club asked me to participate in a club tournament in which he had already enrolled me. I was to form a doubles team with Dr. C., with whom I work in health, but the day of the match, Saturday, he was ill. In a drawing of names from a hat, I was given a Rwandan partner who was good but unknown. It was a doubles tournament. To my big surprise, Saturday morning at Nyarutarama there were only Rwandan males. Not even a little European bird on the horizon, not even a single woman. I was just about to try to get out of this trap, which seems internal, when the president of Rwanda comes up to me and shakes my hand expressing his pleasure that I am participating in the tournament. It is as simple as all that. Here I am obligated to the tournament for two days. I reach the quarterfinals. Then, we elegantly and diplomatically lose. The big shot he was playing with was a bit of an introvert. I was able to attend the final with the head of the country and the president for the distribution of prizes and brochettes Sunday evening. And then I was called on to give a speech and hand out the trophies. I had thought for some time about what I wanted to say for this big occasion. I didn't want to deal with politics. Finally, I decided to say something about gender. Next year, I pleaded, looking straight at the first lady sitting in the first row, please do something to reinforce the women's section because I felt all alone at this gathering of male athletes. Everyone laughed and I didn't say anything about politics or the clash in Kisangani (in the Congo) between Rwanda and Uganda or a lot of other topics that were on the tip of my tongue. It was an extremely pleasant weekend with the leaders of the country. I realized the extent of the great simplicity and solidarity that held them together. Without expressly wanting it, I had the impression for just a weekend that I was just a bit accepted, even if in a Rwandan way: with a smile and a certain distance. At any rate, thanks to a tennis racket I was with them, and I had a great time. Tennis is really a diplomatic sport.

3 February 2000: Those who speak constantly about ethnic identity

Life often unfortunately confirms my first intuition. I always though that we should never have hired that man, but when we voted the other colleagues felt that he seemed so honest.

It was a question of a Rwandan director sinisterly called Cursius, a head agronomist who made fun of us. He didn't do anything that we asked him to do and acted a bit like a broom closet. He always knew everything and was continually interrupting the rest of the staff to correct them. He is basically square and says incredible things about the villages, paedophilia, the Rwandan regroupings, cooperatives, beans, AIDS and human rights. Everything and nothing. The type of person who would immediately join the other side whenever there was a conflict. He gave me goose-flesh and frightened me because I can see him creating conflict among groups. I wondered how many people like Cursius are left in the country. The kind that raise a fuss over everything in the name of ethnic affiliation. A nightmare? Not to that extent, because he worked together with another NGO that also complained about his bellicose nature. He lied like a trooper. He told endless stories on the hills. We were finally obliged to let him go. The only thing that interested him at the time of talking about his leaving was to know whether in the event he tried to set up his own project we could finance it. I think that he never understood why we fired him. It's always a bit difficult to tell someone that he is spreading hatred, when he is in fact that. I told him that he created tension and arguments among team members. He didn't understand what I was talking about. Administering Rwandan employees is not easy when you want to maintain certain neutrality. Still, it's a very strong cultural shock. You have to be careful about communications, about the words that are used and fairness. In the end, you have to take into account reciprocal expectations.

At the end of the week, the international community organized a round table with the British secretary of state for cooperation, a very confident woman, quite sharp in her analyses. She supported Rwanda in its efforts at reconciliation and was very convincing with her arguments. If we want to avoid a new conflict created by poverty and ignorance, we have to help development, she proclaimed. Only economic development will reconcile all the people: not famine. She forthwith announced publicly substantial aid from the United Kingdom over ten years.

14 February 2000: Four lovely women

Saturday, I organized a diner between four women, a meal that I was giving to my colleagues because two of them were unfortunately leaving. One was the ambassador of Egypt, the other the representative of Swedish development assistance and the third the German ambassador. It was a very lively and relaxed female quartet. We dined with sparking wine from Dubai in a good restaurant in Kigali and chatted until late at night. Each person told about catchy situations for which they had found very feminine solutions. Sometimes you have to go through that. We reached the conclusion that female representatives have an advantage in Rwanda when they think rationally, exchange their experiences and know how to reply emotionally to events. They obtain rather impressive long-term results. They have a more concerted approach, more comprehensible but, nonetheless, very critical. Among the four of us, there was support at all times. We were able to combine our experiences and analysis in order to understand better the functioning of the country. The friendship that joined us under these rather difficult circumstances where information is filled with malicious rumours is the best way to avoid making mistakes. There is always someone to say to another that she is off the track and that she should rethink this idea or that approach or carry a query further. The next day, I tried to put into practise what they had taught me: try to transmit a message of truth and my opinions about Rwanda, communicate what I know without compromising myself and without lying. I learned to show compassion for this torn country without being blind or overly compassionate. The Egyptian advice is to get rid of my fear of not having the approval of others. It is a programme that I have taken to heart for the future.

Zen philosophy consists of living in the "now", fully as if it were an eternity and to be happy. Sometimes, for instance right now, I succeed. At other times, I spend a lot of time thinking because things do not happen as I would like. By nature, I am rather calm, but my bronchial-pneumonia has probably brought out definitively the remains of a certain anguish. In the meantime, I spent the time working again like an ant, but I did take time at the end of the week to invite the Prosecutor of the ICCTR with 19 other guests. The diner took place at my house on Friday with representatives of the government and persons in the field of justice. The meal was not lively and very detailed questions of domestic and international law and the analysis of the circumstances of the violations of human rights dominated the conversation. A guest argued that development was part of human rights.

19 February 2000: Kleenex, please

Days pass and are never the same; they spin like a top. We drew up a gender concept to be incorporated into equitable development for men and women. It will be applied in all the projects. A female Rwandan intellectual told me one day: This idea of gender that you keep putting forth, it's a bit like Molière. It is as if we spoke in rhyme without knowing it, but when we are with our husbands, there is no longer any talk about gender. It's all just on paper and never in the huts. She is a primary school teacher in rural Kigali and knows what she is talking about.

Between receiving the evaluators who find the case of Rwanda very difficult and the heads of project who look everywhere to find a way to include something about the needs of women, it was a full week. There were also diners for friends who are leaving Rwanda at the end of their mission. Those are always real rites. Sweden, Germany, Canada, France, Egypt, the representative of the European Commission, all of them are leaving. This week was filled with moving

177

farewells, and we all took out our white hankies, either at the apostolate nuncio's, the Egyptian embassy or at the embassy of France. At the nuncio's diners I am almost always seated next to the ambassador of Libya or that of Russia. Just try to understand the logic of seating and signs for the church. I really like the nuncio. Sometimes, he tells me that I could go a bit more often to mass on Sunday. He is right. I'm going to think about it.

But right now, I am spending a lot of time with the evaluators dealing with problems of local staff and giving a turn of the handle to the field projects trying to pass an idea about self-financing for an association of women, and so on. In short, it's high trapeze work. The past Monday, we lived through real chaos with the evaluators. We had to prepare dozens of meetings, meet with many people and visit several projects. In a single day, we had to organize three different and varied programmes of two weeks. Sometimes the evaluators wanted to go alone on the visits, but often they wanted to be together, but not necessarily with the same persons in the ministries. It was a real puzzle. We spontaneously prepared very tight schedules to finish the programme finally succeeded. A real Chinese puzzle. How can we present a true picture of Rwanda?

7 April 2000: The photos of Marie-Arménie

Today is the annual day of commemoration of the genocide. Even if we visit all the common graves and feel a deep pain along with the Rwandans, the number of dead is so great that we are never able to mourn concretely. Just the thought of the family of Marie-Arménie and the photos that she showed me of her father and brothers and sisters, gives me a feeling of closeness at this time of national mourning.

13 April 2000: The villages of Cameroon

I was invited to the birthday of the Cameroonian, Charles, the head of a mission. Except for Kamel who works for the ICTR, a Lebanese, I was the only European. What a funny feeling it is, to find myself suddenly surrounded by some fifty Africans from the whole continent. We drank, ate and danced the whole night. We chatted away like at a mill. The women were dressed in beautiful dresses made from cloth from West Africa. They were wearing dresses embroidered in yellow and red with beads. The men moved about like floating dancers in bright blue boubous making flowing gestures. In Rwanda, it is in good taste to recall the other Africa, that of the sound of feet in the desert sand of Djibouti or that of the thirty-three saints of Timbuktu or the mud houses of Chad. Mythical Africa is far from the hard reality of Rwanda. I especially liked the confidence that they all showed me during the party. Charles regaled us with a long speech in which he explained how he saw Rwanda. For him, it is difficult, rough, but honestly looking for its way. He also paid tribute to his African brothers. Charles told me that I was working too hard and should travel a bit now, otherwise I would become too café-au-lait. Charles represents for me a sort of African father. He is an impressive very protective traditional village chief, always giving good advice but also authoritative. He took me a bit under his wing and spoke to me for a long time about traditional villages in the Cameroon, where the chiefs provide order to daily life. In addition, he has real gifts for seeing the future. We ended up becoming very good friends despite the enormous cultural gap that separates us and brings us together at the same time. The European and the African, there is always a bit of holding back, the fear that history has unfortunately confirmed.

I can feel that the Rwandans are still thinking, very softly, and even if they find me nice, that I am above all a European and that I am going to abandon them. At any rate, when the day comes there will be no one to help us, they often repeat. Unfortunately it's true. If they start killing each other

179

again, will we leave the next time? Yes, most probably. Nonetheless, I hope that this drama never happens again. We must not be hypocritical about our potential cowardliness.

24 April 2000: The Ikirezi bookshop

I went to visit the Ikirezi (Good news) bookshop and the African artists exhibiting there within the framework of the Fest'africa festival. This event has travelled all around Africa and Europe. It gives Africans a chance to speak out and asks artists on the continent to write books or theatre plays in honour of Rwandan drama; books of memories. I went to have a dozen books signed that had already been written about the genocide. The book by Babacar Boris Diop, for which Pro Helvetia paid for three months of writing in the Tessin, *Murambi: le livre des ossements*, which tries to describe daily life on both sides in 1994, was one of the most touching. I also loved *Mareketete* (May She Live) a story written by a Burkinabé lawyer. She describes a fable impregnated with restrained emotion. It's the same for the superb book by the Cote d'Ivoirian Véronique Tadjo, *L'ombre d'Imana*, the history of children who witnessed the genocide and that of an impossible mixed love. The artists were received and welcomed by Rwandans from the University of Butare. I attended their dances, and we talked for a long time about whether the typical Rwandan dances with the dancers spreading their arms open like the beautiful cow horns have a royal ethnic connotation and whether they can represent all of the people of Rwanda.

This week, I participated in another activity that was formerly very common: I was invited to a concert, a very unusual event in Rwanda. The second secretary of the German embassy, the chancellor of the Belgium embassy, a physician and a lawyer with the ICTR had formed a quartet. They gave us a beautiful concert of piano and violin music: Schubert, Mozart, Chopin. It was a real treat. The Mille Collines Hall was filled with about 500 persons who had come to encourage the skilful amateur musicians. It was not bad at all for a beginning. In Rwanda, European culture is a bit lacking for all of us. Sometimes, we dream about a music festival or a film cycle or even a painting exhibition.

3 May 2000: Eating *ingera*

This past week with the evaluators was really exhausting: drawing graphics, summarizing everything that had been done since 1994, summarizing the aid of the international community since 1997, describing the basis for a strategy to reduce poverty, explaining how we had established priorities and so on. We had to focus on the political dialogue, discover that micro projects are almost never sustainable, emphasize justice and give less support to NGOs working in human rights, introduce our partners, re-do a description of the activities and services of the various ministries. In one word, it's a full-time job for everyone here. Fortunately, the evaluators left very satisfied. They saw a lot of things in Rwanda, travelled throughout the country and spoke with all the participants in our projects. They were able to see the vigour and the good will in the rural area.

We finished Friday evening by going for diner with the evaluators and our Rwandan staff at an Ethiopian restaurant. It was an excellent idea because everyone took advantage to give their last recommendations and exchange opinions about the difficult process of being evaluated. We ate a typical Ethiopian diner, fingers in the *ingera*, (an Ethiopian dish of crepes and minced meat with spices that you roll in your hands). I found myself sitting in front of the chief evaluator. It was interesting to talk with him and understand how he had become an international consultant after 25 years of work as a development coordinator. He knows Rwanda very well from before. Humbly and in a constructive and critical manner, he tries to understand today's Rwanda. He is fully seduced by the willingness of the women's associations.

5 May 2000: A tea plantation at Ngarama

It was a fun evening at the house of a French development worker. Although strongly criticized here, France continues to carry the torch of the French-speaking world with programmes in health, education and the reopening of the French cultural centre. They are supported by all the West Africans from the United Nations. I danced along with an official from UNHCR who had attracted around her all the East Africans and West Africans, especially the Malians. I found old friends from Mali and Senegal. We spoke for a long time about northern Mali (Ségou, Timbuktu, Gao) and the new Malian democracy. I like this other Africa. The party gave me nostalgia for Rwandans because for them dancing still seems to be a bit premature. It's another world here. Perhaps one day they will come out of their mourning and the fog. Will it take a whole generation?

I spent this weekend with the Stanleys after a week of monitoring projects and visiting government offices. He is the director of a tea factory in Ruhengeri where we had a party on the occasion of the departure of one of the foremen. Their concession of tea fields is enormous and magnificent. The landscape rolls like in a film: a panoramic view, an idyllic house on the mountains facing the volcanoes, flowers, frangipani and hibiscus as well as pine trees and oaks because we are at a relative high altitude. We are struck by the luxuriant abundance and overwhelming mass of green shrubs, jonquils and mountain broom. The food was delicious: good Indian food. There was a tennis match for the young people and music for the older people. It is a distant world, like in *Out of Africa*. The contrasts you find here are incredible and you will never eliminate inequalities. Sometimes, I feel guilty, then I tell myself so what but with a pinch of regret because the inequalities remain shocking; Including the salaries. To come here to help means exactly what?

10 May 2000: Egypt as *loukoum*

The departure of my colleague the ambassador of Egypt really broke my heart. We used to go dancing with her and have a few drinks surrounded by well-intentioned people but she is leaving us. She is a really thoughtful woman; like *loukoum* but really fun. We are now going to have to close ranks around the remaining persons. The World Bank seminar was interesting because of the review of their portfolio of directly administered projects. They are going to concentrate on agriculture, income-generating projects, transportation, trade, rural markets and modernization of infrastructure. We are preparing with the government a plan for reducing poverty called a poverty reduction strategy paper. This name makes it sound like a magic potion. We work a lot with the British and the Dutch in the Ministry of Finances and Economic Planning. It is a good and very important project. I saw Terrance, the head of the Great Lakes Department at the World Bank. I think we have a good understanding between us. He is still optimistic about the incredible potential of Rwanda, but he is also aware that Rwanda has not only friends. Opposition of Rwandans outside the country to the current government is, for example, very active. It has to be taken into account. It is as if the 1959 schema was being repeated, but in the opposite direction. It is a question of not making the same errors.

Disgrace *by J.M. Coetzee*

I received a book I fell in love with. I discovered the fascinating book of the South African J.M. Coetzee, the winner of the 1999 Booker Prize. His book is *Disgrace*. It is a small masterpiece of literary construction where levels of language fit into each other like Russian dolls. The rather simple story is voluntarily realist and trivial, but slowly it becomes symbolic. The narrator begins a long descent into hell, but the book ends

183

with a touch of hope. The action takes place in South Africa, which is a place of all sorts of complications between Europeans and Africans. The narrator is a university professor. One day there is a break in his life. He is unable to enter into communication with his students and with women. Not even with his own daughter, with Africans in general or with anyone else in particular. He loses his grip on life, but finishes by finding a sense to his life by busying himself with putting abandoned dogs to death.

This novel evokes, in a metaphor that is only slightly disguised, the loss of many references in South Africa. Former references have not yet been replaced by new relations between Europeans and Africans. There is a heavy atmosphere of immobility in relationships that leads to extreme physical and verbal violence between the characters in the book. The narrator is a professor of English romantic poetry. He explains the difficulty of establishing relationships between Europeans and Africans, Europeans and Europeans, and African and African after apartheid. Nothing is simple. Nothing is ever really resolved. People seem no longer to speak to each other, but on the contrary they speak to each other a bit less awkwardly. A world suddenly emerges between the explanations of national reconciliation and the personal life of individuals whether they are European or African. Obstacles rise as impassable mountains. Coetzee makes an allegory out of this mountain. He speaks of Mont Blanc, majestic and distant, which covered in white snow and mist year round appears inaccessible, as if captured on a post card. This book is magnificently constructed. *Disgrace* has really renewed my desire to write and speak out about communication in Africa.

24 May 2000: South Africa after Mandela

I have just spent a few days in Johannesburg for a seminar related to my work. Cape Town, Johannesburg and the Transvaal have always been places for me that I dreamt about and wanted to escape to. I devoured all of Breytenbach, read Wilbur Smith and discovered Nadine Gordimer. I had the clear sensation that part of my personal history already took place there. I had met Mandela, whom I admired right away, in Beira, Mozambique. I saw only the outside envelope of Africa, just one part of the continent. I suspected that in South Africa everything was hiding a secret. We are certainly not prepared for a clash with Africa. Africa remains enclosed in descriptions of war handed down by settlers, soldiers, adventurers and missionaries. Some are honest and passionate people that are really looking for something. But in general, the hope of discovering other cultures, communicating with them and respecting them has not really been the case. During the past two centuries, Africa has been the theatre of conquests, pillage and massacres. One day, human relations were fixed in accordance with the most basic criteria: that of skin colour. In the end, in place of becoming acquainted and understanding each other, the two worlds became hostile. The weight of European history is very heavy in Africa: intolerable in South Africa and inexcusable in Rwanda. For me, the whole question, from the beginning of the time I began to work in Africa, has been to know how to behave as a European; fully assuming a responsibility without reproducing old stereotypes regarding Africans and not adopting the discrediting attitude of an angel. This brings us back to my initial concern of trying to find the right focus. My attitude has been one of respect, refusing to accept any guilt for my skin colour.

26 May 2000: Sartre's idea of *engagement*

I also read Wordsworth, Heine and Ponge. For me, literature has always stumbled on the question of *engagement*. Contrary to an author like Sartre, I find that literature and *engagement* mutually exclude each other. The freedom to write cannot be burdened by wild militancy. I hung up my hat a long time ago. To write seems to me to be the opposite of my

185

humanitarian commitment but Coetzee made me think about how he resolved this dilemma. He quite simply evokes daily life, which he later transforms into a symbolic manifestation of his own career. It is his own way towards creation. I often ask myself how what I try to communicate in Africa is perceived and which are the values are my priority. After thinking about it, I feel that loyalty, authenticity and transparency are the most important values for success in opening real dialogue in Africa, which is pompously called intercultural. If I start from the principle that I cannot advocate anything different from that of reconciliation with the others, which begins with acceptance of one's self and a philosophy of tolerance (which is completely opposite of laissez-faire), I think I am sufficiently universal to hit the right note. You have to put into practice precepts without proselytising, simply giving proof that these feelings are in the end more profitable to all of society than the race for profit. Coetzee showed this in a very sober manner as if in a fable. I have been intrigued by this author for a long time. The structure of his novel is divided into two parts. The first part is a mirror image of the second; as if the life of the narrator was functioning in a mode of give and take. There are only necessities; nothing is left to chance. His actions have to be put into perspective. Coetzee is an author that I highly recommend. The question of roots and allegiance comes up often in Rwanda, as if everyone were looking for their real roots on the hills. A Dutchman is neither a Belgium nor a Swiss. This seems to me to be obvious. But how are they different if we take away the clichés of the windmills, the dark chocolate or the milk chocolate?

27 May 2000: Diamonds for diadems

In Rwanda, things are slowly fitting into place with the new government and new president. A director of an association that I asked how he liked his new president told me that at any rate he was already in charge before and that it was a good idea for him to be officially responsible. And then, after a moment of silence, he added that it is not easy to be president of Rwanda. He hoped that now that he has come out of the shadows he will be able to represent everyone, including those who were in Rwanda before. At any rate, there is a serious shadow across the board: the presence of Rwandan soldiers in the Congo and the clash between Rwanda and Uganda in the Congo. There was a lot of opposition to this fighting among the international community, although we tried to understand that Rwanda, at least in this case, does not seem to be the only country responsible. Hey, just a minute! How are Congolese civilians involved in a difference between Uganda and Rwanda? And why does the Congo have to contribute with deaths? The struggle against the Interhamwe, who want to continue eliminating Tutsis, is still the dominant goal of Rwanda and that is used to explain their presence in the Congo. It is a justification and a motivation that has never changed since 1959. When will the threat be eliminated? The area around Lake Kivu is a strip of land occupied by so many parties that we ask ourselves how the parties identify each other when they are fighting. Friends, enemies or allies? Eastern Congo has become dangerous. On the other hand, Rwanda seems to have become calm, but we are never sure. The enemy could wake up one day within Rwanda. Everything in the region hinges on Rwanda. Its stability is essential, but what is hidden behind occupation of the Congo? Regional alliances change rather quickly: Kabila seems to be joining Museveni. President Moi recently visited Rwanda. There was a meeting in Mauritius between Rwanda and the Congo. Namibia is joining up with Kenya. The region is splintering into myriad interests, negotiations and partnerships. Everything seems to focus on the diamond mines at Kisangani and M'Buji-Mai. International journalists talk about the first African World War involving more than ten countries. The diamonds being fought over will end up on the diadem of European queens, they write.

28 May 2000: Democracy or dictatorship?

We have a real dilemma: our capitals are repeating right and left that it is still a dictatorship. But in Rwanda, we see things differently. Apparently all countries have this problem of how things are perceived within a country and outside it. In Kigali, we are all very careful to coordinate our meetings in order not to be blind or fall into the trap of denial of reality, but simply to try to be factual. And that's when we realize that in Rwanda there are of course big difficulties and enormous disfunctioning. The government may use very authoritarian approaches but it is not a dictatorship. The nuance is important, even if it is flimsy. For centuries, Rwandan society has had the habit of obeying orders. We think that Rwanda should be understood and not forgotten. These two contiguous realities are very informative.

30 May 2000: The international community backs the judicial system

The international consultant Yvan Dutoit has returned. He is a specialist in legal procedures after large conflicts. At the request of the Rwandan government and several donors, he has returned to talk about Rwandan social policies and a programme of poverty reduction during a week devoted to the topic of justice. He is great at presenting a synthesis and knows how to establish priorities and integrate everyone's opinion. He helped me focus my approaches and renewed my energy. It is wonderful what we are doing, he said and commented that there is a real sign of quality. We spent an evening coordinating among development agencies during a meeting that I organized at my house. We were about ten decision-makers sharing a diner with our Rwandan partners gathered around Yvan Dutoit. The topic of justice was what we talked most about. How could we apply justice in the first meaning of the word? Is the Gacaca (traditional justice) an acceptable method? The discussion was very lively. Everyone was able to express their ideas on the risks, the question of compensation, the concept of truth in Rwanda and that of the confessions as well as that of reconciliation informally. The cost of operating the Gacaca, which was to take place in 154 communes to judge the 120,000 prisoners by groups and by events will be 100 million dollars. Because classical justice does not work, Rwandans say that justice was stolen from them. There absolutely has to be a steering committee to monitor and administer the Gacaca, especially the questions of prisoners, logistics and their protection, especially if the trials are to last for several days, even weeks.

I am leaving next week with representatives of the Justice Ministry to understand better the procedure that Rwanda has just put into place on the possibilities of promoting confessions, which prisoners accused of complicity in the genocide can volunteer to make. As a result, their sentences can be reduced by up to one half. They also have to ask publicly for forgiveness on their hills of origin. The international community backs the Justice Ministry in this step forward that seeks to reduce the number of prisoners stagnating in overcrowded prisons, where there are still more than 120,000 prisoners. Like the truth and reconciliation commission in South Africa, Rwanda is trying to find a solution adapted to its own culture.

Chapter 8

Justice

The Confessions

I went into a small hut where a prisoner was quietly sitting facing an interrogator. Wearing a pink shirt, the prisoner had the usual smile on his face. He seemed to be in good health. He didn't reveal anything about what he felt but it is known in Rwanda that it is a positive quality not to show emotion. There is no chance of seeing a tearful scene like in a Fellini movie. Impassive, the prisoner was sitting facing the interrogator, who had sheets of white paper in front of him and a sharpened pencil in the event that there might be a brief declaration to record. The accused spoke in disjointed sentences: one sentence, then nothing for some time. They were sitting facing each other with indifference and stoic fatality. Nothing was happening. How can we know whether the attitude of the two protagonists is pretended or real?

Invited to a confession session within the framework of legal procedures, I discovered tense and unexpected situations. It all seemed unreal and was not what I had imagined in advance. We arrived in the morning at the court in Kibungo in eastern Rwanda where judicial police inspectors (*inspecteurs de la police judiciaire*) were beginning to interrogate prisoners. I have been accompanied to Kibungo by the chief judicial police inspector who is also my translator for the day. His name is Nepomucène. The procedure is carried out in rather impressive silence, let's say at a stiff whispered level.

The confessions take place in small offices next to the court in small houses that had recently been quickly whitewashed. The floor was earth, and the furniture was very bare: two metal chairs and a table. A light bulb was hanging from a bare wire from the ceiling. Outside, women were sweeping the courtyard with branches from a eucalyptus tree for lack of brooms. Children were chasing each other in a continuous game of hide and seek. Life went on as if everything were normal. To my surprise, there was no sense of emotion in the air. It's normal, daily life, probably like during preparation for the genocide. When I entered the house, Nepomucène pointed out that the prisoner was there for the third consecutive day. The inspector carrying out the interrogation had just been appointed to Kibungo. His name was Mukarambazi. He explained that the process is long because he has clear instructions to avoid any recourse to violence. The prisoner can take his time.

Nepomucène, my faithful translator for the day, sat down beside me. He seemed to be as astonished as I was about the course of events. Inspector Mukarambazi explained that the first day the prisoner stated that he had asked to be part of the group of those who had decided to confess but that he had done nothing. He was there just to proclaim his innocence. Inspector Mukarambazi had experienced this same scenario more than ten times. He picked up his file and pretended to take the prisoner back to prison. At that time, the prisoner said only a few sentences. The second day the prisoner said that he was willing to tell two or three things but that he needed more time. He was still wearing the same satisfied and innocent smile.

You can easily imagine a process of justice that would take one hundred years to try the cases of 120,000 prisoners of which only one tenth would agree to admit certain events at a snail's pace. At the rate of three sentences per day, the course of justice would take two centuries in order to see a bit more clearly. The prisoners understood the deal well: they can exchange bits and pieces of truth against a reduction in their sentence. Today, we were attending the third day of this man's confession. The prisoner's name is Tharcisse, and he remained completely silent. He seemed rather satisfied about his importance, because even people from Kigali had come to hear him. He is silent not because he has forgotten the events, but the contrary. Every Rwandan can well remember all the events of 1994, which are engraved in their memories forever. The memories are permanently there, printed and marked with a red-hot iron. This is true both for the killers and for victims, Nathanaël had explained to me. For the killers, however, a veil hides their actions because it is very difficult for them to accept the horror of it all. It is as if the memory of the events had voluntarily erased the crimes so that the killers would not go mad. In the analysis of Dr. Nathanaël, denial of the facts is a protection for survival.

Tharcisse, the prisoner, wanted to take his time. He wanted to be able to confess his crimes calmly. He agreed to denounce and name all the persons implicated with him in order to adjust a bit the sentence. Inspector Mukarambazi waited. He listened to the flies buzzing around and looked at the ceiling where the light bulb was swinging on its wire because of a light wind, like the movement of a slow pendulum of a clock. Minutes went by. Tharcisse began: "I was at a barrier in the commune of Mugesera, but I had only a little wooden stick. All I did was to separate the people who were passing by. I was supposed to stop them so that they didn't continue walking." About five minutes went by. Silence. Neither of them moved, like in a game of hide and seek, to see who would give up first. The instructor asked again how he had stopped them. Silence. Another five minutes passed. With an absent look, the instructor insisted: "How were the people stopped?" Tharcisse thought and without hesitation explained that he had to hit them on the head, those "cockroaches", but he didn't hurt them at all. It was the others who killed them with machetes.

Inspector Mukarambazi quietly explained that Tharcisse's mates, among those who already confessed their crimes at that place and that barrier were quite adamant. It was Tharcisse who killed the most. Tharcisse had been specifically pointed out by the others as having been a particularly zealous killer. Coming back that night after diner with a few beers under his belly and singing to finish the work. Silence. Tharcisse explained that he used a machete during only a few days; otherwise he had only a stick. He added that he had been forced to do it because the militia came regularly to check whether they had killed a certain number of Tutsis per day. The militia had even told them that they were well below their daily-required quota. At the beginning, they were rewarded but later at that barrier they had received nothing. The inspector asked him whether he had been at other places before manning that barrier. Tharcisse insisted that he had been only there. The inspector asked whether he had been only there for four months. Silence. The inspector asked for how long, from when to when. Tharcisse waited and then answered: "A few days, a few weeks, maybe, I do not know. I had only a stick, a little tiny stick." Inspector Mukarambazi said that there was a number of persons who had reported that Tharcisse killed many people. Silence. "Two or three, but nothing more." "Two or three during several days?" "Yes." "During a few weeks?" "Yes, maybe, but it was an order." To prevent the proceedings from becoming bogged down in petty accounting, the inspector asked whether he had killed several dozen. No answer. After another long silence that seemed to last an eternity, Inspector Mukarambazi asked him whether he would like to ask for forgiveness from the family of the survivors and have his imprisonment decreased because of his confession, regardless of the exact number of dead that he had on his conscious. The prisoner became obstinate: "I don't have to make excuses to anyone. The only thing I did was to obey orders and anyway the Tutsis are a dirty race." He paused for a moment. "I do not see how what I did was wrong. Many others should be on trial and locked in this damned prison, but they are free. To admit guilt doesn't mean I have to ask to be forgiven at all." Silence from Inspector Mukarambazi who turned towards the inspector general, Nepomucène. Both of them seemed slightly discouraged. Suddenly, the questions of confession and decrease in sentence seemed to have lost their meaning. They had the impression of playing the pardon game. Inspector Mukarambazi looked at us: "If no one tells the truth and doesn't want to admit the number of people that he killed and that in addition he doesn't have anything to say, we are going to have to find another method for the question of the overpopulated prisons…"

After having carefully listened to this dialogue, I intervened and asked the prisoner a question: "You have been here for three days, how do you think your punishment can be reduced?" Very sure of himself he answered: "I do not know why I am in prison. Basically, I did nothing. It's all unfair, I had only a little stick and, furthermore, I was just following orders." His frozen smile was empty. I left the little house stupefied.

Chapter 9

Justice

The Law Courts

That same afternoon, I went with Nepomucène to the court next to the little houses for confessions. The trial of one of the prisoners who admitted having been behind the gathering up of 580 Tutsis in a shed, located in a commune in the prefecture of Kibungo. He was accused of having carefully organized the massacre. We entered the court through a heavy wooden entry, whose two doors were open. The inside resembled that of a church. Outside, the sun was warming up the courtyard paved with red bricks. At least a hundred persons were seated about. Way in the front in a single row, were the 15 prisoners, all wearing pink shirts. The prosecutor calmly read the accusations. The attorney for the defence, sent by an international organization, was noisily searching through his papers. The court was listening. The judge covered a yawn. It was the third trial of the day, and the stories were all the same as though it were a play all written out, acted out and repeated ad infinitum. All the conversations were the same: there was not a single regret to be found. It was *Waiting for Godot* to the third degree. We were waiting for God, but it was always the devil who arrived first. Not a breath of air circulated in the courtroom. The accused prisoner turned towards the public. He gave us a false smile, rather pleased with himself. There was not an inch of fear in his gestures. The doors of the courtroom were wide open. Passers-by could see inside and like at mass, some people were still quickly taking their places because they had missed the beginning. Others, tired of the very slow procedures, left discretely.

You could hear the same children that were there in the morning playing hopscotch in the courtyard. They were jumping around between the small houses. A few of the older inhabitants of the commune were sitting on wooden benches following the reading of the accusations. We will never know whether there were survivors in the crowd. We will know only the identity of the main accused and that of about 15 fellow prisoners brought to the trial with him. The main accused ended up admitting a few crimes, but he rejected the label of "leader". His fellow prisoners were closely following events. They were hesitating. Should they tell everything? What should they disclose? The 15 prisoners, their heads shaved for questions of prison hygiene, were packed together like sardines, viscerally dependent on each other and used to the close proximity and the warmth of a group. They looked like people who had been used to doing things together for a long time. The pink shirts, clean and neatly ironed, gave them a childish look. Some of them seemed to be swimming in their shirts. They joked, elbowed and swore at each other.

The head of the court asked for silence. Soon, they would have to give testimony. They would have to say whether or not it was true that they first killed the children with machetes, then raped the women and then finished off with a bullet those who still seemed to be alive. The other question would be to learn whether events took place under the eye of the main prisoner, Aaron. The Aaron in question was the head of the area. Each of the prisoners testified and explained that they were forced to obey him. Aaron had joined the militia with special enthusiasm. He was a good leader, they said. He paid for beer in function of the number of people they had killed. They were even forced first to do away with the local mayor. He didn't want anything to do with it, and Aaron always returned in the evening to see whether the work had been done. The prisoners were going to nicely behave themselves, exploding with laughter. They give the impression of being at a football game. Now, they had to guess when they should try to score. They didn't want to let out even a little bit of information. But the charges against Aaron were growing. Little by little, the other prisoners were realizing who was the captain of their team. You could sense that they suspected a trap and no longer knew where to put the goal posts. Their only criterion for playing was the possibility of a few years less of detention. Finally, it was less a question for them of being close to the truth than ensuring that all those who participated that day in the massacres received the same sentence. That was one of the mechanisms of the killing machine that the militia had built: implicate everyone so that no one would come out innocent. The "football players" wanted the head of the region to be assigned more responsibility than them for the massacres. A sort of internal justice about a crime was taking form. Also hidden behind this reality, was the settling of all the accounts inherent to the prison world.

The main accused, Aaron, realized that he was now the star but that at the same time he was losing his fellow team members. He turned towards the court where the wigged heads were trying to reconstruct calmly the chronology of events. What is disturbing was that Aaron continued to deny any responsibility despite the obvious lie he had constructed out of nothing. Nonetheless, he insisted in recalling abundant and macabre chronological details. He was able to all of a sudden tell the details of events within a day of accuracy. He even gave obscene and precise details. He asked that the detailed facts of the killings in the shed be minutely recorded; not for his amusement but in order to explain fully the carrying out of the orders given and the care that was taken to apply them. He acted as though he was not at all involved in this story.

At a given moment, he realized that a white woman (*muzungu*) was present among those gathered. He began to look at me regularly, as if he wanted to explain to me how unfair it was to have been imprisoned under such catastrophic conditions during the past five years. He did nothing but bravely serve Rwanda. It appeared that the presence of a foreigner should be enough to in his eyes to re-establish a former truth. The reality that led to all the misunderstanding about events, this imbroglio where the Hutus are imprisoned, is

197

just a terrible mistake. They did nothing but obey orders and eliminate what for Rwanda represented real danger. "That propaganda", he shouted, "you accepted it at that time, right? And now you pretend to be surprised?"

Aaron told that he was one of the "accused perpetrators of genocide", quickly arrested after having been denounced. He recalled the unfair arrest and was very angry about this relentlessness that was following him about. And what about the others, all those who did things much worse than he and who are walking about free? He shouted at the court. He didn't feel that a legal system should be able to arrest him. And all the others?, he made a gesture that included everyone. Was that fair? I was very uncomfortable and had the impression of being singled out because of my skin colour. Nepomucène continued to interpret, but didn't want to tell me everything. I insisted that I wanted to hear all the details of this drama that, although a bad performance, speaks so poignantly about the difficulty of rendering justice. Rendering justice? Was it ever rendered? I want to understand.

Aaron, the leader being interrogated, once again mercilessly related the facts in chronological order. He often became angry because he said it was the tenth time that he was telling this episode. What was not said was clear. There was certainly no reason to make a mountain out of this story about the shed. He wanted to get on to the essential. By how many years would his sentenced be reduced? Sitting next to me, Nepomucène continued to interpret the events of that 25 April 1994 from Kinyarwanda. He explained that the attorney for the defence was trying to decrease the sentence of the leader by showing that he was not the only person involved. The others had been just as wild as he had been, even more so. The judges are calmly sitting, their faces expressionless. The public prosecutor read out once again the charges and the people who committed them. On the front bench, the other prisoners continue to move about nervously without speaking. The question of individual responsibility compared to collective responsibility was debated for a long time. It can't be decided on. It was too hot in the courtroom. The doors of the courtroom were strangely still wide open. It's as if it were an invitation to some unknown person to appear miraculously to help unscramble the judicial mess. The prisoners don't even try to escape. They know that they could not go far. The only thing they could do was to return to their commune, where they would be immediately recognized.

Finally, I asked to leave the courtroom. This thing was going to last for some time. We began everything from the beginning. I can still hear the defence attorney repeating that his client didn't really give any orders. The situation was hopeless.

Jordan the journalist

In the courtyard, the children continued to run about. A grey metallic Land Rover had just pulled up in a hurry with screeching tyres. The door opened suddenly and a journalist from the Nouvelle Vérité got out of the car all out of breath. He had come to cover the trial, one of the first under the system of confessions, but his car had broken down. He made vague excuses and distractingly extended his hand and introduced himself. He knew Nepomucène well, the inspector general of the judicial police and asked him whether he had been with me since the morning. The answer was yes, we came together. How were things going? Nepomucène answered casually that it was another of those days, filled with silence and a lack of regrets on the part of the prisoners. They had come only to buy fewer years of prison. They regretted nothing and were going to have a terrible time setting up pardon sessions on the hills, which were, nonetheless, so necessary for reconciliation.

When Jordan Brown, the sharp journalist, heard the hint of discouragement behind the inspector's story, he let out a loud diatribe about justice in the world, in Africa and more specifically in Rwanda. "I told you, you people who represent justice, you will never succeed in eliminating the bad seeds from these hopeless people."

We were obliged to bide our time because these two wanted to talk about philosophy and ethics. The Nepomucène had studied law in the Congo. He is French-speaking, while Jordan studied humanities and philosophy in Uganda. Jordan speaks perfect English. In order to talk to each other, these two men have to speak Kinyarwanda. One or the other of them then interpreted into French or English what had been said. Not really practical, but that's the way the new Rwanda works. Rwanda has taken in former refugees from so many different places that that is the only way to communicate. Jordan looked at his watch. He realized that he had better listen to the trial, but his desire to talk indefinitely was stronger. "To understand well what the word justice means, he began, you have to understand that justice is a quite different and very theoretical concept in Africa." He wiped his forehead. "Often, it is based on traditional ideas and practices. Sentences are usually linked to punishment set by the ancestors or the spirits. Decisions are taken by the elders or religious leaders, who take decisions about crimes, whenever there is conflict within the clan in order to preserve the clan's unity. They give more importance to the group than to rendering justice to a single individual. In Africa, many countries have lived for hundreds of years under monarchies, dictatorships or even "fathers of the nation", who were sometimes well intended, but not always Usually, they were corrupt and autocratic. Examples of totalitarian nations propped up by the West are numerous. The so-called international community is not sufficiently burdened with deep questions about their support for one or another of the dictatorships. Sometimes, there is a bit of pretence in meetings of being offended, but nothing ever comes of it. On the other hand, the word "justice" is thrown about as the indispensable ingredient for good governance", Jordan catches his breath and looks at me. "Isn't the concept of good governance just a new European thing?" I can only raise me eyebrow.

He went on, "In Rwanda, the question of justice is doubly sticky. First because for more than 50 years there was a culture of impunity. You could kill people because of their ethnic affinity with total impunity. Some people burned houses and then sat around a table with the victims. Little be little, people no longer saw anything wrong. Justice never punished criminals for their acts. That was the situation that became normal. At no time in Rwanda was it ever stated that it was reprehensible to attack a group of people and try to eliminate them. The judicial system functioned as a form of administration, with an empty content." He looked away at the hills and threw back a boy's ball that had entered the courtyard. "They should have a basketball net", he grumbled. "Then there was the genocide. It rolled on like wildfire, like a trail of powder prepared for a long time. The government tried everything to involve everyone. And it succeeded. There was a sort of official line that hid the activities. There was no justice to punish anyone; no rules; no Sword of Damocles. Some excuses were made for certain Europeans who timidly spoke of violations of human rights. If justice existed, it was completely blind and its eyes were covered. There was just a pretence at having rules. The system worked that way and whoever resisted was immediately eliminated."

Nepomucène agreed. "This situation led to the Rwanda of post-1994 spread over a mixed social landscape, disturbed, broken and divided. We are now a nation that has to reinvent completely the word justice. That word can no longer signify the same thing as before. We are trying to paste together the pieces, but we don't have any magic remedies. That's why when the international community reproaches us for the crowed prisons and tells us that we should do differently we always react by huddling up. How else can we render justice?"

Nepomucène goes off on a litany, as if it were the hundredth time that he was discussing this problem. "Those who survived are suspect in the eyes of the Rwandans who returned after 1994. Those who left for the refugee camps are necessarily all guilty. Even if that was not the case. Those who committed crimes are sometimes in prison. But others are in prison, who did not actively participate: just a little bit at a barrier like the accused declared just now. And then there are all those who were unfairly arrested. The proportion of guilt is difficult to measure. The genocide invariably led to much settling of accounts between families, between hills and clans. How can we verify the veracity of pain or madness?" Nepomucène agreed completely: "You see, we are in a phase of pure experimentation, which allows us to be a bit forgiven. Nonetheless, we completely depend on handouts from others. As you can see, we don't really have any room to make a mistake."

Nepomucène looked at me. "Furthermore, every donor has its own idea on how we have to solve the multi-headed problem that is the prison population. There are those who argue for expanding the prisons and those who want to decrease the prisons; and then there are those who simply want to open the doors and let everyone out. There are still a large number of participants in the genocide who are walking around the country or abroad. All of them have not been arrested, and they will perhaps never be arrested for lack of witnesses even if they are on the official lists."

Jordan agreed. "It is impossible not to get it all wrong from the outside looking in. And he added: "In Rwanda everyone knows everything and is spying on others and denouncing others. Every guilty person well knows that one day, he will be found out or recognized. The country is sufficiently small, and that small group of architects of the genocide is too well known for them to escape easily. At least we hope so; likewise we hope that the innocent will be exonerated."

Nepomucène sighed and frustratingly added: "It is becoming even more complicated, when we learn that in a commune, for example, a local mayor was completely capable of saving a few Tutsis whom he liked. He did it either for family reasons, affection, personal convenience or historical cohabitation. He saved a few people while participating vigorously in the chasing down and murder of other Tutsis in accordance with the strict instructions of the militia. The word "guilty" in this context takes on a special tinge, as if a chemical reaction depended on this essential ingredient. All of a sudden, the colour can turn dark green or even violet. The test of truth here is the test of history and its course. It is more meaningful than isolated acts."

Nepomucène paused then said, "It is difficult to imagine how we could set up an adequate judicial system. Half the magistrates were killed or left. How can we put in prison those who committed crimes fairly and with justice without any acts of revenge? At least for a while, the question of categories of killers has calmed things down without really solving the major problems of detention. The organizers of the genocide have been clearly separated from the small-time killers. Women and children have been placed in different cells from those of the men, but the number of persons killed was not taken into account as a criterion for the length of their sentence."

Jordan added, "In fact, the Rwandan government is more and more caught between the very demanding claims of associations of survivors, complaints of NGOs working in the field of human rights about the inhuman conditions of the prisoners and the need to reconstruct the country with educated persons."

I asked him a question: "Will the international community ever build four-star hotels and increase the number of prisons?" Nepomucène answered: "That's why at the end of 1998, the Rwandan legal system tried to find a new approach in order to reduce the prison population of more than 120,000 persons stagnating there. That's how the idea of tradition courts came about."

Nepomucène became enthusiastic: "The prisons create a serious problem for us, because we don't have enough labour for agriculture. Yes, the international organizations visit the prisoners, but feeding and caring for such a large number of persons cost too much for the families living tens of kilometres away and that have to travel to the prisons, as well as for the government. The economic cost of having to feed so many mouths is enormous. You can see that we have tried, but we don't have a choice. We have to believe in this crazy idea of reconciliation."

Jordan countered: "The government has decided to propose to the prisoners to confess in exchange for a reduction in their sentence. It is a fact that the judicial police inspectors were trained for this. The prisoners who want to confess their crimes are separated from the others and can begin to confess in the small rooms next to the courtrooms. In the courtrooms, the prisoners are tried as a group in relation to a single event at a specific place, but I am worried if you think that the accused recognize their guilt by asking for forgiveness. The question of collective responsibility is central, right Nepomucène?"

Nepomucène defended himself: "The cycle is closed. We have a new experiment of confessions and traditional jurisdictions, which is criticized by everyone on the basis of its form and substance. But I believe in it. It is like pounding on a nail with a hammer. Anyway, the president himself said that if it had been possible to make a nation of wolves, we can succeed in making a nation of sheep."

Jordan answered: "Be careful. Sheep are docile for a time, and then they are eaten by other wolves." He picked up his leather briefcase and waved good-bye. What does it all mean to be an African intellectual and return to Rwanda after having been a refugee for thirty years and having to solve, after the genocide, the problems of others? Jordan shouted that he was going to see for himself and entered the courtroom.

Nepomucène asked me what I thought. An avalanche of questions was spinning around in my head, like the music of Spike Jones. I was struck by the willingness of the new Rwandans to want to do things differently, in their own way and in good faith. I thought quietly to myself that it was not easy and admired that they are willing to try new approaches. I turned to Nepomucène and thanked him for all the trouble that he had gone to since this morning to explain to me the twists and turns of justice so devotedly. "I am very touched that you have given me the possibility of entering the small rooms in order to listen to the confessions, observing the court session and listening to the prisoners. You have helped me to understand. Thanks to you, I was able, to follow the reading of the accusations and testimony and attend a collective trial. It was impressive but a bit ridiculous to see the prisoners dressed in pink and see them sitting in a row. Seeing this has allowed me to understand better this mechanism of killing and the group effect. I was able to detect in the character of the main prisoner a sort of defiant bravado but no sign of regret. He was calmly listened to by the prosecutor and defended by an attorney. These episodes are very important to me. You have shown me Rwanda's hidden face. Thanks for your confidence in me."

"But we have hidden nothing", he exclaimed. "We are rather pleased to be able to share problems that seem to have no solution. Let's go. Don't be so serious. We are trying to do our best to continue to live and laugh. Tragedy has never led anywhere. You have to know how to be light." I told myself that it was fabulous that we worry and they try to encourage us. I had learned a lesson and resolved to smile and relax. He was right. Where does it come from that I often have the impression of having to solve all the world's problems? We left that commune and the area of the courtroom for the prison, which was about five minutes away by car. We were going to visit a prison. Nepomucène gave me a gentle slap on the back and said, "I hope you are not too sensitive because in the prison it's going to be a different story." I reassured him that I had visited hundreds of prisons in another life. He seemed to say: "Really, then you know about them?" Like almost always, the weather was beautiful. There was a slight haze above the hills. The twisting red track of the main road made the car sway. It's just unbelievable, I said to myself. It's just marvellous when I wake up in the morning with the birds singing or when I travel throughout this country from north to south, from Butare to Ruhengeri or, like today, in the eastern part of the country. I find Rwanda quite simply magnificent. I feel nostalgia for a lost paradise, like it probably was years before.

Nepomucène gave me a nudge with his elbow. "Are you here or far off? I am going to tell you a joke to cheer you up. Have you heard this one? It is the story of a Tutsi who arrives in Heaven. Saint Peter praises him for his life of hard work but remarks that he still could make an effort in the field of reconciliation. He gives him one more chance to make amends. Make a wish, he said, but remember that whatever you choose there will be a Hutu that will receive the double. Disconcerted, the Tutsi thought for awhile: if I ask for a beautiful car the Hutu will have two of them, if I choose a house, he will have two houses, if I choose a beautiful woman, he will be doubly lucky. After thinking for some time, the Tutsi had a bright idea and announced that he had it. He would like to have one of his eyes dug out. Saint Peter shook his head disappointedly and said it would be done as he wished. But he was forced to send the Tutsi back to Earth, more precisely to Rwanda, because he had still not learned the meaning of the word reconciliation. And the Tutsi is forced to come back to Rwanda with only one eye." Nepomucène breaks into enormous laughter. I am sitting on the rear seat of the four-wheel drive vehicle and wonder whether it is me who is totally out of step. I laugh a bit, just to please him, but sincerely I do not find this joke at all funny.

Chapter 10

Justice

The Prison

We arrived at the prison, where an iron gate marked the entrance. It was 4 p.m. Nepomucène greeted two or three colleagues, the prison director and several soldiers. As inspector general of the judicial police, he was owed all the deference due to his rank. People bowed to him, greeting him *à la rwandaise*, in other words they held him with two hands at a discrete distance and absently, avoiding looking him in the eyes, as if this expression of emotion should not be visible, just feigned. We entered a prison that with a capacity for 3000, held 8000 prisoners. Everything was organized and measured out. No space was left vacant. The overpopulation was obvious through the sense of smell, physically and through the skin. There was no sign of rebellion in the prisoners' eyes, just a bit of weariness. Many were even smiling with a bright expression. How much longer? And all these Europeans who come regularly to observe the problems of nutrition and health and then leave?

"At the beginning, these visits gave us a bit of hope", explained a prisoner who was a section head with the incredible name of Innocent. "Over the years, we have accepted that the Europeans come to see us, offer us a few words of general encouragement: like "everything will be all right, you'll see". They come to feed us with a few additional scraps of meat in the common pot, then it's forgotten for the rest of the day. In the end, we realized that these inspections are better than nothing, but it is unbearable to be crowded in like this. We are crowded in like animals, don't you think?"

He must have given this speech a hundred times. His tone of voice was very jaded. I didn't say anything because I probably would have said something stupid, like "and you think you merit what?" Innocent added that by now they had told each other all their stories. It happened just like that, like a way to pass the time after having spent at least a year staring at each other. It's not part of their culture to tell personal stories. Now they know the whole story of the other prisoners. And in the end, what does that change? Nothing. They were all locked in here for the same reason.

Several other prisoners came up and formed a circle around us and asked as if they were chanting: "Do you believe in the categories 1, 2, 3, and 4? Is that the democracy that you talked about in the 1990s? I caught on right away that it was the same s… for everyone. Justice from the bottom up." The prisoner laughed openly, pleased with his words. He was not at all aggressive even a bit philosophical. He spoke French well. "The boredom is fatal, even more so that being locked up", he explained to another prisoner, also visibly accustomed to speak to foreigners. He came over to join Innocent.

Nepomucène was standing straight as a ramrod a step away, ethereal, playing the bodyguard and slightly bored. I told him not to worry because I never felt in danger in a prison. The prisoners know that we come to help them not to harm them." Nepomucène said, "Really, that's a strange way to think."

We had to find our way through the prison, which was a real maze of alleyways crowded with men in rather good physical shape because they were made to do gym exercises every morning. The women, fewer in number, were kept in another part of the prison. The prison was a miniature version of society. Everything was ordered, the very few clothes that there were carefully folded, and the few personal possessions were piled in cages by level. The prison was very clean. In a corner, a group was waiting in a queue to take a shower. The water was used sparing. There was a constant background noise. The prison society was hierarchical and structured like in the communes before the war. The section heads had heads of cells under their command, who in turn controlled a group of ten persons representing ten blocks: the *niumbakumi*. Because of a lack of space, the prisoners could not always sleep lying down. They took turns. This organization of daily life had become a business that was negotiated and that made up all aspects of prison life. And for six years that was it.

Nepomucène explained to me that the prisoners themselves manage the prison's entire internal administration. There was a very strict internal order imposed and no need for the administration to become involved. "Of course", he said, "these arrangements create a sort of law outside the law, which includes ransoms and extortion, but they make for a better arrangement than at the beginning when the government was involved. Before, it always ended up with fighting. Now, they have found a balance among themselves", he grinned. "Nonetheless, it's a bomb that is building up for when they get out", I ventured to say.

"Do you have a better idea?" Nepomucène retorted. Then he added: "whole families queue up during hours in front of the prison. Some have to travel tens of kilometres to bring a bit of food to a brother or father. They also bring money, cigarettes or batteries for a radio. The tradition is not to let down one of your relatives who is in difficulty despite whatever shame you might feel. Is it possible to measure the consequences that long hours of obligatory visits represent for the present Rwandan economy? An economy in which, small farmers have to feed and encourage their parents locked up for six years when their fields should be cultivated?" Innocent entered the conversation: "Can you imagine the shame of having to visit a relative, cousin or father who has killed in front of everyone three times a week? In addition, you have to pretend that nothing has happened."

He stopped a moment because he realized that he was beginning to reveal what he really felt. He was drifting a bit from the practiced speech for prison visitors; something that was unpardonable for a Rwandan. Nepomucène got carried away. "At any rate, we can't take care of everything. The prisoners, the consequences of the genocide, the debts and even provide them with a cosy house. You should be pleased that we have stopped executing those in categories 1 and 2. You know, the minor killers, the others, we don't hate them so much. They are the poor guys who were disgustingly manipulated. I don't mean that I excuse them, but at any rate I think they were really tricked. They were forced to participate. Furthermore, the survivors are adamantly opposed to any blanket liberation. There should be no mistake about policy, if we want to satisfy everyone." Nepomucène thought it over and categorically declared: "In the end, I wasn't there, but I want the pain to be sharper for the others. When we think about it, that is all they deserve. If we can make them understand that with a touch of regret we could accelerate the reconciliation process."

I thought about it. The comment of an important government official came back to me. It was on April 7th, the day of the commemoration of the genocide at Gisori near Kigali. There was a common grave of about 25,000 persons. The international community had gathered to pay tribute to the dead. P. was with me. He had realized that I was rather disturbed and said to me, "If one day the small-time killers were willing to simply ask for pardon and recognize that they had killed and regret what they had done, the government would be capable of freeing all of them. Those are not the ones who should be locked up. We do it because the survivors need strong symbols. But it is the architects and the brains behind the genocide that are walking around your capitals that are the real monsters. They have Mercedes and have been granted exile." This comment stuck with me for a long time. What does it mean to appropriate a genocide?

"Hey, are you listening to me?" repeated Nepomucène. "You know," he said as if he had heard my thoughts, "We are having a tough enough time giving just a little bit of hope to the survivors. They feel that it is totally inadmissible that any radical measure of compensation has not yet been established.

It is not the little survivors' fund that is going to satisfy them. Many of the survivors are extremists because the prisoners are really making no effort to ask for forgiveness. It is not easy to run this country. There will always be people who will find that such and such a thing should not be done. Let them reconcile and repair the damage themselves. They will see that it is a nigh impossible and gigantic task."

Nepomucène almost got carried away. He coughed lightly then softened a bit. "It's for this reason that we are now trying the confessions. But this idea too does not seem very promising, as you have seen." Nepomucène motioned to me to walk on through double ranks of prisoners standing still. They were standing at attention, a calm but empty look on their faces. It is true that the international organizations regularly came to visit them and that they are used to seeing Europeans. It doesn't stop me from wondering how they have spent their days for so many years. And how do they accept the discipline? We were moving towards a corner that was prepared for the morning gymnastics and then between 10 and 12 a.m. a course in Kinyarwanda was given. Most of the prisoners are illiterate. They may come out of prison with a primary school certificate. The little corner also serves for holding Sunday mass. During the week, it is used to make announcements regarding work duty and internal organization. Nepomucène had just met with the local low authorities (*chefs de rang*) to explain in Kinyarwanda how the confessions were to take place. He was trying to convince a few others. The prisoners' faces were attentive but revealed nothing. When it was a question of food they could say something, but about other things they had to be careful and remain silent. First of all, they had to talk about it among themselves. At the end of our round, the head of unit number four, Jean-Bosco, came forward. He was acting as messenger and explained to his buddies that he had confessed his crimes and had found God. A rumble could be heard among the prisoners. Just like a homily, he went on about the advantages of forgiving, the

211

wonderful feeling he now had and his hope that had been renewed. You would think that he was acting in a theatre play, something by Beckett. Jaws dropped in disbelief. Who would still believe in what he was saying? Jean-Bosco came over to me and asked me to be a witness before Almighty God. "You see", he said with a strong voice, "that is how to rise from the ashes." A bit like an actor carried away by his text, Jean-Bosco swept the crowd with an ecstatic look. It was like in *M, le maudit* without sound and in 18 millimetres. Suddenly, the main guard, another head of sector, found that that was enough for the day. He moved forward and asked the crowd to break up. It was intermission time.

Jean-Bosco was alone with Nepomucène and me. I asked him whether I could ask a question that was a bit personal. He nodded yes. "If it were to happen all over again and you were in among the killing, now that you have found God like you say and you felt you were on the right path, would you be willing to die instead of killing others?" Silence. It was not a question of interpretation. Jean-Bosco spoke perfect French. He looked at Nepomucène who didn't move. He looked at me in desperation and then after a long pause that seemed an eternity, he said in a loud voice: "I don't understand your question at all".

We left the prison at Kibungo to return to Kigali. We wanted to arrive before nightfall although there has not been a curfew for about one year. It was not like in 1998 when the Interhamwe attacked the local inhabitants regularly once it was dark. It was just a precautionary measure. Here, you go home quickly at night. Africa is funny: "No matter what, a proper woman does not go out alone after nine o'clock at night", Nepomucène told me. We wanted to pass through Rwamagana on the shores of Lake Mohazi, which is very beautiful. Nepomucène and I were no longer chatting in the car. I ended up asking him to be a bit more relaxed and to tell me another joke. "Do you really want to hear another?" he said, delighted to break his train of thought. "Yes."

Here's one, he began. It's the story of a Rwandan who is on the point of dying. He knows that the end is near. He has difficulty breathing and in order to relax a bit (you never know what you might have to account for in the other world) he decided to call for his wife. He wants to tell her two or three things about his love life so that she will forgive him his errant ways before beginning on the long voyage. He asks that she be brought to him. She arrives all dressed up and in a cloud of sweet perfume. She leans over his bed, and her calm look strikes the bedridden husband. It is getting late and he has to speak. He blurts out: You know, dear, I have to admit to you that I have not always been faithful. I even had several rather long lapses. Well, one with your sister and another with your cousin. There was a little something with the neighbour and then another, a bit longer, with the cousin of our uncle from Butare. His wife looked at him tenderly, waited for an instant and gently took his head in her hands. She whispered sweetly into his ear: You see dear, that is why I poisoned you. "A typical Rwandan joke, don't you think", shouted Nepomucène.

We entered Kigali. All those pardons, confessions and mistakes were enough for today. Will we some day break this spiral of the killers considering there confessions like a comedy of the Catholic Church and the link to the celebration of mass and the religious practices of the Catholic Church?

Chapter 11

Justice

Gacaca: Grains of Hope

The Gacaca system of justice is a wild bet to empty the prisons. Gacaca (it is pronounced *gatchatcha*) literally means "justice on the grass". Given the enormous difficulties linked to the detention of prisoners, investigation of charges and the question of reparation for victims, Rwanda is trying to find a unique solution adapted to the circumstances, although risky and original, to judge the accused "on the grass". The accused will be tried either in their sector, cell or commune of origin where they committed their crimes. This system of justice could be used to try more than 100,000 prisoners. They will appear before the local inhabitants who are asking that the truth be publicly elucidated. Trials will come later according to a system of categories. A confession will make it possible to decrease a sentence by one half. Sometimes, the sentence can even be cancelled if the prisoner is declared innocent or is cleared of any crime, but only if he asks for forgiveness. Months of promoting an understanding of the local population and pilot trials have shown that this type of system of justice, the result of a process of local and traditional justice, could function and create the basis for true reconciliation.

The Gacaca system would allow better reintegration of those who have committed crimes and who have already served part of their prison sentences. The unknown is the reaction of the victims. Nonetheless, everything makes it possible to believe that existing cohabitation outside the prisons with people who have tacitly been recognized as killers but not yet arrested has accustomed the local population to accept the situation and has removed any desire to be restricted by the past. If an accused prisoner publicly confesses and explains what he did, people are ready to reintegrate him. The local rural population knows that there is no choice because so many killers are implicated in the genocide; almost the whole population. It is now time to start reconciliation. There are about 120,000 prisoners in Rwanda. Why is there still that many in 2001?

The genocide lasted from April to July 1994. It took place over 100 days and led to the death of about one million persons. You need a large number of killers to carry out such a large massacre in so little time. No one knows the exact number of criminals. Some historians estimate that there were at least one million killers because the previous regime made certain that all the population would be implicated in the killing. The 120,000 prisoners would represent only one tenth of the total number of participating killers. Other participants are living in Rwanda but have not been arrested for lack of a complaint or have fled Rwanda. They probably represent the majority. In the meantime, prisoners have been held in prison for the past six years. About one quarter of the total number of persons arrested has been freed or tried and another quarter has been arrested for the first time or arrested again. The total prison population has been rather stable.

Among the prisoners are those who will never speak out; those who will never admit to anything; and there are those who refuse to say anything more. A slight hope exists for those who confess their crimes. Their prison sentence will be reduced or transformed into work of general interest, which will perhaps incite others to do likewise. The current government is betting that social pressure will oblige prisoners to tell the whole truth and nothing but the truth. The fact that the local population will judge the criminals publicly represents a whole new challenge. The government has given guarantees that the police will protect the accused. The difficult part is making the local population accept after the verdict reintegration of a person into the commune so that the freed prisoner can begin a normal life and have an activity that will produce income. That will be the price of reconciliation.

"Gacaca" has become a word that represents hope, an open sesame that even the prisoners end up demanding loud and clear, although there was at first strong resistance inside the prisons. Then, the prisoners separated themselves into categories. In general, they are imprisoned in the same parts of the prison as their former heads of neighbourhood who continue to give them orders. Because Rwandan society has always been very hierarchical and the prisoners are not aware of the changes that have occurred outside during the past six years, they remain obedient. The prisoners are still potentially dangerous because they have been cut off from the world for more than six years. Furthermore, they maintain their 1994 mentality. Despite these obstacles and despite the fact that there could be an outbreak of a cry for vengeance from the local populations, the prisoners have backed the idea of the Gacaca. At any rate, they see no other way to accelerate their trials.

The combat of Jean-Emmanuel Gasana

Jean-Emmanuel Gasana is a high-court magistrate posted to Nyanza in southern Rwanda. He is an ardent defender and one of the Rwandan originators of the concept of the Gacaca. He is also a member of the national commission that is studying the principles and effects of the Gacaca. His role is to make proposals to the government, but he has nothing to do with their application. We agreed to meet in Butare at the National University of Rwanda. He had travelled from Nyanza to Butare at about the same time as I travelled from Kigali. We met in the university car park, which is located at the end of a tree-lined avenue shaded by oak and eucalyptus trees.

We were meeting at the university for a day of reflection on the concept of the Gacaca system of justice. From the time he left his car, Gasana chatted with me as we advanced towards the main entrance. Right away, we were talking about essentials, and I asked him why justice did not advance faster.

Gasana patiently explained to me in a controlled and kind voice that three years ago the idea was first tested of the possibility of offering prisoners the possibility of confessing their crimes. They thought the process would take place quicker because sentences would be decreased. After a promising beginning in 1999, confessions dried up a bit. Only about twenty per cent of the prison population participated. There are still about 100,000 prisoners who have not confessed, of which one quarter have cases pending that have not been investigated. Maybe they can be convinced to speak out. Nevertheless, the majority of the prisoners continue to say loud and clear that they did nothing and that they have been mistakenly arrested. They often laugh when attorneys who try to help them become confused. I asked whether many of them are in prison although they did nothing. Gasana said, "yes that was sometimes the case and that the numbers are difficult to estimate because they can be arrested on the basis of the testimony of three eyewitnesses. Later, their case is investigated. If there is no proof, they are released. It is difficult to know who did what because witnesses often retract their accusations out of fear of reprisals and family pressure from outside the prison. Don't forget that everyone has to live together year round in their commune. Unfortunately, there is a great deal of settling of accounts that happens without the judicial system being able to intervene in time. This is regrettable and, unfortunately, inevitable. Sometimes, witnesses disappear. I asked whether there were human rights associations that promote and monitor the arrests and trials by groups of prisoners. Up until then the sentence has been individual. Facts declared in any accusation must be proven. An event has to be reconstructed. In principle, an accused person declares that he did nothing, which does not help at all, or he accuses someone else. That requires the investigation to take a turn in another direction, which takes a lot of time and money, a need to travel, automobiles, salaries and attorneys who accept to defend those accused of genocide." He asked whether I knew a lot of people who would like to take on that task. I shrugged my shoulders and didn't know what to say. He explained that's why they had been obliged to call in foreign attorneys, who were even more expensive. After a genocide, justice is a vicious circle. He would not say that there was no corruption or payment under the table to speed up cases, but it was minimal, taking into account the breadth of accusations. Often, it is the lot of poor countries that money is made wherever possible. He looked at me and asked whether there wasn't corruption in my country. I nodded my head, and he smiled and added that the administrative means, the typewriters, computers, paper, court clerks and everything else, was lacking in Rwanda. Three quarters of the staff of the judicial machinery were killed in 1994. You cannot train lawyers in a few months. The international community should be satisfied that the government did not let all of them starve after 1994 or at the time of their return from refugee camps in the Congo at the beginning of 1997. A list of killers had been put together on the basis of testimony and archives, and those who prepared the genocide were identified. The International Criminal Tribunal for Rwanda (ICTR) is taking care of the big shots. Using just a few means, the judiciary is obliged with few means to know in which category a killer, a little fish, should be placed. Because the prisoners declare themselves innocent, the classic justice system is inefficient. I asked whether the international community pays a lot of money to support the judicial system. They had received a lot of money, but it was insufficient. Above all, they needed to reconstruct the whole judicial system and train new judges to bring the 120,000 prisoners to trial. There was not enough time.

We joined the other members invited to the seminar at the main door, where there was a small table with coffee, refreshments and raisin buns. The coffee, Rwanda's main export, was delicious. We were a small group of about twenty persons who had come to Butare from Kigali to spend the day discussing the origin and feasibility of the Gacaca system. Representatives of the government, civil society and NGOs, a representative of the prisoners and international legal consultants were participating. It was to be a roundtable, like they say, but we would most certainly be seated at a rectangular table. The public was mixed. From the time of their arrival, people were arguing around the coffee. The discussion was already lively. It is true that the question of justice in a country like Rwanda immediately provokes passions and strong opinions. Gasana had invited judges, prison directors and representatives of prisoners' families as speakers. There were also associations for monitoring released prisoners, the well-known association of survivors, *Mémoire vive*, and foreign attorneys. As you can imagine, not all had the same point of view. There were those who thought that the prisoners should simple be released. There was an association of survivors that immediately declared scandal, explaining that that would just be perpetuation of the law of impunity. The best solution was perhaps somewhere in between, but the established judicial system had not functioned under these difficult conditions. Something else had to be found. That was why we were there.

Gasana is a tall and serious, quite person. He wears round gold eyeglasses. He is very thin with long legs that swim a bit in his grey-flannel trousers. He seemed a bit tense before the session and said that it would be difficult to assuage all the fears of the human rights organizations that had come to express their reservations. Under his arm, he carried the latest edition of *Loi rwandaise*. An NGO representing women's rights began to make a fuss right away. The representative introduced herself as Hyacinthe. Everyday, she visited female prisoners, their families and abandoned children. She did not mince her words. She was wearing her best green dress covered with a beige poplin shawl thrown over one shoulder like all women do in Rwanda. Hyacinthe was tired of the lack of tangible results from established judicial system. She declared that this slow process was a nightmare for the judicial system. Nothing was ever solved. Problems just continued to pile up. Judicial independence is a difficult concept to practice in reality. Arrests were running at about the same rate as releases. The few confessions that were being made did not free any space in the prisons or in solitary confinement. It was, however, a beginning, which might someday lead to a wave of confessions. The female prisoners were as tough as the men. If only at least the women regretted what they had done, if even only a little bit. She sighed. Benoîte, a small Rwandan nun from Kabgaye, her cup of black coffee in her hand, agreed: "Yes, according to all the specialists from South Africa the question of confessions (more or less sincere) is crucial. The genocide must be recognized first by those who committed it in order to initiated a process of forgiving and real reconciliation." Gasana stopped them. "You are not going to debate all that now. Everyone has to hear what you have to say." He gently pushed the two women inside and called us in. We entered the main building and sat down in a small rear room off the law faculty at the National University of Rwanda, which is located on a beautiful plot, right among huge trees and avenues of flowering jacarandas. The discussion was to be led by Gasana. That day he was representing the Justice Ministry.

Charles-Edouard Despont, a practiced, top-drawer attorney from Paris, was not pleased. He did not like the idea of the Gacaca system, which raises the fundamental issue of the right to defence. In his opinion, a prisoner would find a defence attorney only within the framework of a general assembly that represents everyone, which he considered inadequate. Despont commented as he sat down that it was meagre consolation, almost a masquerade. I told him to be quiet with a finger to my lips. I could sense that he was ready to take on everyone there.

Gasana had brought slides with him and tried to make us see how the local inhabitants on the hills, the court and the prisoners were going to interact. Outside, the weather was mild, the windows were open, and we were all trying to understand. "A short history is in order," he began. He adjusted his eyeglasses and stood next to the overhead projector. "After the genocide, a new government of former exiled Tutsis took power dominated. They inherited a completely destroyed country, debts and an impoverished, traumatized population. The government had collapsed, and the infrastructure was looted. Now, six years after the drama, the infrastructure was partially rehabilitated. Rwanda's economy was partially back together, sometimes operating even more efficiently than before, sometimes hastily patched over with a real lack of competence. It had been difficult to rebuild the economy in a few years. The big rupture in the social fabric had still not been repaired. In order to render justice, attempt reconciliation and end the culture of impunity, the question of the prisoners and guilt must be resolved more systematically and quickly." He paused, and we could sense that his main argument was still to come. "We have reached such a degree of overcrowding in the prisons that it is simply no longer possible to manage it. This problem will be a real time bomb for the future if we do not attack it now. Can you imagine the mentality of prisoners who have been completely out of touch with the reality of the country since 1994?"

There, we are in full agreement but where was the magic product that he was going to present? Perhaps, I was underestimating Gasana's determination to promote the Gacaca system. He didn't state all his arguments at once. He was patient and let the accusation speak first. He hands the microphone to the specialist in international law, the very-same Charles-Edouard Despont, who adjusted his necktie before speaking. He looked determinedly around the room and began his attack. "Thank you, Maître, for having invited us and given us this opportunity to comment on the preposterous idea that you call the Gacaca," he began. "Mr. Gasana," he proclaimed, "we have to change the level of our discussion. We have to speak about law and the legal order. Law is law. We cannot mix everything up. We are not trying to sell an agricultural project, to talk about improved seeds or repairing a road. We are talking here about prisoners—120,000 of them—who have

221

been locked up for six years under inhuman conditions. Stacked up for lack of space, they cannot even sleep lying down and sometimes have to queue up for six hours to shower. They are waiting for their trial, but nothing happens. A law is a law, quite simply that, and as a law it cannot be avoided. Every person accused of a crime has a right to a defence. As long as the prisoner has not been proven to be a killer, he must benefit from the presumption of innocence. Laws exist in order to take us out of the jaded law of an eye for an eye and a tooth for a tooth. The Rwandan government is obliged to respect a minimum number of conditions for human detention. We have to free them little by little and simplify the trying of cases."

His resounding voice could be heard clearly. The context was set. Now, we knew. He was going to explain why the Gacaca system was not going to work. The amount of trouble we have in initially accepting something bold that was based on a logic other than ours is strange. The idea of the Gacaca system of justice may not be immediately clear, but it is a proposal by Rwandans for a Rwandan problem. It is a remarkable development representing a new response to an insoluble problem. What if we can give confidence back to this country? It is true, I tell myself, that a prisoner must always be defended. Seen from our Western perspective, the Gacaca could end up in a massacre.

Despont's voice brought me back from my thoughts. He went on: "I would like to explain to those present that justice has nothing to do with morals. The same laws must be applied to all citizens. We must carefully ensure that a state of law is truly created in Rwanda and ensure that Rwanda does not become a …republic." He was going to say banana republic, but caught himself and said bana…ba, corrected himself and ended up saying "a republic of vengeance".

He paused a bit to assess the number of supporters that he could attract. Several heads nod affirmatively. "It should be noted," he began, "that under circumstances as violent as post-conflict Rwanda, a system of formal justice guarantying adhesion to the standards of human rights is impossible. If the prisoners are harshly sentenced, a new coup d'état could take place. On the other hand, the cost of maintaining several tens of thousands of criminals in prison would seriously affect the whole economy. Currently, the income of a prisoner's family is low. In addition, it is obliged to help a relative instead of farming its land."

Despont paused again because he wanted to change the subject. "This country also cruelly lacks competent police, judges, prosecutors and investigators that are above corruption and that are neutral. Complete re-building of these resources is highly improbable in just six years after three quarters of the intellectuals were killed or fled to exile. Since you lack everything, how can you imagine for even an instant successfully applying "fair justice" in rural areas? In short, I am against the Gacaca unless you succeed in creating guarantees that the prisoners will have a right to a fair defence."

This time, he took a long pause. He wanted to be sure that we had followed his reasoning well. It's clear that secretly there are defenders of his theory, but it must be remembered that it is against tradition to say those things in public. He continued with details, "In the whole world, there are three fundamental rights to which an accused has access" (he then made a theatrical flourish like Vergès). "First of all", he thundered, "There is the fundamental guarantee of knowing the charges and, second, of having access to the evidence. The third right is that of benefiting from a defence attorney, paid for by the government if the accused has no resources. In Rwanda, this third right is not always guaranteed. And the Gacaca risks letting loose collective revenge."

A survivor sitting next to me asked quietly: "These laws, are they also applicable to genocide? Does a killer have to know the charges against him when he has systematically killed people at a roadblock because of their ethnic affiliation? What do you think?" I told her that in all cases what Despont was saying was true and formed part of international law, which unfortunately had nothing to do with the pain that survivors might feel.

Gasana thanked Despont, who had come expressly from Europe. Despont thought that by mentioning this favour a discussion about it would begin, but he did not take into account the Rwandan mentality. In Rwanda, there is no possibility of discussing this question, even at a theoretical level. There is only prudence. No one moved. Despont returned to his seat, a bit perplexed.

Gasana went on all alone, "Allow me, Sir, to clarify several points. Over the past six years, we have seen for that it is the followers and the small fry who are caught rather than the architects of the genocide. This does not really represent justice, I agree. However, with a list of killers that was revised in 1999, a classification of the guilty drawn up by the prisoners themselves and the considerable efforts made by the donors, it has been possible to improve the application of justice between 1998 and 2001. As a result, the situation is less catastrophic than you make it out to be. Put simply, we will need two hundred years, at the current rate to investigate all the cases." His words reflected the tragedy and hopelessness of the current situation. Gasana continued, "Unfortunately, as of the end of 2000 only about 3,000 persons have been brought to trial and about 10,000 persons have been freed. About 4,000 persons have been re-arrested or arrested for the first time, and many released prisoners have returned to their communes of origin. There, other witnesses have recognized them for crimes related to events other than those for which they were charged the first time so they are again incarcerated under new accusations." Despont furiously interrupted, "And you think that we have to allow that and accept it, even if it is one of the consequences of the genocide? Even if the quality of the decisions has improved, the neutrality of the prosecutors, the degree of corruption of the judges and the intimidation of the witnesses are still important problems. This is inadmissible." Gasana did not appreciate at all that the term "corrupt" judicial system was continually brought up in public. He said, "Given the extent of the genocide the situation could be worse, right?" He continued, countering Despont's insolence, "We shall see. The current classical justice system not only is confronted with a nightmare but is also facing insurmountable difficulty in promoting economic and social recovery and reconciliation."

The floor was given to Constance, a member of the NGO *Mémoire vive*. Using a neutral tone, she explained that it had been vividly brought out by several specialists that to massacre about one million Rwandans with knives and machetes in three months, the whole population had to be involved in one way or another. Those who refused to participate were killed on the spot. Many of the guilty have left the country. Others have taken refugee nearby in the Congo and continue their dastard programme. The Interhamwe (the militia of the former regime) still existed. Many innocent people also returned in 1997. Some are in prison, while others have been reintegrated into society for better or worse. Others are still unfairly incarcerated for reasons of revenge or access to property. Others should be in prison but have not been arrested for lack of witnesses or proof. The 120,000 prisoners represent a small part of the problem. At any rate, their trial is more symbolic than fair. We all agreed on that point. The problem had to be dealt with differently.

Gasana continued, "In such a large and terrifying drama, no classic source judicial system can render justice, bring back to life those who died, compensate families or oblige the killers, most of whom are very poor, to pay compensation. Already in 1998, several government officials, seeing that the judiciary would take at least a century to investigate all the cases and try 120,000 prisoners, put forth the rather audacious idea that if we could devise a sort of collective justice inspired by the traditional Gacaca, we could mover closer to the Rwandan mentality. After all, Rwandans are the ones who have to reconcile themselves with each other. For centuries in Rwanda, the traditional Gacaca used in some regions has made it possible to resolve problems in a friendly way. Questions of civil law, land disputes and marital disagreements have been resolved in that way on the hills. The Gacaca is based on decisions by elders asked to decide local disputes because they have the advantage of knowing well the people and their clan. Justice is rendered at the problem's place of origin. It is a local response to a local problem, resolved by respected members of the community designated locally by the local population itself."

Immaculée added: "The South African model was at one time envisaged for Rwanda but it caused a stir among extremist movements of Rwandan survivors. They explained that only when the guilty have been convicted can they ask for forgiveness and not the reverse. But in Rwanda, there is still not a sufficient trend among the prisoners indicating that they regret their crimes."

"In order to be forgiven", intervened another survivor with the name Consolata, "a guilty person must recognize that he has committed a crime and made a mistake. This phenomenon of personal recognition of a mistake is essential. It is impossible to attribute all the crime to the government or to orders that were given. In a question of genocide, the question of individual responsibility should be dealt with first and only then that of collective responsibility. It will take a long time for this distinction to be recognized. Perhaps, it will never come to pass. A killer must acknowledge that what he did was not correct. He must also know that he has personally broken a taboo. Up until now, the persons seem to have joked about it. That's how the idea of the traditional Gacaca has little by little been accepted by the Rwandan government. Out of the question of confessions, pardon and punishment came the idea of the Gacaca courts. It is for that reason that the population immediately accepted it with the condition that the truth be determined loud and clear. A crime must be admitted publicly."

Gasana added maliciously, "At the same time that the idea of the Gacaca began to grow, obstacles and resistance began. What is most important to understand is the idea of proximity, not the idea of vendetta or a form of collective vengeance. Traditional courts are considered to be a mechanism for resolving conflicts at the local community level. They imply a local approach where persons accused of having participated in the genocide and massacres are judged exactly there where they committed their crimes."

Consolata agreed, "On several occasions during preparation of the Gacaca in the prefectures, legal specialists introduced the Gacaca system in public meetings. We were positively surprised by their correct functioning." Gasana explained that he had personally attended one of these debates in Kibuye.

Despont intervened, "At first, the local inhabitants were sceptical but little by little they became enthusiastic for a procedure that finally gave them a say in things?" He urged us to be careful of traps of participation. "It is possible to be in agreement publicly but to think the opposite collectively and secretively. And then Rwanda is not particularly known for its freedom of expression. Far from it."

There's another of those European flights of fancy, thought Gasana, a new understatement implying that Rwandans lie all the time. They really lean on their clichés, those *muzungus*, he said to himself. He was not the least intimidated or influenced and said: "Let's give a chance to all the prisoners to tell publicly the truth and in that way promote reconciliation." Furthermore, did we have a better idea? No one up to then had expressed one. He resolutely continued his presentation and explained while he changed the transparency on the overhead projector: "Throughout Rwanda, Gacacas will be created composed of the irreproachable elders elected by the local inhabitants at the level of cells, sectors, communes and prefectures. Their distribution will depend on the number of accused in categories two to four. Category four includes any

227

act of looting, vandalism or ransacking without death. Category three includes physical aggression, but not murder. Category two, in which have been placed 75 per cent of the accused prisoners for small-scale to large-scale repeated killing in pursuit of a plan for extermination with premeditation." Gasana caught his breath, "Do you follow me?" Those who were listening nodded yes. He took out another transparency and adjusted the overhead projector. "Category one will not be dealt with by the Gacaca. This category includes the architects of the genocide and high officials of the former government who knowingly participated in the preparation of the genocide. The established courts and the International Criminal Tribunal for Rwanda (ICTR) will be responsible for that category of crimes. According to the estimates and projections, more than 200,000 persons are going to participate in more than 10,000 Gacaca courts. At first, they will try prisoners who have confessed, and their sentence will be reduced by half or even more."

Despont interrupted and Gasana showed impatience for the first time. Despont emphasized, "I would like to recall that the new penal code has already decreased the sentence for murder by half; from twenty years before 1994 to ten years after 1994."

Gasana thanked him and without moving continued, "If we take a category-three prisoner who confessed and has already spent six years in prison, he will already have served his sentence. He would be immediately freed at the time of the Gacaca and would have publicly asked for forgiveness. If we take a category-two prisoner who has already served a certain number of years, his sentence will be reduced by half or more depending on the specific Gacaca. Thanks to his request for forgiveness, the rest of his sentence can be commuted to work of general interest."

Despont was almost in a rage: "That's exactly what I wanted to say, slightly causiously. Ok, Ok, but the Gacaca system very seriously compromises international principles of justice accepted under principles of human rights and penal law. Under your Gacaca system, there is no separation between the prosecutor and the judges. There is no legal counsel or legally defendable verdict. In addition, there is a certain risk and strong pressure for the population to magnify the crime. The door is open to major differences in fixing sentences and punishments. No instance will reconcile the lies on one side or the other. This system would become a real battlefield and lead to interminable discussions that no law would be able to stop. In that case, you won't take a hundred years but a thousand years, unless, of course, in the meantime everyone has killed everyone else."

Our Mr. Despont was pleased by his diatribe. He turned to look for a bit of support in the room, but the audience did not appear to follow him at all. The audience's faces showed bewilderment. The shock was too brusque. It is not advisable in this country to express things so strongly. On the contrary, the audience began to consider Despont a bit like an animal in a zoo. The temperature in the room rose. It was definitely becoming too hot in there. How was Gasana going to react? How would he defend himself with regard to principles of international justice? It was a bit as though we were suddenly at a trial under the Gacaca system, while all we had intended to do was to see whether that process would be viable. We looked at each other with expectations. Instead of a roundtable, we were attending a trial, and no one really dared to intervene. We were following this duel with interest.

Very subtly, *à la rwandaise*, Gasana dodged the blow and added a spoonful of sweetness and smoothness to his answer. "We can understand that during an initial period the presentation of this new idea that is unique in the world annals of justice, the Gacaca courts, revolutionary and risky for everyone, both for the prisoners and the government, has caused a general outcry. We are gathered here to find the best guarantees possible for secure and peaceful operation of the Gacaca system. We have to make positive proposals, and it is easy to criticize." "Art is difficult, Maître…" Suddenly, the audience had the impression that they didn't count. The exchange had been biting. We were willing to let things happen as they might. Despont raised the tone: "You can see that everyone is resisting your idea of Gacaca. It frightens people. It's going to create disorder. Resistance first began internally within Rwanda throughout the judiciary system and the government, according to my sources. Then, there were questions raised in parliament that stopped things. Finally, the international community declared its reticence: it could already image scenes of lynching. The international NGOs, attorneys and human rights workers received a great deal of negative mail. I am not speaking at all of the Rwandans outside of Rwanda who are publishing pamphlet after pamphlet of abuse." "You know," interrupted Gasana, "things need time to work out, and we are very determined. Rwandans have let people speak and act, and they have incorporated the fears and proposals of everyone. Two national reconciliation and human rights commissions have been asked to carry out feasibility studies on the transition to traditional courts. Just have a bit of patience and will shall succeed." Despont had no reply.

Gasana began an interesting comparison: a national study had been carried out at all levels. It had produced a real laboratory of discussions and study of risks. Symbolically, it had given the impression of carrying out comparative research on possible links and transpositions between an African medicine using traditional plants concocted by Rwandans for Rwandans and the classic Western medications that often heal symptoms but not the illness. He was willing to grant one thing to us: if the potion were used incorrectly, it could become lethal like a poison. But he was arguing for use of a homeopathic dose of the local medicinal plants and the local healers were well known. The Gacaca courts are Rwanda's own medical formula and that's why it is going to work.

"That's the way it is", mumbled Despont. Gasana went on: "The sessions held to promote awareness, participation, integration of the aspect of gender and other aspects dealing with society in preparation for the Gacaca courts have all been confirmed positive. Prisoners have organized themselves into various categories. They have begun to talk about it. The law was finally passed in August 2000. The sixth Gacaca court was created and the Constitutional Court is studying the feasibility of the project. The government has always argued that the Gacaca was a specific way to advance prisoners' cases. If everything goes well with the initial Gacacas, the prisons and solitary confinement cells will be emptied of their current occupiers in three years."

"And what will you do with those who are recognized as killers—those who are accused and arrested for the first time? How many of them are there, any way? Are you not afraid of being overwhelmed? Despont asked incredulously.

"No", replied Gasana, "I think we are going to be able to start a cycle of releasing prisoners that will clear the prisons using an approach of innovative truth. This is going to console the survivors and those who no longer want to live in silence to the point that they will not want to exteriorize their frustrations in a few years. We do not run that risk."

Despont soften up a bit. "It is true that Rwanda has always been successful where we least expected it," he remarked, nodding his head. "Yes", answered Gasana, "we have reintegrated more than one million persons who returned from the refugee camps in Bukavu and Goma in 1997 with incredible discipline and shown a willingness to reinsert them quickly into society in their home commune. In general, This task has been successful. We also integrated hundreds of ex-FAR soldiers (Forces armées rwandaises from before 1994) into the regular army. They fight along side each other without too many difficulties. We succeeded in creating a form of security propitious to development within Rwanda. Why could we not succeed, six years after the genocide, AT trying and releasing prisoners who confess and whom we are willing to pardon for their crimes? "It's a duty to understand better what

231

happened and to learn better the names of the people who disappeared," added Immaculée.

Despont calmed down. He was finding this discussion interesting and was beginning to understand the Rwandan mentality. You could feel that he was slowly moving towards a positive frame of mind. Gasana was secretly very pleased. Despont added: "Without wanting to dampen the enthusiasm, but taking into account a number of impressive advances since 1994, we are probably right to think that everything could function well. I insist, however, that the accused must be defended. We have to find mechanisms that provide the accused with recourse to a proper defense. We have to try things that work. We have no right to make mistakes."

Gasana continued, "Yes, we agree. We are aware. In the Justice Ministry, we are working out all the logistical and administrative questions. One of the attorneys explained one day how he saw the concrete operation of the courts. This is how we see it. The prisoners will be brought before the Gacaca courts in the following categories: categories four and three in the cells and sectors; category two in the communes. The prefectures will serve as appellate courts if we do not reach a consensus on the facts. The prisoners will be brought before these courts of local community which represents the general assembly. They will discuss the charges and listen to witnesses and counter evidence, arguments and counter arguments. Persons elected in the courts at the level of the cells will classify the prisoners using the 1996 legal categories, about which we have already spoken. During a second phase, the Gacaca courts at the level of the cell (about ten houses), the sector (about ten cells) and the commune (about ten sectors) will decide the sentences depending on the categories. They will apply a scale of reduced sentences that will have been established for the new Gacaca courts."

"There we have it", exclaimed Despont. "Where is the legal advisor? Who will guarantee that the sentences are not going to be handed out uniformly?" Gasana replied, "You cannot mix traditional justice and classical justice. At a certain moment, you just have to trust in the wisdom of the people. The local community will explain how that happened. All the pilot trials that we have carried out have shown that they tell the truth in public before other members of the community. They also want to learn better what happened and the circumstances of the crimes. We held a trial Gacaca court with a group of prisoners who had confessed in one of the prefectures. We took this group before the local inhabitants of their sector. Surprising but true, the population described exactly what those persons had done for the events for which they were eyewitnesses. The local population clearly said that one there (they pointed to the person who had confessed) he has had enough prison; he didn't kill many. Furthermore, the guy standing next to him was incarcerated for nothing; he fled and joined the APR soldiers. And that one there, they designated another one standing next to him, you can release him right away. He didn't do anything. But the other one, in the back, he was especially active and killed very many persons. He deserves to spend a few more years in prison. They even added that if the one who had killed many asked for clemency from the survivors and his own family, his *mea culpa* would allow him to cleanse a bit his shame. In that way, he could be released and assigned to public work to participate in the development of the commune. In the end, what good is it to still keep all the prisoners who have already spent six years in prison? A woman added that the commune needed people to work in the fields. "The survivors are not at all in agreement. They are willing to decrease their sentences only if the local inhabitants speak out and the prisoner tells his version," added Immaculée.

Gasana commented, "The Gacaca will also be very symbolic. We cannot arrest and correctly and equitably punish everyone. The local inhabitants will be able to speak out and say whether they would agree to live again with these people in their midst. This is very important. Six years further on, they realize that they have to live together; sometimes very close to those who killed their families. They have begun to live together again. They all say that they have no choice and some say that there is no reason to continue to lock up the prisoners who have already been imprisoned for six years. Many widows farm the land of friends who take food to a husband in prison. Everyone helps each other. It's incredible, but true."

Despont listened very closely and stared with his eyes wide open. He told himself with a shudder that it was unthinkable for Europeans to have to think of living next to a executioner. But that is just what they do in Rwanda for six years and maybe longer. Despont became thoughtful. What a thorny question, he whispered to himself. At any rate, he agreed about one thing: "A general amnesty was neither politically nor socially feasible. That would mean that the killing could start again with impunity and that part of the prisoners paid unjustly for others. Perhaps the Gacaca would allow a form of parole and reconciliation. He asked Gasana what was happening to the prisoners who had not been arrested but who will be identified and recognized by the local inhabitants during the description of an event at the Gacaca trials? He had already answered this question. Gasana repeated, "It is very difficult at the present time for us to know how many persons in the country should still be arrested. We have the impression that over six years most of the persons in category two have been arrested. Many have fled. Some are still active in the Congo. Nonetheless, if a Gacaca court, for example in a commune, considers a new person guilty then that person must go to prison. If he confesses his crime, his sentence will be reduced." To finish, Gasana summarized the spirit of the Gacaca. "The aim will not be to render classical justice, but rather to start a mechanism of reconciliation and better knowledge about the truth throughout Rwanda. It is conflict resolution using a local approach. This method, we hope, will loosen tongues and allow people to live together better. They will have spoken of the past and have had the possibility of asking for forgiveness. It is impossible to foresee all the cases, and that is why the Gacaca courts will certainly be very different from hill to hill and in the towns. If we succeed in reconciling the country, we shall all be more conscious of the 'never again that'. The Gacaca system can be a strong instrument for better justice."

Immaculée interjected: "We have been struck by the increasing enthusiasm of the local inhabitants. They all want the truth to be revealed. Small farmers do not want to remain silent; nor the women, nor the children. It has been clearly established that the prisoners want to be questioned and that means must be found to investigate their cases. They prefer to face justice under the Gacaca system rather than continue to stagnate in their cells. The result can be only positive. Finally, for the survivors, part of the problem will be dealt with: that of the crimes." Immaculée then asked if she dared read the deposition of a survivor who had left a written testament before dying from malaria a month earlier, who left her papers to the association *Mémoire vive*. Immaculée looked around at the participants in the forum. She explained that she would like to read in order to show how important it was to the families to recover the ties of neighbourhood and good understanding. Rwanda is too small for people to be enemies. We all said yes out loud. Gasana sat down and wiped his forehead. Despont pushed against his chair. Immaculée took out several lined pages from her small leather briefcase. The pages had been torn out of a school notebook. She told us that the person's name was Angeline.

Here is the posthumous story of Angeline. "In the Rwandan commune where I come from, a neighbour is someone important. He knows how I am, in which mood I woke up, what I need. We have always helped each other because that's the tradition. We take each other an ember to light the fire in the morning to warm us up. When something is not going right with the neighbour, it's best to leave. It is a very bad sign. One day, I realized the Hutus did not like me.

They could no longer look me in the eyes. I wondered whether I had some marks on my face or body. I wanted to know why all of a sudden it was like we had the pest. Since the genocide, I have met Hutu widows or sisters of prisoners, my neighbours. They regret what the men did, but they say rather casually that I should forgive them because they were told that by killing the Tutsis there would be more houses and land for the Hutus. I can't forgive or forget, but I can envisage reconciling myself to living again with my former neighbours. But they must tell me why they did what they did and tell me all the truth. Justice is meant to do away with the survivors' fear, but it is always within us because we do not understand why we are different. Things are changing a bit on the hills. We talk to each other timidly. I agree with reconciliation, but they have to explain it to us."

"You see", said Immaculée, "the Gacaca is first of all going to allow us to talk, to say a bit of the truth." We were all very touched by that story. Visibly moved, Despont got up and shook Immaculée's hand. Gasana, straight as a ramrod on his chair, looked at his watch. "I think the meeting has reached an end and we have had an interesting discussion. I propose that we now discuss informally among ourselves on the terrace during the lunch break. It is really too hot in here. Let's go outside." He suspended the meeting and thanked the participants.

Despont was reconsidering the whole story and called out again to the audience that was getting up to leave. "In the end, your Gacaca could work well. Pay attention, nonetheless, and carefully elect the elders acting as judges, especially those for the cells where you have a large number of local people. You have to think about protecting the prisoners."

Gasana smiled a bit sadly. He was pleased although he knew that his struggle was just beginning. He told himself that he had to use all his energy at every session and for each group because he was going to be dead before the Gacaca trials began. We walked with him to the exit and gave him a slap on the back. "A very interesting discussion", I told him, "even if we did not participate much. I think we were able to gather a lot of pertinent arguments." He smiled and said that the struggle was only beginning."

Chapter 12

Diary (2000)

An End-of-the-Century Feeling

3 July 2000: The hour with ninety minutes

The war between Uganda and Rwanda on foreign soil at Kisangani is beginning to annoy many foreign observers and the great foreign powers. Rwandans' ability not to speak clearly frustrates more than one. Some critics thunder and declare that Rwanda's behaviour is beyond any understanding. One day, I also had the impression that I was being told tall stories. I became angry and went to see an important government official to complain about this opacity. He listened to me, shook his head and said that he would see what he could do but clearly he could not do much either against the system of favours and skirmishes between Rwandans and Ugandans and their disagreements in the field. The war was expensive, and the Lusaka agreements were not being implemented. Cooperation is always tied to a context, and the current context was unfavourable. In addition, there is always a delay between action and reaction. It was a question of adjusting rhythms with available resources in order that between demands for speed and immediate tangible results made by the European donors and the relaxed African rhythm, we are able to function. There are really two different measures of time used in Africa and Europe. There are minutes and hours, but they don't pass at the same speed. There are two separate spaces with different dynamics. I often have to remind very impatient Europeans about that. Here we are in Africa using a different clock; not the one with sixty minutes in an hour but one with ninety minutes in an hour. This diluted African time is sometimes difficult to understand. I remember a diner with a European visitor who wanted an accounting of the expenditure of his money. He considered that things were all right here. Of course, he saw that there were poor people here, but it wasn't that bad. He told me, "You know they are very lazy." That was one time when my discretion protected me. I said to myself to be careful and not start off on a crusade; don't try to be right about everything and at all costs. I kept quiet. He asked for confirmation of his opinion and the only thing I said had something to do with things taking time in Africa. I listened during the whole diner and only at the end did I mention that 75 per cent of the population in Rwanda lives in poverty. My visitor was a bit surprised and wanted to know what the other 25 per cent did.

4 July 2000: The sacrosanct Day of Liberation

This 4th of July is both the Rwandan Day of Liberation and the American national holiday. Pure coincidence? It's the sixth commemoration by the Front patriotique rwandaise (FPR) and the third for me. A lot of progress has been made: for once we have translations, which changes everything. The speeches of the president and other dignitaries now make sense. We watched a military parade that was perfect, with a touch of humour at the end. A small circus unicycle closed the parade. I interpreted that wink as progress in this country; progress that reflects a capacity to be able finally to relax a little, to ease off a bit. Can a touch of humour even be included in Rwanda? What a revolution. At the reception after the parade, I had an explanation from a friend over a glass of Coca Cola. "You know", he said, "you cannot abandon us, the Rwandans. Give us a chance. We are barely beginning to get to know each other." Six years after the genocide, those are encouraging words. It's true they no longer know each other, and they no longer recognize themselves. There are no longer any reference points between those who have returned and those who stayed. Often, those who stayed no longer know what happened to them. This is also true most of the time for those who have committed crimes and who cannot admit it. I realized that for these Rwandans who have all had a different destiny, who have returned as refugees from various countries and speak other languages, quite often badly, than their own mother tongue, Kinyarwanda represents a real undertaking. When I asked that friend what it meant to be Rwandan, he answered that it means belonging to a country where a genocide occurred. That is the essence of being Rwandan.

10 July 2000: The Jewish woman from New York

I have just returned from a seminar on justice given by an international NGO. In the evening, there was a diner for the participants with the minister for justice and an American Israeli, the head of the Jewish Holocaust Fund. The diner was very touching and also very instructive. We learned a lesson: similarity is not the same as being right. Jews in New York are very interested in the question of the Rwandan survivors. What is a little bit annoying is that they often see only that part of the population. It is important, of course, for Rwanda, but that is not the whole story and it is far more complicated than it seems.

All evening, the woman frequently shouted at me. She was picking on me. At the beginning, I stayed aloof and adopted an attitude of speaking about the victims and the whole country that had suffered from the genocide. I advocated a slightly more global approach, but she insisted on comparing the Tutsis and the Jews. In the end, everyone felt ill at ease. She was aware of nothing and kept insisting morosely. I know from experience that Rwandans detest persons who come to commiserate with them publicly over the genocide. They are very reserved about the drama that affected their country. The Rwandans seated at the table began to shuffle in their chairs and to speak to each other.

At a certain point, I decided that was enough: "There were also many moderate Hutus killed. It is important not to divide the victims, and an approach too tied to ethnic affiliation should be avoided." She looked at me furiously. Not to chose victims? What did I mean? I think I upset her a bit. After that, she didn't speak to me again. A bit later, that same woman broke into tears while listening to an account of an event during the genocide. Two Rwandans sitting next to me broke into hysterical laughter and said: "You see", she cracked. "You cannot express just like that feelings of compassion. Is she crying for us or for herself?" It is a taboo here to break down. You have to hold your head high and continue and continue with dignity at the risk of not solving anything.

I think what the people of the Great Lakes Region need more than anything are peacemakers and not persons who come to explain after the fact what should have been done earlier. Rwandans are allergic and deaf to any lessons. They know that there is still too much tension between them. They want to find for themselves the way toward reconciliation. Unfortunately, it is often stronger than they are: they hate each other in a friendly manner. How can you fight the negativity and distrust in Rwanda?

Tensions also exist in our countries but they are muffled and, nonetheless, tempered by a democratic system. Everywhere in the world, no one wants to be taken for an idiot. Everyone wants to have power. Rwandans are ashamed of their history. We must rethink new ways for a new diplomacy that must be honest inwardly and outwardly. I have learned to be conciliatory and not swim against the current, to be part of a whole and to take interest in those who initially appear to be in disagreement. I have learned to be patient, patient and gentile, but an idea should never be abandoned. You have to find the right moment to express it, to evaluate when the listener is ready to hear it. Its implementation can sometimes take a lifetime. I think Rwandans do not always know how to appreciate the little things that are close at hand, the handy friends, for instance. This country is still really in a survival mentality, with its nose just above the water lever. It is fragile, but you have to believe in its future. We have all gone through phases of great hope, then deceptions between Mondays and Fridays interspersed with feelings for and against Rwanda, just like the up-and-down of the hills.

11 July 2000: The boomerang effect

I had to fire the new Rwandan computer expert after two days on the job. He had just come out of prison after stealing 15 million Rwandan francs from the Banque de Kigali. He didn't tell me anything about it. I was alerted by an anonymous telephone call, and then I checked his story. This turn of events created a real problem for my conscious. He left after I explained to him that I was prepared to give a second chance to someone, but I expected to be told of the circumstances before. The hidden side of things always comes back to the surface. When you give too much freedom, things always turn sour right away because temptation is too strong and salaries are too low in relation to the money that is dealt with. It is a tiring situation to live with, but you have constantly to begin again with supervision and controls.

Having gone to Europe for a holiday, the former computer person simply stayed there. Rwanda is facing a big problem of capacity and abilities. In addition, there is almost no middle class; no specific professions such as computer expert or electrician. They are just not there and are not trained. We have noticed that there are more and more people leaving the country, especially survivors. They are declaring loud and clear that they have no freedom, no work and that they have been left out of their share of the pie. Is that true or is it the result of the after-effects and disappointed hopes? Is there any way of actually making reparations? This part of the population is very fragile and difficult to please.

27 July 2000: A stiff meeting

The Americans have organized a large "Women's Peace Forum". They want this forum to lead to a declaration of African support for women and for monitoring peace negotiations, especially those being held in the Congo. African women often participated in the discussions. Each told her unbelievable and difficult life story. Often, they were female refugees; women who had become lawyers, physicians or economists and who were now fighting for democracy in their own countries.

Those from the Sudan talked about a domestic conflict in the South that is political and religious, which has been completely forgotten. Those from Ethiopia argued for a lasting peace and against a ridiculous war with their Eritrean sisters. Those from Burundi wanted the international community to recognize the 1993 massacres as a genocide. And the Rwandans cried for help because the United Nations system was becoming disinterested in the region. The United Nations is very divided in its support for the new Rwandan regime.

My surprise, which led to my early departure rather than my becoming disagreeable, was to see the United Nations regional representative explain to us what Rwanda is as seen from outside the regional level. He essentially spoke of the naughty Rwandans and Ugandans and the sweet Congolese. His presentation was made in the presence of a large part of the Rwandan government. We had the impression of waking up from a bad dream. He created real hostility. While his words might have been very courageous and provocative, at that time there in front of 450 persons in Rwanda, it was an especially undiplomatic speech. It's a shame, because the question of the Congo should have been the object of a calm and sincere discussion. Not a single Congolese woman spoke out. Like the rest of the audience at this forum, I swallowed and tried to smile as least stiffly as possible. I left telling myself that was one diner I was willing to give up. I don't know whether I missed something, but there are days when I have trouble being a pleasing diplomat, all smiles and asking how the family and the little dog are. While to have been welcoming would have been useful, that Friday it was beyond my strength. It is true and inadmissible that the war in Kivu province sometimes leaves the Congolese population forgotten and subject to the demands of all the parties to the conflict. The challenge is with complete neutrality to find what outside assistance can really do to prevent future conflicts. This week, time flew by to the point that I forgot to go home at noon. I confused Thursday with Friday and forgot the American 4th of July. Thank God that my friends at ICRC came for me. They had rung and were worried, but picked me up at my office at 9 p.m.

13 August 2000: Would you like a bit more *franglais*?

We just inaugurated the Kigali Institute of Education (KIE), the teacher training school in Kigali. The television people and students were there. The World Bank paid for the buildings. We contributed to the construction of the kitchens, the library and the biology and biochemistry rooms.

There was only one little problem…hum, like the physician said in *Docteur Sachs*, a book I loved that tells the story of a rural physician in France—"hum" was his tick in the book. The little problem was that the director who had been hired is English-speaking, while about 75 per cent of the students are French speaking. This means that everyone must learn Kinyarwanda, French and English very quickly. The three languages must be learned simultaneously in order to obtain the teaching certificate in three years. Given that most of the subsidies—right now—are American or British, I wonder whether it is still possible to keep a little bit of the French-speaking world. I doubt it. It's a sad state, but that is the way it is. The hotchpotch of languages does not always raise the level of grammar and spelling in any of the three languages. In addition, verbal use of the languages does not allow focusing on anything. Welcome to *franglais* in Rwanda. August is going to be a bad month; there is so much work. I am going to have to spare my efforts and keep a watchful eye. In the whirlwind of activities, we are beginning a new training session for Rwandan general physicians in the field of mental health.

14th of July, the French national holiday. It is curious, but many Rwandan children are called Fetnat (*Fête Nationale*). Of course, they were born on the 14th of July. France and Rwanda still have obvious reasons for misunderstandings.

20 August 2000: Free elections?

Visit of Renato, the special representative of the European Union. He paid me an honour and invited me to diner. He wants to present a new plan for the Congo and organize a meeting with the non-Congolese belligerents to try to move the monitoring of the Lusaka agreement along. I was invited to a diner meeting of the European Union where a high official of the Ministry for Decentralization spoke to us about the holding of the elections scheduled for October. Each of us was able to ask questions and compare elections in Europe with elections planned for Rwanda. Each country tried to promote its own form of democracy. The discussion was chaotic. We ended up arguing about the regional approach based on the Great Lakes Region and the quickly changing alliances. We could all sense that Rwanda was having difficulty in overcoming the crisis. Fighting in the Congo risks lasting for some time. Rwandan occupation of the Congo has led to many complaints.

20 September 2000: Those who become angels

"In order to become an adult, a child must separate from its parents by mourning the past and the parents it would have liked to have. Nothing ever happens in life as we think it is going to happen." For me, it is almost impossible to write it, but my mother died on September 18th; a Monday morning at 7

245

a.m., several hours after we had left her, wishing her bon voyage. She left loved on the anniversary of my father's death. All the time I spent with her was both a sort of tunnel, emotional gift and deception, but also of learning. I am very sad. Her most beautiful parting gift was that of having waited until I returned to Geneva before her last breath: the funeral, the reading of a text at the church, visiting mother for the last time at the chapel. Everything happened so quickly. And then here I am in the plane returning to Kigali. My birthday was lost in the sorrow of her death. Her death was a deliverance for her and an indescribable depth of feelings for me. It was a feeling of love towards a person that I had never felt before. In Kigali, the welcome was very warm. All my colleagues came out to the airport to give me their support and offered me flowers.

24 September 2000: Life after death

The day after I returned, I had to go to the International Criminal Tribunal in Kigali for the inauguration of their information centre. Then I spent ten hours at the office dealing with the pile of papers. I was sitting at my desk when I suddenly heard on the radio that the Netherlands was giving substantial assistance for development in all of Cyangugu prefecture and was going to establish a large programme for the Rwandan judiciary system. That evening, I was again invited to the Chinese national day celebrations. We drank Chinese wine, which tasted a bit like a juice of marinated frogs, but that's all right. The Chinese cuisine makes you dream of nights in Shanghai. At the Chinese buffet, several new members of the Rwandan government were present. They welcomed me warmly, presented their condolences and talked with me about their new jobs in the government. You can have a very critical attitude and at the same time have an interest in the enormous efforts being made in Rwanda.

3 October 2000: The sweet-and-sour policy

In life, you always forget too quickly the good side of things. In Rwanda, the good aspects of life often make us forget that the bad side unfortunately also exists. Hot and cold always live along side each other. One day, we think that the government really wants to begin a new era and wants to do well for its people. The government is rather democratic, from bottom up as in the case of the elections. But the next day, examples of violations of human rights, proof of a closed, frightened regime, inwardly clinging to power, hits us in the face, making us doubt their good intentions. We ask ourselves how people who are subservient and at the same time want to believe in it, still hope for better days, while all the time the degree of poverty continues to worsen. And yet proof of solidarity and enthusiasm is there.

There are also, unfortunately, examples of the contrary. Everything is a question of overall evaluation and a capacity to see events in their whole context over the long run. This ambivalent reality often creates problems for my conscious. How to be effectively certain of being able to contribute to progress when you also see the horrors, violence against individuals and flagrant lack of freedom. Can we say that the country is on the right road but it is forced to still drag the sequels of the genocide? Or should we pack our bag and say, "Nothing is working out here?"

In the same order of ideas, my night watchman, Sebastien, was arrested for driving a borrowed motorcycle that was then stolen. He was tortured and accused of having organized the theft himself in order to have the money. He was beaten and then locked up. He is having difficulty recovering from the shock, especially the humiliation. I am flabbergasted to see that a government allows the police to treat citizens so badly. I feel helpless and wonder once again what the presence of foreigners with our glowing reports can do to stop outbreaks of violence.

Fortunately, my friend from Djibouti came to see me. He wrote me a wonderful poem in memory of my mother. His collection of poems *Pèlerin d'errance* is very moving. He is one of the rare persons I met in Rwanda who gave me back the taste for culture and literature. I miss that world here so much. All our discussions hinge around development. They end up hiding art, culture and, quite simply, human relations.

This Sunday, I was even able to play several matches in the new tennis tournament. I reached third place with my new Rwandan partner. He tried very hard to make our team look best. He is a young Rwandan of 17, passionate about tennis, with the name Jean d'Amour. A beautiful name, don't you think?

18 October 2000: The pot has boiled over in Burundi

Departure with two specialists for Burundi. The three of us get along very well. We are on the same wavelength. We participated together in all the official visits, meeting at least 25 persons in Burundi. I think I learned a lot about cooperation and methods for negotiating with partners. Epiphanie, the painter, gave us a warm reception. I bought one of her oil paintings. It represents a black face looking at an orange and yellow abstraction. Sandra, the American, gave a large party in our honour and invited the international community. It is strange; despite the difficulty of living in Burundi, which is slipping slowly into chaos, we have to admit that there is a more extravert attitude here than in Rwanda. People seem to speak with greater ease. The city of Bujumbura, located near Lake Tanganyika, is almost enclosed. The lake is the scene of regular fighting and gunfire coming from the surrounding hills. The contrast is striking: the inhabitants continue to live almost normally, recovering from a long regional embargo while repeated gunfire takes place on the hills in rural Bujumbura. Can you become accustomed to war?

I received my old friend from Krakow who knows the region well. We had not seen each other for ten years. We looked each other over like two cocker spaniels and then shared memories of field visits, especially in Mozambique. We were like two old legionnaires. It was very important to be able to talk about my early years in Africa and to compare Mozambique with Burundi. We exchanged our opinions about Mandela's mediation in the Burundi conflict. Then it was back to Kigali in a hurry and back to the desk.

1 November 2000: All Saint's Day

Today, like almost every day, I think about my mother up there in peace. I hope so very much. She helped us to face life with affection and confidence. We must remember the dead every day. This knowledge I gained in Rwanda.

17 November 2000: Fighting poverty

My stay in Rwanda was becoming an analytical voyage inward. I decided to go to fewer diplomatic diners and political meetings. After a long struggle for acceptance, I can now sit out and think and quite simply follow the Rwandan rhythm. I meet more Rwandans in the field; for example Théogène, the head of the programme against poverty with whom I exchange impressions once a week outside Kigali. The problems of the transitional government have not ended, but I now understand the outlines better. I am much more relaxed, like after an exam when finally you have the impression of really knowing the subject matter. "Just relax and laugh", an American friend repeats to me endlessly. This laugh has become an ancestral laugh reverberating at the beginning of time. To be less serious in order to be serious at the right moment has also been a lesson.

Like most women, I always want to do well, to be as fair as possible and to be perfect. But now I have changed.

Now I accept my errors because I also accept the errors of others. I have become more indulgent. If I am able to let go of everything that depends on my personal will and replace that with a universal logic, I shall pass my life exam. Gradually, I can succeed in leaving a positive souvenir for my Rwandan friends. I am proud of my personal progress. That's where victory is; at that level. While remaining discreet, I think I have been able to form lasting relationships among Rwandans themselves. I have developed a real friendship, even a complicity, for many Rwandans that I have met. The struggle against poverty on the hills and the hope of reconciliation have been my two main motivations.

This Friday evening, I spent a wonderful time with two Ethiopian friends. I have rarely met persons who are so attentive and thoughtful. They do everything they can for me and want to explain to me everything about the conflict between Ethiopia and Eritrea. They are lawyers and refugees, a man and a woman. They are exiled and work for the United Nations. I wonder how many conflicts there will be in this Africa so torn apart. Countries come out of one war to start another. The end of the fighting in Eritrea raised great hope for everyone. Why, then, another war? And why is Africa becoming a continent of refugees? Well-educated Africans, men and women, with so many abilities and university training that can be used in their own country. They are exiled, here or somewhere else, occupied counting grains of rice in warehouses for humanitarian emergencies.

19 November 2000: The status of African women

The word "gender" is in fashion. It is everywhere and represents the willingness of international assistance to promote balanced development between men and women. It is a wonderful idea, but it is culturally delicate to introduce it concretely into projects. It is a bit as if you wanted to settle the question of the inequity of women with one word. Magical word, right? Let's say it is a new awareness about an old issue. During a weekly meeting of the heads of national programmes, there was a discussion about balanced development between men and women. Two women, a Rwandan and an Englishwoman began to speak kindly to each other then very quickly they were tearing each other's hair out. They were not at all in agreement about how to make women aware of their unhappiness. The Rwandan was very theoretical after having attended many seminars in Europe. She was looking at the intellectual side of the issue. The other, the Englishwoman, was on the contrary down to earth based on years of experience as an anthropologist and midwife. They spent hours talking about experiences that they had found with women who suffered bad treatment. The men sitting around the table remained politely silent, as if this discussion did not concern them at all. Nevertheless, implementing a gender policy will take time: first to understand fully what it means and then to convince men to participate. I became aware that to ensure this balance between men and women in development programmes provides a better balance in income-generating projects. The attention given to this balance makes it possible to generate a more healthy general economy, especially in the micro projects where women do not have the same access to money, an inheritance or an income and, therefore, no credit.

A dinner for the Burundi ambassador. I am preparing the diner and desert, a tiramisu prepared with a local sort of cream. The recipe comes from the papal nuncio. The diner was a success, and all the guests thanked me warmly. The most pleased of all was the Burundi ambassador in Rwanda. His job seems especially difficult, even gigantic.

25 November 2000: African children adopted in Europe

Today, we were urgently invited to the ministry to solve a problem concerning Rwandan children who survived the 1994 genocide and have been adopted in Italy. The radio,

251

television and newspapers are all talking about it. It is a real ethical case of conscious: several distant Rwandan family members want them back, but the adoptive families do not want to return them. I think this time the Rwandan government reacted too quickly. Discussion of the background of the problem between the two countries would have been better. Here are the facts: 41 children, adopted in Italy after the genocide, are now claimed by the Rwandan government who speak of a legal void at the time of the genocide that did not allow legal adoption of the children. Must these children return to their country where their families are often too poor or can they remain with their adoptive families in Italy? Often, it is their expanded family that is asking for them. The government is talking about kidnapping, which is perhaps too strong a word, but that is how this event is seen by the Rwandans. The real debate about the adoption of Africans has unfortunately not taken place. The government wants to recover the children who still have relatives in Rwanda—no discussion. They want the support of the whole international community to settle this conflict. In their eyes, these children will be happier here with their relatives, even if the living standards are lower, than far away in Europe with wealthy foreigners.

Beyond the legal debate about the children who were taken at the height of the genocide to save them is the question of happiness and money. It is a question of point of view. I fully agree that an attempt should be made to find a solution to bring several back if they have close family, case by case, but through bilateral negotiations between the two countries. The international community, for once, shares that opinion. The difference in interests should be settled case by case, but not be treated as a question of principle that must be settled as a whole. Italy is concerned about the drama of separation from the host families.

6 December 2000: The eucalyptus of Kibuye

The big positive news this week was another visit to Kibuye. We visited several education projects and those started by local initiatives of the Ministry for Gender and Advancement of Women, just by chance. During our visit to the prefecture, we discovered that international organizations were deforesting the surrounding forests at a rate of about 8000 trees a month. They are doing this to help refugees in a camp make firewood. We discussed with them deforestation and reforestation. The environment should be better respected under the framework of outside assistance, especially at the beginning of projects. Lake Kivu is really beautiful; there is a feeling of lost pleasantness. The government again received me very kindly. Near the water in the evening on the terrace, there is something that attracts people passing through. About 10 p.m., all sorts of people gathered around a table to eat brochettes and drink beer: people for the parliament, the constitutional commission, businessmen and Rwandan NGOs. Reflection of the lake makes everything appear as bronze, smooth, majestic and secret. This lake is really an element that brings people together. It recharges your neutrons. During the meal, I ardently defended the trees, trying to convince people not to cut them down.

7 December 2000: School desks

The next day, we were still in Kibuye. We visited a project for building school desks and benches for schools in the prefecture. The plan for building desks is rather good. We were at Gishita, a very outlying commune. An apprentice carpenter working on a bench told us that the making of the desks had been slowed down because of the lack of experience of the head of the project. Out of 75 desks, 25 wobbled, but not all in the same way. All were unusable but each was different, a bit like the wood had been cut in any which way for imaginary pupils. Their heights varied as well as their dimensions. When I asked whether the age group of the pupils for whom the benches were being made had been chosen, all hell broke loose. No one had ever thought about it. We had disturbed this little world: the technician, the head of education and the government. Often a whole project is ill conceived, not just a small detail. We patiently prepared new objectives for the project and set a timetable for the activities. All the benches would be measured, worked on and checked. Children would be put in them to determine needs. In the end, everyone was pleased. Sometimes, we are blocked by a lack of ability and lack of willingness on the part of Rwandans to take responsibility with regard to their own country, their ecology and their schools, as if these priorities were not really their problem. It is part of the post-genocide syndrome of indifference. There is also a question of using other people's money, negligence and probably very low salaries. How can we motivate society and give it a sort of civic pride? I returned from Kibuye a bit astonished and disturbed by the extent of poverty and lack of diligence in undertakings. It will be a long process to heal the wounds of the genocide. Is it possible to reform one's own country when you are completely dependent on outside money? A European development worker once stated it well: you sometimes have to force yourself to be indifferent. It is often better to pretend to want to aid when you know that in reality you cannot do much. Especially in a context where it is desirable that Rwanda reintegrate its local talent. Rwandan intellectuals are often disappointed when they return to their country. They expect an eldorado, but they find only its ashes. Everything has to be done again here and basically in the mentality of people. That's why throughout the country there is an attitude of waiting-and-seeing. Everyone is waiting for a change, but no one sees how to produce that change. What is the difference between pre-1994 Rwanda when we thought we were helping honest people, and that was not the case, and now when we are trying to help people who really don't know whether they want to be helped?

11 December 2000: A Rwandan named Rudolf

I had several beautiful experiences this week. One morning, a clear and lively voice called me: "I have to see you right away." It was Rudolf, the former director general of the Agricultural Institute in Rwanda. He had even been secretary-general for agriculture until 1989. He is a calm person who says little but selectively and in a controlled manner shows that he has experience. He refuses to talk about former times. He tells me that it all started because of a political error and not as a war between ethnic groups. He is a pleasant and educated Rwandan Hutu living in Madagascar after discreetly fleeing in 1992 and predicting the catastrophe. He is the father of seven daughters and works in Antananarivo. He wants to come home and thinks that it is the right time and that everything will work out. He calmly sat in my office because he wanted to see me. His expertise in agriculture and agronomy is impressive. He feels that agriculture is still not doing well in Rwanda, but Rwanda is his country and he badly wants to return. In addition to the usual structural problems in agriculture, there are other problems. He went to see his old friends and came out a bit disappointed. When will the country learn to assimilate returning intellectuals with fear of loosing face? Why are there so many incompetent persons or, even worse, people who create obstacles that block the ministries, preventing access to those with technical abilities or who are not of the right ethnic affiliation and who don't dare say anything? Rudolf left saying that as soon as his last daughter had finished school, he would return to Rwanda. He would at least have offered a future without hatred to his children. I introduced him to everyone in order to prepare him for his future return and give him a little advantage. He was delighted.

14 December 2000: Forced to go to school

Here is another beautiful story, that of an African who receives an education, despite himself. It occurred one evening, during a diner during Ramadan at the house of Yvonne and Ahmed in the company of Mourad. My friends were talking effusively about solidarity among Africans. Some of them were from the Maghrib; others were from the Horn of Africa. Writing had brought us together. That night, all of us had brought parts of stories, a novel or short story to read. Yvonne and Ahmed talked about a beautiful blue terrace with flowers and red roof tiles in a large house near Carthage. Mourad slowly and timidly began his narration. Then he began to read eagerly. When Mourad speaks, the whole of Africa seems to come out. All the stories of Hampaté Bâ, all the stories about the little Europeans who impose their schools and their values seem to come to life. Mourad began: I was born in a large family on the edge of the desert. He was writing about his mother who has just taken her seventh child, himself, to school. He was still a young boy. It was against the will of his father. The mother dreamed about a better future for her son, brilliant studies and moving out into the world. We held our breath. In Africa, in the evening, people tell wonderful stories. The story of his mother fascinated us. One morning, she had dragged him screaming out of the house. They walked for several kilometres in the desert. For a long time, they could hear the shouting and swearing of the father. "I don't want you to put our son in a European school; he will loose his identity," he shouted. His mother stood her ground. She had decided to find a school for Mourad in the town. They reached the doors of a white large building where there was a sign "Ecole des Pères Blancs". For a Muslim, it was a bit of an affront. Nonetheless, she left him there, looked at him for a last time and went away. That was how Mourad began his studies. He was a good student, received a scholarship and left for Europe where he became well integrated. He never returned to his father's tent in the desert. He knows only that his mother received a serious scolding upon her return. Then one day, the image of his mother came back to him in a dream. This image haunted him. Mourad had no choice and dropped everything. He took the ship in the other direction and returned to Africa where he took charge of his mother who was then a widow. She received him with a simple statement: "You have come back. I was waiting for you." What could we say when our children will ask us one day: have you tried to help Africa or have you or have you given in to enslaving Africa even more, tying it to the yoke of your models and your schools? Mourad became part of my literary consciousness. He often guides me with his poetic words. They are soft and nostalgic. They speak of an Africa continually looking for meaning and purpose.

20 December 2000: A literary evening with Rwandans

We founded a Mutual Admiration Literary Society. I organized the first literary evening Saturday with 16 persons at the house; all sorts of nationalities and a majority of Rwandans. The guitarist and the director of the national theatre led the evening. They sincerely wanted to promote culture in Rwanda. The evening clearly answered a need in everyone. For some, like my wonderful Hungarian friend, it was the opportunity to read extracts of his memoirs to us. He had written about the dark years through a story about his mother in the 1950s in Hungary. He described the humiliation, nationalization of their personal property and the lack of individual freedom. That evening, everyone had to talk about his or her texts or accept a slip of paper and talk about something for two minutes. It was a remarkable evening, with moments of silence and interventions by one person or another. There was lively discussion about African dance, the culture of the Rwandan kings and the search for Rwandan culture. The magnificent extracts of travel stories of a Belgian friend thrilled the audience. The atmosphere was a bit nostalgic. There were moments of silence and thoughts that drifted away; sometimes sluggishness, sighs and laughter. Emmanuel from the radio,

Gratien from Festafrica, Atom from the theatre and as many Rwandans who gave us spontaneous and natural comments and some that were even comical. The guitarist illustrated Mourad's poems with his music. The love poem of a Rwandan who dedicated his sorrow to his readers at the time of an unbearable absence of his wife won first prize. It is completely rare to listen to a Rwandan talk about his personal life.

Grégoire wrote one for me. His poem describes a girl at the edge of a lake rescuing a drowning person. It so well reflects what I was experiencing in Rwanda that I became completely upset. I was crying to myself. I was not only flattered to have been the object of a poem but also pleased that he had been able to capture a certain sensitivity beyond my daily activities. The poem brought out my deep conviction of a world that can be improved by showing empathy and embracing the universality of culture; especially in the case of Rwanda. The lines referred to my spirited defence of this so complicated and infuriating nation and to my enthusiasm for their ravaged and yet touching society. Rwanda is catching. It brings out in each and every one of us our own contradictions, our hypocrisies and our strengthens. Rwanda is a telltale, a warped mirror, grimacing and reacting to our own inconsistencies.

A public library in Kigali

Just before Christmas, an evening to gather funds for the American Rotary Club "Virunga" was organized. In a very relaxed and very simply manner, a typical mixture "made in USA", the Americans succeeded in launching a project for a public library in Rwanda. The bidding went well. All the Rwandan businessmen were there dressed in neckties. It was an amazing diaspora. The president of Rwanda, also there, had opened the bidding. I raised him, just to show him, but not disrespectfully. Europe is not yet the United States. Each person had his say by ricochet. Who bids for a bag of cement, for electrical work, for two library assistants or an accountant? Numberless people promised books.

Another chapter in a busy week: the three days spent with a consultant specialized in training project leaders. Marco is a deadpan Jew, as he describes himself, working for a Catholic NGO. He teaches extremely subtle and catching methods for monitoring development projects. It is exactly what we need. He has not disappointed us. We have been doing role-playing exercises: each of us is alternately a minister or a small farmer. In just a short time, he has us in the palm of his hand. The training course went very well. The participants learned how to form a team, set objectives and manage projects. Among the participants were gifted Rwandan project leaders. Of course, there was a slight hitch: the Rwandans wanted to eat something other than sandwiches. It's true I should have thought about it before. Our food is not necessarily to the taste of the Africans; especially sandwiches. On the other hand, they declared having learned a lot.

24 December 2000: Christmas Eve: emotion in the hearts of Rwandans

Although I had the impression that I managed the twists and turns of this third year better, the road of 2000 was still very difficult. To spend Christmas in Africa is singular; like the contrast between sweat and sour. I decided again this year that I would stay in Rwanda. My Rwandan friends and their desperate efforts to cheer me up were probably the reason for my decision. I admire their courage in the face of all the difficulties they have every day. I find them unshaken and willing. Even if they are not always transparent, they are proud and capable of expressing many hidden emotions. They gave me a desire to spend Christmas with them. Advent was spent in the best of humour with Madame the Prosecutor. I was very pleased to organize the evening. The theme was "black and white". More than 50 persons in all turned up dressed in black and white. At the table for the place sittings, there was only one obligation: a European had to sit next to an African and inversely. This situation made us laugh a lot and led to a continuous hubbub of talk about dressing and skin colour. Finally, we were all able to find our right places.

25 December 2000: Christmas in Kibuye, a haven of peace

I spent Christmas of the year 2000 in Kibuye. My escape to there worked like a real detonator, a touch of the magic wand. I was once again sitting facing Lake Kivu and had the impression that I saw the three years in Rwanda go by like a film that had been accelerated. The time had come to look back and evaluate my accomplishments during the past three years. Kibuye and Lake Kivu made me want to tell the story of my adventures and to put them on paper. It was then that I decided to re-read them and complete my diary.

This Christmas Eve, I had the enormous pleasure of quite simply taking in the landscape, of finding myself in a large tropical garden surrounded by entangled vegetation. This landscape just enchants me. In Kibuye, you can see palms, banana trees and coffee trees growing everywhere. There are also high grasses and climbing plants. They invade the landscape with such vigour that man seems to be excluded, and I enter a wonderful world. I feel like Alice in Wonderland. The bushes are weighted down to the breaking point from Nature's contribution of vigour and sap. Will Nature be able to oblige the Rwandans to seek greater harmony? How do Rwandans see their own landscape, their country? The friends of Théoneste warmly welcomed me in Kibuye, and we prepared a huge barbecue and a boat ride. It's wonderful to be able to relax and forget the omnipresent death in the country. Every week, every day and every minute, people are struggling feverously to reconstruct Rwanda, the land of a thousand hills; this former paradise.

End of the journey

I decided that now, in this new millennium, I would change my skin. My old skin, well I'm going to leave it behind to the 1990s. Those years were marked by incredible adventures, deviations symbolized by that long march in Mozambique or even in Mali. But those years were also filled with wonders. I have the impression of having matured. A whole forest of events spreads over ten years, and I patiently cleared it. Rwanda renewed my hope. What happened there is inconceivable. Rwandans are looking for themselves and continue to ask us how to live after genocide. How do they continue to go to church every Sunday?

Thanks to Marie-Arménie, Nathanaël, Ephraïm and Nepomuscène, I learned what is the modesty and kindness of a different Africa, but at any rate Africa.

The slow cicatrisation

It was on the road to Kibuye and finally by the contemplation of Lake Kivu that all the terrible history of Rwanda came back to me like in the cinema. That was where my drive to write about my time in this country in mourning began.

My adventures in Rwanda have no meaning unless they can transmit the weight of this story. My peregrinations are the result of a strong encounter: that of a woman together with a devastated and violent people. It could be said that this country seems to call out to the world. I never met anyone who came to Kigali who was not touched by Rwandans, by their overflowing charm backed by an enormous inner violence. Will this tiny country be able to withstand the healing process? Those who returned to the country or those who stayed there must survive. They are struggling for a new identity. There are still many Rwandans in exile and many others who are members of the opposition while many killers are walking about free somewhere else. The right to dignity and to recognition of the wrong seems to be a priority. It is the hard reality of Rwanda. It shows the work of God and the work of evil. The rumours, superstitions and Christian faith, they all mix together here like superimposed layers of beliefs on which we grab like a life board.

At Christmas 2000, I was on the road to Kibuye. There the lake murmured to me that I had to write homage, and I did it because I loved and accepted this country in its desire to have an international voice. Rwandans act as though they are damned and chosen at the same time. From the time of my arrival in 1998 until I found myself again on the way to Kibuye and towards Lake Kivu at Christmas 2000, the meanders of daily life in Rwanda have taught me many, many precepts. The first was certainly that of not making quick judgements about events that I witnessed, but to learn to look behind realities into the invisible world, there where you cannot see because of the bright light.

My stay in this country is a wonderful voyage of initiation. The road to Kibuye is an emblem. The small dips and rises of the steep road will always give me a deep feeling of happiness; that of having known this corner of the world. I was able to share the concerns and the impossible challenges. Lake Kivu has a blinding reverberation that brought me back to the waters of my Lake Leman. But the resonance of the Rwandan lake is sad and metallic; this lake that has decomposed and rejected so many corpses. It has swallowed the history of the country without digesting it, but it has not yet revealed all its secrets of the gas and the hardness. Its water is dark blue, impenetrable. Nonetheless, this lake fascinated me and attracted me to the point that I wanted to sink all my thoughts there. They came back to me in the form of droplets, spurting out of the water like jumping dolphins in the form of memories and moments of painful sharing.

I think back to the New Zealand mountain climber, who after his historic climb of the Himalayas wrote that before being totally committed, hesitation squeezes us. There is still a chance to give up the challenge and the same powerlessness before God. At the base of all acts, there is a basic truth, the ignorance of which kills numberless ideas and projects. From the moment we are totally committed, providence also moves. The road to Kibuye continues to wind. The hills climb and descend. From the crests, you can see the lake; in the valleys you are a prisoner of the hills. I hope that Rwandans will gain a bit of ground towards the work of God and not that of evil. The shades of green are an invitation to hope for the future. The memories of stories of reconciliation and solidarity are advancing on the obstacles. Rwanda belongs to the Rwandans and they must make it grow.

Bibliography

1. Cahiers Africains No. 12. Rwanda. Appauvrissement et ajustement structurel. 1995 (96 pp.).

2. Courtemanche, Gil. Un dimanche à la piscine à Kigali. Montreal, Les Editions du Boréal, 2000 (novel).

3. Desforges, Alison. Leave None to Tell the Truth: Causes of the Genocide and Direct Consequences on the Population. Human Rights Watch/Africa Division, 1998.

4. Dialogue: Revue d'information et de réflexion. Les chantiers de la reconciliation. Brusselles, Number 219, November/December 2000.

5. Diop, Babacar Boris. Murambi: Le livre des ossements. Paris, Stock, 2000.

6. Gourevitch, Philip. We Wish to Inform You that Tomorrow We Will be Killed with Our Families. New York, Penguin Books, 1998.

7. Guichaoua, André. Les origines des conflits au Burundi et au Rwanda. Paris, Editions Gallimard, 1996

8. Guillebaud, Jean-Claude and Depardon, Raymond. La porte des larmes: retour vers l'Abyssinie. Paris, Editions du Seuil, 1998.

9. Halsey Carr, Rosamond. Land of a Thousand Hills: My Life in Rwanda. New York, Viking Penguin Group, 1999.

10. Hatzfeld, Jean. Dans le nu de la vie. Récits des marais rwandais. Paris, Editions du Seuil, 2000.

11. Joris, Lieve. Mali blues et autres histories. Arles, Actes Sud, 1999.

12. Kapuscinski, Ryszard. The Shadow of the Sun: My African Life. London, The Penguin Press, 2000.

13. Lamko, Koulsy. La phalène des collines. Paris, Editions Le Serpent à plumes, 1999.

14. May, Patrick. Quatre Rwandais aux assises belges. La compéence universelle à l'épreuve, 2001 (130 pp.)

15. Rusimbi, John. By the Time She Returned: A Refugee's Tale. London, Janus Publishing Company, 1999.

16. Sebasoni M., Servilien. Les origins du Rwanda (Collection Points de Vue), 2000 (240 pp.).

17. Tadjo, Véronique. L'ombre d'Imana. Arles, Actes Sud, 2000.

18. Ben Jelloun, Tahar. Le Racisme expliqué à ma fille. Paris, Seuil, 1999.

19. Uvin, Peter. Aiding Violence: The Development Enterprise in Rwanda. Bloomfield, Conn., USA, Kumarian Press, 1999.

HOW TO REBUILD A SOCIETY FROM ITS ASHES?

After the genocide in Rwanda, what should be done? Here is an attempt to answer that question in the form of a diary written by a European diplomat and development coordinator in the "Land of a Thousand Hills". The author uses the testimonies of survivors describing their trauma and the difficulty of reconciliation between people whose destiny was broken in 1994. Rumour and superstition, against a background of the question of the existence of God, play an important role in the accounts of daily survival of the very humble; the challenge of the struggle to survive despite everything. Reconstruction of the society torn apart and the destroyed economy are described. One generation will not be sufficient to fill the void left by the massacre. This is a work of fiction interspersed with fact.

THE AUTHOR

Brigitte Kehrer is a trained and practicing journalist, who was formerly a delegate of the International Red Cross Committee (ICRC) in areas of conflict. She is now an international consultant specializing in sustainable development and conflict resolution. This personal description of her work during the period after the genocide in Rwanda is her first book.

Printed in the United Kingdom by
Lightning Source UK Ltd., Milton Keynes
142645UK00001B/58/A